Doing Time

Jack N. Lawson

authorHOUSE®

AuthorHouse™
1663 Liberty Drive
Bloomington, IN 47403
www.authorhouse.com
Phone: 1-800-839-8640

First published by AuthorHouse 8/16/2010

ISBN: 978-1-4520-3953-4 (hc)
ISBN: 978-1-4520-3954-1 (sc)
ISBN: 978-1-4520-3955-8 (e)

Library of Congress Control Number: 2010908725

Printed in the United States of America
Bloomington, Indiana

This book is printed on acid-free paper.

For Chris, my wife and best friend—whose encouragement helped me to give these stories their voice.

Acknowledgements

My sincere thanks go to Bill Mahood, both for his encouragement as well as joining me on the journey; to Louise and Steve Coggins for adding their professional points of view; to my niece, Elizabeth Casimiro, for her critical eye and patience with my many questions; and to Ron Bayes—poet and lover of the eternally expressive word— for his inspiration.

You can simply serve time or make time serve you.

Inmate proverb

Prologue

"Defendant, please rise." Frumpy had to be helped to her feet—she couldn't quite grasp that *she* was the defendant. She was still flummoxed that *she* was here, in a court of law, at all. *And on trial.* Except now the trial was over. The judge was reading out her sentence: "For knowingly aiding and abetting her husband Carl Locklear in common law robbery on June 16, 1975, Annabel Lee Locklear will serve three to five years in the Correctional Center for Women in Fairborn, North Carolina…" Whatever else the judge intoned evaporated as Frumpy fainted, collapsing into a heap on the floor of the defendant's box.

Perhaps it was the shock of the sentence, but in her swoon, Frumpy—or Annabel Lee Locklear—was many miles and many years away. Frumpy wasn't 'Frumpy' at that place and time. She was, in fact, who her birth certificate said she was: "Annabel Lee McNair." In the mansions of her mind she was quite small and tightly clutching her favorite ragdoll as her mother recited the eponymous poem that bore her name.

It was many and many a year ago,
In a kingdom by the sea,
That a maiden there lived whom you may know
By the name of ANNABEL LEE…

Long Time

Time travels in divers paces with divers persons...
As You Like It

Annabel Lee had been named by her mother, Colleen Watkins— 'fallen woman' and former English teacher. After leaving her teacher training college in Raleigh, North Carolina, during the late 1950s, Colleen had gone to teach high school in the western part of the state: rural Appalachian, Bransford County, on the eastern slopes of those ancient mountains. She had wanted to bring her love of the English language and literature to people that the times, culture and economy had seemingly passed by. It was her vocation—and her mission. It had all started so well, but ended ingloriously. In later years Colleen blamed it on Edgar Allan Poe—Poe had been Colleen's favorite American writer. The romantic in her was attracted to Poe's freely dabbling in the darker side of human nature and his tragic sense of life. She always harbored the thought that had *she* been around during his time, Poe's literary light would not have been doused in a bottle, and that his weak and sensitive heart would have enchanted the world for decades to come. However, Poe was long dead when Colleen Watkins, newly qualified English teacher, found herself moving to Bransford County and renting the small garage apartment owned by county sheriff, Wyatt McNair.

Wyatt McNair had been sheriff as long as anyone in Bransford County could remember. With each passing election, the office of sheriff had become something of a birthright, such that no one dared run against him. Generations back, the McNairs had come to North Carolina as a result of the crofters' clearances in Scotland. And like so many immigrant families, they gravitated to areas in North America that resembled their former homelands—and not always to their advantage. The McNairs had left the western highlands of Scotland, where stony earth grudgingly yielded any harvest and north Atlantic salt winds tortured whatever managed to grow or live there. But even with the Atlantic between them and their dispossessed crofts, they still managed to trade one difficult living for another: trying to grow corn and burley tobacco on the stony mountainsides of North Carolina.

Although Wyatt and family still eked out a small living from their one-hundred-and-fifty acres (of which thirty were under cultivation), it was as sheriff that he made his living. Perhaps the name helped: 'Wyatt.' It had the ring of the American west and one of its most famous lawmen. Being sheriff in a rural county in the South had its advantages as well: Wyatt didn't just uphold the law—he *was* the law. Thus whatever he chose *not* to see wasn't illegal. As the McNairs were good Scots Presbyterians, alcoholic wine never passed their lips at Sunday communion. Moreover, Bransford County was a 'dry' county—since before the days of Prohibition. Yet delve far enough back into the woods on an old logging path, find a good source of spring water and—if the breeze were right—the sweet smell of sour mash and wood smoke would betray the existence of a whiskey still. What the sale of burley tobacco at the warehouses down in Winston-Salem couldn't buy, corn whiskey could—and even more—*tax free.* Wyatt himself benefited from the moonshine trade, as his ne'er-do-well son and namesake, Wyatt Junior, ran a still just off their property and into the territory of a state forest. As the term 'moonshine' suggests, this illegal distillation of corn liquor took place 'out-of-hours.' Farmers and tradesmen by day became moonshiners by night.

Wyatt McNair, Jr.—or 'Junior,' as he was known—had tried many jobs since leaving high school eight years earlier. Intellectually lazy, but handsome and physically gifted, he had relied on looks, charm and one hell of a throwing arm to get him through high school. With his six-foot two-inch frame, Junior was the quarterback during football season and pitcher during baseball season. These were the perfect reasons for rarely having his homework in on time and for having his choice of pretty girls. As Junior didn't give his teachers any *real* trouble, and as his daddy was sheriff, Junior was allowed to 'drift with the breeze.' He graduated in 1949, just missed being drafted for the Korean War, and had hoped to go to a state university by means of a sports scholarship. However Junior's arm wasn't up to university conference standards and his brains even less so. Plus universities were still full of enthusiastic young men seeking an education on the GI Bill. So Junior worked the family land, and along the way failed at various attempts in local business. The natural fall-back for any such mountain lad was moonshining. The fact that his daddy was the county sheriff was his insurance. And McNair senior never *ever* let Junior drive the whiskey; it was just too big of a risk; and besides, there were dozens of hot-headed and lead-footed mountain boys eager to prove their prowess behind the wheel of a stripped-down Chevy or Ford.

The McNairs still churned out less whiskey than most of the family operations in those parts. This was, in fact, intentional. McNair senior might be outside the law on this account, but he wasn't a *bad* man. Far from it. Hell, everybody *knew* and could *see* that Bransford County was *poor*. And it wasn't as though the moonshiners were opium dealers, selling to mind-addled addicts. Besides, most of the call for 'shine came from the more prosperous Piedmont—Winston-Salem and Greensboro—and even the state capital, Raleigh. It was all just a case of supply and demand; after all, if people didn't *want* moonshine, there'd be no reason to make it. Nevertheless, as the local law and a Presbyterian elder, Wyatt senior had to be seen to be playing fair with Federal law. There would be the occasional visits from agents of the Federal Bureau of Alcohol, Tobacco, Firearms—or ATF, as it was referred to sometimes. Everybody knew that there was 'shine being produced from North Wilkesboro to Asheville and nearly all points in between. The film "Thunder Road" was far from pure fantasy, and NASCAR, still in its infancy, was largely the domain of the fast-driving young men who transported the illegal liquor. So Wyatt senior had to produce results from time-to-time. The ATF men, or 'revenuers,' as they were called, were serious men in dark grey suits and they brought with them an arsenal of revolvers, shotguns, dynamite and axes. The former two for personal protection and the latter two for destroying any stills they should find. By mutual agreement with other still operators, Wyatt would arrange a schedule of whose still would be raided from year to year. It was a fair system. Suspected by—but unbeknownst to—the revenuers, the moonshiners would always be alerted to their arrival. As the revenuers approached the arboreal lair of the whiskey distillers, a shot or two would often be fired by the 'shiners—and in the general direction of the raiders. This lent an air of credibility to the raid and whilst the revenuers were ducking for their lives (there were human hearts within those grey suits), the 'shiners would make good their escape. The axes would come out for puncturing the whiskey vats and a stick of dynamite would then be tossed into the boiler to dispatch the still. Photographs would be taken of the raid, before and after, and the revenuers could take the self-congratulatory evidence of a job well done back to the state office.

Junior McNair was twenty-five when Colleen Watkins first set foot on their farm in answer to the newspaper ad about their garage apartment. It was July 30, 1956. More than one person later had cause to rue that day, month and year. The McNairs had been used to having old maids, the occasional Forestry man (probably a revenuer!), and ex-GI rent their apartment. But here was Colleen: twenty-two years old, an aspiring high school teacher—but no old maid! Colleen was a shapely five-foot five-inches tall, auburn-haired, with striking green eyes. Junior was walking back from the barn where the family kept their tractor when he spied Colleen leaving the apartment with his mother. He stopped in his tracks, just out of their sight, and let his ravenous eyes devour her frame. He liked what he saw: the front, the profile—and he damn sure liked watching her walking away to her car. He whistled softly to himself, muttering, "Man, there oughta be a law!" Like the Magi of old, following their guiding star, Junior McNair—failed business man, part-time farmer and ne'er-do-well moonshiner—now had a goal in life. He had to have Colleen.

Ever appearing in his role as Southern 'gentleman,' Junior made his play for Colleen on the day she came to move into the apartment. Over breakfast, and in an uninterested sort of way, he asked his mother, Ginny, whether the new tenant might need any help shifting boxes and furnishings; as he'd already taken care of the tobacco priming up on the allotment, there wasn't much to keep him busy today. Ginny reckoned she knew the priming was done because, *if Junior remembered*, she'd *been there* to help him. Ginny was a woman of her culture: strong, once attractive, weathered and shaped by the mountains, with skin color somewhere between bronze and ruddy brown. She wore no make-up and possessed knowing, patient eyes, which also betrayed more than a little world-weariness. Her younger son, Frank, had left home at seventeen years of age, joined the Marines and been killed in Korea. His body was never returned. But the look in Ginny's eyes betrayed more than a mother's grief; rather it was a loss of her self. As the only remaining child, his parents' hopes and expectations for him rested heavily upon Junior. More than once, when Junior drove his mother into town for shopping, he had seen her lingering eyes search the faces and features of the infants of local unwed mothers, as they shamefully went about their business. And on each occasion, Ginny would turn that same unhurried gaze upon Junior's face, and—guilty or not (how could he be sure?)—he would feel the blood rising to the surface of his skin. He wasn't sure either.

Junior knew he had better not linger over the question of helping the new tenant move in. He shuffled over to the humming refrigerator and fumbled for the milk bottle; and then over to the cupboard for a glass. As he poured, Junior yawned and asked: "What time you 'spect the new tenant to arrive?"

"About four," Ginny replied.

"Another Fuller Brush salesman?" snorted Junior.

"Not this time," his mother responded. "Got us a teacher for the county high school."

Junior had to bite his tongue not to betray his interest. Instead he swung about, put the milk back in the refrigerator and huffed, "I'll be around to help. Gotta check the spark plugs on the tractor now."

"Shit," Junior thought to himself. "It's only 8:30 a.m. How'm I gonna get through 'til four? Guess like any other day—they're *all* about the same."

Still in the midst of the 'dog days,' the clouds had boiled up as the summer heat increased during the course of the afternoon; they had released their moist content in a short—but fierce—thunderstorm. Such storms were common during mid-to-late summer, and brought much needed relief from the heat in these days before air-conditioning.

When the pick-up truck bearing Colleen's belongings arrived, Junior wasn't long in meeting it. He picked his way around the lingering mud-puddles, greeted the driver, and helped him reverse up to the outside staircase that led up to the apartment over the garage. There was some wheel-spinning in the slick, red clay, but the truck successfully negotiated the short distance to the outside staircase. Although Junior had supposedly been working around the farm all day, he was amazingly fresh and clean. This didn't escape his mother's notice when she came out to greet her new tenant. Junior was releasing the tailgate as Colleen got out of the cab. She accepted Ginny's outstretched hand.

"Afternoon, and welcome," offered Ginny.

"Thank you; it's good to be here," replied Colleen, as she noticed Junior at the back of the truck, his carefully chosen T-shirt revealing his still-athletic form.

"This strappin' young'un is my son, Wyatt; but we all call him 'Junior.'"

"Pleased to meet you, Junior. I really like your place."

"I'd be glad to show you around it," interjected Junior—a little too quickly—so he added: "When you're all settled in, that is."

"That'd be nice," Colleen replied, dipping her eyes.

"Well, come on, girl, let's get you moved in before supper, which I *insist* you have with us."

Ginny's words—though friendly and motherly—came as more of a command than a suggestion, so Colleen simply laughed and said, "I can see it's no use my saying 'no.' I'd be delighted."

Junior was already hefting boxes of books up the white-washed wooden stairs. The apartment came partly furnished: small sofa and two chairs in the sitting room, and a modest dining table and four chairs in the eat-in kitchen, a bed and dresser in the bedroom; so there were only books, two small bookcases, clothing, dishes and kitchen utensils to move. "You got more books than anything else," puffed Junior.

"Guess I should," laughed Colleen, "I just finished my teacher training."

"What d'you teach?" fired back Junior.

"English. Do you like to read?" queried Colleen.

"Ha!" interrupted Ginny. "That boy coulda got a high school diploma in *avoidin'* readin' or doin' homework!"

"Thank you, Mama," grumbled Junior, "I *read*."

"Read *what*?" asked Ginny, "The corn flake box?"

Junior wasn't used to being put down in front of women—especially those he was trying to impress. And he certainly wasn't used to having his mama around when he was trying to chat up an attractive young lady. He would have to make his pitch for Colleen later. "I'll leave y'all to do the unpacking. Heavy work's done. Time's supper, Mama?"

"Same time it *always* is; when you're father's home from sheriffing: six o'clock. And could you pick some extra collard greens for supper?"

Junior was already halfway down the stairs: "Sure," he mumbled, half to himself.

Sheriff Wyatt arrived home at his usual time (when not on a call): 5:45. Junior was already hanging about the kitchen. "What've you been doing today, boy?"

"Worked on the tractor some—oh, I helped the new tenant move in the..."

"I *bet you did*," interrupted Wyatt, giving stress to each word. "Your mama says this teacher is quite a looker, so between you and me, son, don't you go shittin' where you gotta eat—*understood?*"

"Hell, Daddy, what d'you think I am?"

"Son, I *know* what you are—you're a McNair and you're a man. And I don't even want to think about the possible number of grandkids I probably already got spread 'round this county. You keep it zipped *tight* with this one, son, 'cause she's a paying tenant, and I got a reputation to uphold in this county." Wyatt's words shot out like bullets. "I can smell supper; so where's your mama?" Wyatt asked, his words coming out somewhat more gently.

"She's with our paying *tenant*," mocked Junior, "helping her fix up the apartment. She'll be back in a few minutes—oh, and the *tenant* will be having supper with us tonight." Wyatt fired his son a warning glance and then went to wash up.

The conversation over supper ranged mainly around where Colleen was born, what her family did, and what brought her to this out-of-the-way place. Colleen had been born and reared in Onslow County, down on the coast. Her father had come from near Asheville, and she still had some family there; but as her daddy had served in the Marine Corps at Camp Lejeune, he had taken a liking to the warmer climate of coastal North Carolina. He had met Colleen's mother in Jacksonville and they now ran a motel on the intra-coastal waterway, not far from Swansboro. As is so often the case, the child gravitates towards what the parent has left; thus Colleen, having spent many a school holiday in the mountains near Asheville, felt she would like to try living in that area as she began her teaching career.

After a brief pause in conversation, Ginny spoke—to no one in particular: "Our boy Frank was at Camp Lejeune…"

"Really? Where is he now?"

"Frank died, Colleen," Wyatt quickly interjected. "He was killed in Korea." Wyatt looked at Ginny, wanting to reprove her for bringing up the subject of their dead son, but Ginny was staring off into the middle distance, pushing her food languidly around her plate.

"I'm so sorry," stammered Colleen, her eyes fixed firmly on the napkin in her hands.

Junior had let his parents do most of the talking and asking of questions. He now took advantage of this uncomfortable pause to change the subject. "So. You're an English teacher?"

"That's *right*," replied Colleen, happy to be rescued from her embarrassment.

"You don't look old enough," offered Junior. Wyatt's eyes fixed themselves on Junior, glowing like caution lights about to turn red.

"I'm *plenty* old enough," drawled a blushing Colleen.

"I might have paid more attention in class if I'd had a teacher like you," ventured Junior.

Wyatt's eyes changed from 'caution' to 'stop.' "What Junior *means* to say, Honey, is that he paid attention to anything *but* his lessons. Ain't that right, son?"

Realizing he had overstepped the mark, Junior quipped, "If you say so, Daddy."

"Well," spoke Colleen, smoothing her napkin on her lap, "it's never too late to learn. And I have lots of good—*interesting*—books I could lend you."

"I might just take you up on that," fired back Junior before either parent could say anything.

Over the coming weeks, Junior took every advantage to watch Colleen's comings and goings. She occasionally had a meal with the McNairs, but Ginny usually arranged it when Junior was off on 'farm business'—i.e. seeing to the loading of the family's 'shine for runs down to the Piedmont of North Carolina. Junior and Colleen stopped for a brief chat whenever they saw one another. It was clear to Junior that she had time for him; but he was chomping at the bit to see more of her than either those lovely green eyes or the windows to her apartment revealed. During those late August nights, Junior lay on his bed looking out the window of his room towards the garage apartment. His window faced the stairs leading up to the apartment, with the curtained door at the top. The only other window into Colleen's private life was the small kitchen window. Junior made it a ritual to watch her washing the dishes or simply going to the sink for a drink of water, where she would often linger, looking out the back window, up the mountain behind the farm buildings. This put her in profile, from her head to her waist; and Junior mapped every inch in his mind—and in his loins. When Colleen's lights went out, Junior often relieved his sexual tension by masturbating; all the while wondering when he could get into her pants.

Junior wasn't bright enough to distinguish between love and lust; as far as women were concerned, one was as good as another. However, he was just aware enough to remember—when he cared to—that his 'love' had often cooled even faster than his lust once he had ejaculated into most of the girls he had known. Junior never used condoms, as he always professed his love to the girls who had sacrificed their honor or virginity to him. His come-on line usually went something like this: "Baby, you *know* I love you; and if you love me, well…you wouldn't make me wear socks in the shower, now would you?" Truth to tell, Junior also enjoyed the 'Russian roulette' aspect of unprotected sex. The thought of one of his little squigglers hitting the bull's eye made him somehow feel more of a man. It added an air of danger to the whole business of getting laid. The girls and—as he got older—young women, usually gave in to his advances. Junior was, after all, something of a good 'catch' in these parts. His father had a good job as sheriff, and Junior's family owned land as well. Junior was bound to make something of himself sooner or later. And so their underwear came off and they opened themselves to Junior's desire. Most of the girls or women with whom Junior had sex waited for another phone call from him, which never came; or, for the ones that it did, the infrequency of his calls soon betrayed his disinterest. For those who had accepted Junior's protestations of love and were persistent enough to drive by the farm or stop him for a chat when he was in town, Junior's tongue was as good as a slap in the face: a certain indication that all hope of a future with him lay in the past.

The school term began in early September, just after Labor Day. As the month progressed, Colleen began staying at school later and getting home when it was nearly dark. She also began staying up later, as she had lessons to prepare and papers to mark. One evening, near the end of September, when the Carolina moon was on the change from summer's pale white to the golden harvest color of song, Junior returned late from the still. As he rounded the woods along the gravel and dirt track that led back up the mountain hollow where the still was located, Junior noticed the light from the apartment door illuminating the darkness between the garage and the house. It was then he saw Colleen sitting outside, on the small landing at the top of the stairs. She had a pile of papers on her lap and was deep in concentration. Junior held a gallon jug of whiskey in his right hand; with his left he rubbed the day's stubble on his chin while he glanced at the house, to see whether either of his parents was still up. Apart from the inside hall light, the house appeared dark. Junior fiddled nervously with the handle of the heavy jug as he made up his mind what to do. The sounds of late summer—insects, frogs and night birds—had masked his approach along the gravel road. In another dozen steps Colleen would be sure to hear his footsteps. With purpose, Junior strode up to within the light's embrace. "You're up mighty late. Ain't you got school tomorrow, young lady?"

"Oh—Junior, hey! Gosh, yes, it is late. But I have to finish grading these papers before tomorrow. But speaking of late, where are you coming from at this hour?"

"Oh, I've been with some friends. They—uh, they gave me this," he indicated the jug in his hand. "Care for a night cap?"

Colleen eyed the jug and with mock concern asked, "Now, Junior McNair. Is that what I *think* it is?"

Junior was now mounting the stairs. He was aware of how hard his heart was beating, and that his mouth was dry. Colleen was barefoot and wearing a sleeveless, cotton summer dress, with buttons down the front. The top two were open, revealing the beginnings of her cleavage. Junior licked his lips, "All depends on what *you* think it is."

"Is that moonshine?" Colleen's voice was both querulous and conspiratorial.

"Well, as your Mr. Shakespeare wrote: 'Does a bear shit in the woods?'"

"Somehow, Junior, I don't think that was Shakespeare," quipped Colleen.

Junior stopped in front of Colleen. "So, what about that night cap?"

"I thought this was a *dry* county," taunted Colleen playfully.

"So it is, but I ain't *selling* this. It's strictly for personal use."

"Is it strong?" Colleen ventured.

"Honey, this stuff will set you free—they don't call it *white lightnin'* for nothing. Got any soda pop?—that way we can mix it."

"We-ell," Colleen drawled, "I have some RC Cola in the refrigerator. Will that do?"

"Sho'nuff!" fired back Junior, now feeling more in control of the situation. They moved inside towards the kitchen.

"Please excuse the mess," offered Colleen as they walked through her small dining area, "I've got all these papers to mark." She waved a hand towards the neat stacks of papers covering the table.

"*They* don't look very appetizing," teased Junior.

"No, but *they* pay for my food—and the rent." Colleen tossed her hair as they crossed into the kitchen. Junior caught a whiff of her perfume and felt a throb in his groin. "Remember, I have to work tomorrow," chided Colleen, "so just a night cap."

"Let's have that RC," responded Junior. He poured the cola first, knowing that Colleen then wouldn't be able to see how much 'shine he put in the glasses—especially hers. Junior handed Colleen her glass and asked, "Got any music, teacher-lady?"

"Well, I do have a few records; but I don't want to wake your folks."

"Oh, we'll keep it low; and besides, their bedroom's on the other side of the house." As soft music wafted from the phonograph, Junior placed himself next to Colleen on her small sofa. Colleen held her glass somewhat rigidly in front of her, so Junior leaned across her, tapped her glass with his and said, "Here's to first times." They both took a drink.

"First time*s*?" queried Colleen.

"Well, yeah," drawled Junior, "your first Carolina moonshine, and—uh, my first time sitting in your apartment with you. Bottoms up!" They both took a drink.

"I can't afford to get too giddy, Junior. Remember, I do have to finish these papers and teach tomorrow."

"I'll help you finish the papers," offered Junior. "Just tell me what to do."

"It's not quite that easy…I wish it were. No offense, Junior."

"None taken, Colleen. Just wanted to be helpful. Enjoying your drink? What do you think of the evil 'shine? Is it everything you've heard it was?"

"Hmmm," came Colleen's reply, "makes me wish I could just lie back, enjoy the music with you and forget about paperwork."

"So, do it!" retorted Junior. "Get up early and finish them."

"S'pose I co-u-ld…" Colleen's words became more elongated and slurred with each sip of her drink. "This stuff really is go-o-d." Colleen slumped back and let her head rest on the back of the sofa. "I've never really drunk all that mush—I mean *much*." Colleen giggled. "Alc-hol, I mean." She stifled another giggle.

Junior got up, taking both of their glasses with him. Over his shoulder he asked Colleen, "So didn't you go to any of them wild college parties—so-rorities, fraternities and such? I'll bet you had the boys buzzing around you like bees around the hive."

"Well, to be honest, Junior, I went to a *girls'* school—Vance Teachers' College, so there weren't too many boys to buzz around me." Colleen laughed.

Junior returned with their drinks and handed Colleen hers. "Well, here's to Vance Teachers' College for keeping you safe from all the college boys." He clicked her glass again. "So are you telling me you didn't *date* during four years of college?"

"I didn't shay—*say*—" another giggle—"that I didn't *date*. I just said I went to an all girls' college—not a convent! We used to go out with the boys from NC State. We held dances that they'd attend and they would do the same for us."

"So did'ya go steady with any of 'em?" Junior was mining for the usual information: Was this young woman a virgin or was she experienced? The answer would make the difference on how he approached the next steps.

"Well aren't you the curioush one?" Colleen was past correcting her moonshine-induced, slurred speech. "Anyone would think *we* were dating wi' all the queshshuns you're asking me." Colleen lifted her hands to toss back her hair; Junior watched the rise and fall of her breasts as she did so.

"You got beautiful hair—anybody ever tell you that?"

"Why thank you. My mama always did tell me I had nice hair and to look after it."

"Well it's not just *nice*," countered Junior, "it's *beautiful…* just like the rest of you."

Colleen blinked her eyes a few times and tried to look straight at Junior, but her head remained cock-eyed due to the alcohol coursing through her system. She pushed herself up straight—or what she felt was straight—took a large gulp of her drink and said, "Zhunyer M'Nair, are you getting fresh with me?"

Junior put his arm around Colleen, pulled her in close and said, "What if I am? God, you're beautiful." He took the lack of focus in Colleen's eyes as the swoon of passion and began kissing her.

Colleen pulled her mouth away, and with Junior still planting kisses on her face and neck, gurgled out: "Yunior, I…I'm not sur' about this."

"I am, Baby. I've been sure since the first day I saw you. And I think you've known it since the first time we talked." Colleen and Junior were now in more of a wrestling match than a love embrace. Junior's hands were roaming freely over Colleen's body, greedily groping the flesh of her legs, thighs and breasts. Colleen was too drunk to keep up with the speed and strength of Junior's explorations. Her hands were flapping about uselessly, like fish out of water. Junior now had Colleen's dress unbuttoned to her navel. Watching Colleen's breasts jostle about within the confines of her bra only strengthened Junior's lust and determination to have her. "Is this your first time,

Baby? Is it?" Junior tried to sound soft and soothing, although he was exerting a lot of energy trying to pin back Colleen's arms. "'Cause if it's your first time—and we've all had one—then it works best if you just try to relax, okay, Babe?" Junior had now pulled down Colleen's dress and bra straps to her elbows, which aided his efforts to keep her from pushing him away. "Nice, Baby, I mean these are *really* nice." Junior was pawing and rubbing her breasts like a pauper who had found Aladdin's lamp. His erection was now more than he could ignore, so in one move, Junior heaved himself over Colleen's body, half-supporting his weight by smothering Colleen's mouth with his own; all the while unzipping his trousers.

Despite her fright and drunkenness, Colleen realized what was about to happen to her. She tried desperate reasoning: "Junior—I'm not saying we can *never* do it, but just not *tonight*, okay?"

Her words were uttered in hopeless supplication. Junior had freed his erection and was now tugging at Colleen's panties. With powerful tugs and the sound of ripping seams, Junior pulled her underwear over her bare feet. For a moment they were both silent: Junior hovering over Colleen and Colleen in stunned muteness at his next advance. Junior hoped Colleen's silence was acquiescence, but as he pulled her legs apart, Colleen started to scream. Junior first muffled her scream with his hand—then thought better of it—and pressed his mouth hard against Colleen's. Meanwhile Junior pushed first one, then a second, and finally a third finger into Colleen's vagina. With the absurd hope of giving her coital instruction, Junior babbled, "Gotta get you wet, Baby. It won't hurt as much that way. It always hurts you girls a little bit the first time...Just try to relax, Honey. Don't fight, you're gonna like it, I swear." Colleen's only response was a vain struggle and a hysterical groan from deep in her throat as Junior pushed inside her. "God, Baby, you're tight!" gasped Junior. "You feel so good…" After only a few thrusts, Junior ejaculated. His ineptness as a lover and his over-heated excitement at the prospect of finally 'having' Colleen, brought him to a completion of his male task. "Oh, Baby; that was good."

Junior rolled off Colleen, mopping the sweat from his face with the shirt he had earlier tossed aside. "Whoa!" he muttered more to himself than to Colleen, "I've really wanted you—*bad*." Colleen had rolled to one side, sheltering her breasts and pubis. She whimpered softly into the seat cushion. Junior hitched up his trousers and draped his damp shirt over his shoulder. He knelt onto the sofa and gently took hold of Colleen's convulsing shoulder. "Hey, now, Baby; you're kinda making me feel bad... It... it didn't hurt all that much, *did it?*" Junior wanted to attribute Colleen's emotion to his manly love-making.

Colleen shrugged his hand away. In a blend of disbelief and despair, Colleen sobbed, "You—*raped*—me..."

Junior bridled at the word 'rape.' "Now hang on a goddamn minute!" Any semblance of tenderness quickly disappeared. "*You* invited *me* in here, remember?" He spat his words like a cobra. "So don't you go gettin' any ideas, *got it?* And just remember who's the law in this county anyway—in case you try reportin' this. Rape, my ass..." Then Junior, remembering his father's warning, checked his outburst and made one more attempt at jocularity. "Shit, Baby; you're just a little drunk. You don't have no idea what you're saying. You'll feel better in the mornin'."

"Get out, you bastard!" Colleen gasped.

"Okay, well fuck you then." Junior turned to the door.

"You already did..." trailed off Colleen's reply from over her shoulder.

Without thinking—not an unusual thing for him—Junior slammed the door of Colleen's apartment and stomped down the wooden steps as he made his way to the house. With his gorged sexual appetite now turning to emotional indigestion, he fought the rising shame of his assault: "Shit... the bitch. Who does she think she is? I don't need this shit." As Junior mounted the three steps to the back porch of the house, a light came on in the kitchen. It was Wyatt senior. He stood in front of the open refrigerator, wearing only boxer shorts and scratching his bare belly, the other arm resting on the door. The light framed Junior in the screen door, and Wyatt saw him. Junior froze, but it was too late to turn back and enter via the front door.

Wyatt peered at his son. "S'matter with you boy? Ain't you comin' in?"

"Uh, sure, Daddy; the light, uh, threw me for a moment—that's all." Junior threw open the screen door, but then remembered that his shirt was off; and he was still sweating. Junior tried to push past his father. "G'night Daddy."

But Wyatt took him by the shoulder and spun him round. "Hold your horses, boy." The law officer in Wyatt made him study his son carefully. Junior began to sweat more profusely from jangled nerves and guilt. Wyatt removed his hand from Junior's shoulder, looked at the glistening moisture on his fingers, and then slowly wiped his hand on his boxers. The refrigerator door swung shut, allowing the light from Colleen's apartment to bathe father and son in its soft glow. The cicadas, crickets and other creatures of the night sang out in cacophony. Wyatt stared thoughtfully at Colleen's apartment and then turned his gaze upon Junior. Still flushed from a near-toxic blend of alcohol, sexual gratification, violent anger—and now—fear of his father, Junior's chest rose and fell heavily. Wyatt pivoted suddenly and switched on the kitchen light.

"Damn, Daddy!" Junior furtively tried to wipe the sweat from his face and chest, at the same time shielding his eyes from the sudden glare of light. Again Wyatt took hold of Junior's shoulder with his strong finger tips and turned his son towards him. Junior jerked away.

"What have you been up to tonight?" demanded Wyatt.

"Nothin'. Just been to the still, that's all." Junior couldn't look his father in the eye; his sexual exploits had usually been conducted away from home—normally on the back seat of his Ford.

"Unh-huh," sniffed Wyatt, "so why're you sweatin' and puffin' like that?"

"I been runnin'..." ventured Junior.

"*Runnin'*!? From *what*?" asked Wyatt.

"I...I thought... I thought I heard something... or someone," offered Junior. Seeing the quizzical look in his father's eyes, Junior continued: "I thought maybe someone was gonna try to rob me—or maybe it was a Federal man. I don't know. Anyway, it spooked me, so I ran."

"And those scratches?" Wyatt indicated the roseate streaks on his son's chest.

"Briars and branches, Daddy. It was dark, so I couldn't *exactly* see *where* I was running." Junior tried adding a touch of logic to his tale.

Wyatt had conducted many an investigation in his years as sheriff; he could be patient and persistent once he began a line of questioning. He scratched his belly once more, took a deep breath, let it out slowly, and looked pensively at Colleen's lighted apartment. Without turning towards Junior, Wyatt asked, "So where's the whiskey? You were supposed to bring us a jug."

"Hell, *I* don't know...I dropped it, I guess. Yeah, I musta done— as I was runnin'." Junior nodded to himself.

Wyatt still looked across the yard at Colleen's apartment. "Yeah, you must have dropped it—'cause *you* were *runnin'*." Wyatt abruptly changed tack: "Colleen's up late tonight, ain't she?"

Falling for this old lawman's trick, Junior piped up: "Yeah, she's grading—" Junior stopped. "I...she... she told me she'd be grading papers tonight." Junior silently cursed himself.

Wyatt now turned towards Junior. "So that door slamming I heard as I came into the kitchen—that wasn't anything to do with you?"

"Naw, Daddy. I don't think *I* heard anything, anyway."

"So your old man is hearing things now, eh?"

"Well, no. I—."

"And your cussin' and talkin' to yourself as you came across the back yard—that ain't nothin' to do with Colleen either?"

"No! I swear! Look, Daddy, I'm tired. I need to go to bed. Can we drop this, *please*?" Junior tried an attempt at humor: "Hell, Daddy, maybe you were still dreamin' when you came downstairs, huh?"

Wyatt turned back to the refrigerator. "I'll see you in the morning."

Junior slinked upstairs. Wyatt poured a glass of cold water and rubbed the sweating glass across his forehead as he stared into the dimly lit refrigerator.

When Wyatt got back in bed, Ginny stirred and woke. "Thought I heard voices downstairs," her sleep-filled voice croaked. "Everything all right?"

"Yeah, Junior was coming in from the still when I went down for a drink; that's all." Then Wyatt added: "I saw Colleen's lights were on... maybe you ought to look in on her tomorrow—just to make sure she's all right."

"Fine," said Ginny as she drifted back to sleep.

Wyatt pondered the encounter with Junior until his thoughts were submerged by the weight of tiredness and he succumbed to sleep.

Two people didn't sleep at all that night: Colleen and Junior. Junior lay on his bed looking at the light in Colleen's apartment, working out different variations of cover stories. As for Colleen, after Junior had left, she remained on the sofa weeping until her eyes were dry and burning from the salt residue left in the aftermath of her tears. When she got up from the sofa, Colleen pulled her dress around herself modestly and went to lock the outside door. She added the chain for good measure. Summoning her courage, Colleen next went to the bathroom and stood looking at herself in the mirror. Her hair was a tousled mess; the little make-up she wore was in streaks down her face; her lips were slightly purple and swollen from Junior's violent kisses. After a brief moment, and as though frightened of further contamination from Junior, Colleen began frantically tearing off her clothes, throwing them into a heap on the floor. She began to run the bath and, while the taps were running, she began to splash cool, cleansing water on her face.

After a few minutes Colleen looked in the cabinet for her hand-mirror. She sat on the toilet seat, opened her legs slowly and lowered the mirror to assess the damage. Slight bruising was beginning to appear on the inside of her thighs; there was a mixture of Junior's semen and Colleen's blood—now coagulated and brown—in her pubic hair and around her labia. Colleen let out a deep, sonorous moan. She let the mirror slip from her hands and fall onto the floor. With purpose, she got up from the toilet and stepped into the bath and attempted to purify herself. But the more Colleen washed away the evidence of Junior's assault, the dirtier she felt. Colleen ran another bath, and then another—until the hot water tank was empty. When she could stand the cooled-down water no longer, Colleen finally got out of the bath; but not being able to bear the thought of leaving the womb-like security of the tiny bathroom, she put on her bathrobe and curled up on the floor mat, remaining there until morning.

Colleen was still on the bathroom floor when the dawn's light came through the milky glass of the window. She lay motionless as she heard first Wyatt's, and then Junior's, cars leave. Colleen was still curled up on the mat when she heard Ginny, first tapping—then calling—from the door. She heard Ginny's footsteps descend the stairs, but then return again soon afterwards. She heard the key turn the latch, Ginny's inquiring call, and the dull clunk as the chain stopped the door from opening further.

"Colleen? Honey? Are you all right? The high school has been ringing and asking where you are. Colleen, if you can hear me, *please* say something!" pleaded Ginny. "Honey, do you want me to ring the ambulance?" Ginny was shouting as Colleen opened the bathroom door.

Colleen pulled her robe tightly around her as she shuffled her way to the door, her body stiff—both from Junior's attack and having lain all night on the floor. She lifted the chain from the door. As it opened, the bright light of day illumined her features.

"Lord, Sugar! What's happened to you!?" blurted Ginny. "Come on, Sweetie. Let's sit you down."

Ginny took Colleen gently by the arm and led her towards the sofa, but Colleen recoiled upon seeing the scene of her violation. Ginny looked from the frozen Colleen to the sofa and its surrounds. She saw the two glasses, still partially filled with cola and booze, and then the gallon jug of moonshine, sitting on the floor. Ginny's mind flicked quickly over the brief conversation she had had with Wyatt in the night: Junior had come in late, Wyatt's request for her to look in on Colleen—*Junior.* "Oh, God. No." Ginny prayed silently.

Colleen shivered as she stood in front of the sofa. "Not *there*," was all she could murmur.

"Okay, Honey. Let's go to the table, all right?" Colleen moved on unsteady legs as Ginny guided her, one arm around her waist. Ginny got Colleen settled in a chair and went to put the kettle on the stove. "You look like you could use some coffee, Sweetie," Ginny sought words—any words—that might comfort Colleen. While waiting for the water to boil, she took a seat opposite Colleen. "Honey. What's the matter?"

Colleen began to weep and simply shook her head. Ginny took Colleen's hands. "Colleen. Look at me. Something's happened, hasn't it?" Colleen's head fell onto their clasped hands, heavy sobs coming from deep within her, and her tears washing over their hands. "What's happened, Colleen? *Please tell me.*"

Colleen rocked her head back and forth and whimpered, "I can't."

Ginny held Colleen's hands, not uttering a word. Her silence was interrupted by the kettle's whistling. Gently, she let go of Colleen's hands and in a near whisper said, "I'll make us that coffee." While Ginny made and poured the coffee, Colleen kept her face pressed into her hands, sobbing, and occasionally gasping air. Ginny rejoined Colleen at the table: "Honey, please get some of this into you." She lifted Colleen's head as though it were made of finest porcelain and then slipped the coffee cup between Colleen's hands. Colleen's eyes fixed themselves on the cup. Ginny noticed the ripples that ran across the steaming dark liquid as Colleen's body shuddered. "Drink it," offered Ginny softly. "Drink it, Hon." The cup slowly rose to Colleen's lips. Jerkily, Colleen sipped the coffee. A clock on the kitchen counter ticked off the seconds as they sat in silence. Not being one for equivocation, after several more moments Ginny ventured to expose her fear in words: "Was my boy—was *Junior*—here?—last night?" The coffee sloshed from the cup onto the table, burning Colleen's hands in the process. Ginny wheeled out of her chair, grabbed the dishcloth and ran it under cold water. In a matter of seconds she was back at the table pressing the cold cloth onto Colleen's hands. Colleen was openly weeping now. Ginny kept soothing Colleen's hands and pleading with Colleen. "Colleen, I'm sorry, but I have to know. Is *that* why you're so upset? I *saw* the moonshine on the floor…" Colleen uttered a noise between a groan and a gurgle, began to nod assent and then dropped her head to the table, not attempting to soften the blow. Ginny rested her strong, weathered hands on Colleen's head. As she cradled it, Ginny slowly lowered her lips to the crown of Colleen's head and kissed her. Colleen's hands slowly extended towards Ginny and pulled her closer. Ginny had her answer.

They spent another half-hour in silence, still in that same embrace. Ginny broke the silence saying, "Honey, I'm sorry, but I got to get up; my poor back's killing me. Why don't you lie down on your bed while I fix you some food?" Colleen simply nodded and waited for Ginny to escort her to her bedroom. Colleen collapsed onto the bed and turned her face towards the wall. Ginny pulled the quilt over Colleen. As she turned to leave the room, Ginny said, "Colleen, I'm going to ring the school and tell them you got the 'flu. I won't be gone a minute, all right?" She saw Colleen's head nod slightly. Ginny left the bedroom door open as she went; then hurried across the living room, out onto the landing, down the stairs and back to the house.

Ginny returned with a can of soup and some homemade bread in her hands. After she had prepared a simple—but warm—meal, Ginny went to Colleen's bedroom. She walked to the end of the bed to have a look at whether Colleen was asleep or not—she wasn't. Her red-rimmed eyes stared vacantly at the wall. "C'mon, Honey," cooed Ginny, as she helped Colleen out of the bed. She took Colleen's hand and led her to the table where a slab of buttered bread and warm soup awaited her. Colleen sat in the chair like an uninvited guest. Ginny had to place the spoon in Colleen's hand and coax her to eat. It was as though Ginny were taming a wild deer; she gently broke off pieces of the buttered bread for Colleen, placing them in front of her. Colleen shivered as from the cold, but obediently took the proffered food and began to eat: first nibbling at the bread and then shakily spooning soup into her mouth. Once she was convinced that Colleen could feed herself, Ginny—though she remained seated at the table—let her thoughts go elsewhere: Junior, Wyatt, whether to say anything, how to say anything. The day was already far spent.

Birthing Time

If you can look into the seeds of time,
And say which grain will grow and which will not...
Macbeth

"I'm pregnant." The effect those two words had on Junior was like the blast of a double-barreled shotgun. His chair toppled over as he shot to his feet, his Saturday morning breakfast half-eaten on the table.

"Like hell you are!" he fired back at Colleen.

"I've missed my period for the *second time*, Junior... and I've been to the doctor." Colleen kept her voice even.

"Hell, even doctors can be wrong. And can you keep your voice down about all this?—'cause Mama's upstairs and Daddy's around somewhere."

"My voice *is down*, Junior. And your 'Mama' knows what happened last month—and I suspect your Daddy does as well. Besides, you're the one who's shouting. The point is: I am pregnant, and I didn't make this baby by myself."

"Jeez, Colleen." Junior turned his head away as if to protect his ears from some harsh noise. Whilst checking the hallway for any sign of his mother, Junior whispered to Colleen over his shoulder, in a raspy voice: "How do I even know it's *mine?*"

"Because *you know.* You know *when*, you know *where* and you know *how.*" Junior could feel Colleen's eyes burning into the back of his head. "You were man enough to father this child. I just want to know are you man enough to do something about it?"

"Like *what*? Take you to one of them doctors that can uh, uh…"

"I am *not* having an abortion!" Colleen's eyes were on fire now as she marched across the kitchen and spun Junior around. She gripped his biceps in her hands as she stated her terms: "You…that is *we*… are going to do what's right by this baby."

"You're damn right." Both Colleen and Junior were startled to see Wyatt standing in the hallway. "You're damn right Junior's going to take responsibility for this child." Wyatt stared icily at Junior and then warmed as he turned to look at Colleen. For once, Wyatt, who was always sure of himself, stammered: "Colleen, I—I wish, for your sake… I wish that I could turn the time back. But I can't. This boy of mine…it's, well, time he became a man and stuck with something he started." Wyatt turned towards Junior. "You *will* marry this girl, son. You'll marry Colleen." Wyatt called out for Ginny to come down to the kitchen. She answered from the upstairs landing and footsteps were immediately heard on the stair treads. Ginny's eyes sized up the situation in the kitchen. "Me and Junior are going out for a while. You two ladies got some planning to do."

As far as *Sheriff* Wyatt was concerned, being stupid wasn't a crime; but being stupid and getting caught *was*. This time the 'criminal' was his son, the 'crime' was committed on his own property and the evidence was growing daily in his tenant's womb. Ginny had indeed shared her knowledge of Junior's assault on Colleen, the night after it happened. The partially drunk jug of whiskey left behind in Junior's hasty departure from Colleen's apartment had been the first piece of incriminating evidence, and put paid to the lie he had told his father. Junior hadn't come home for supper the following night, so Ginny related the events as best she could piece them together. Wyatt had fumed all that evening, but the only words he could muster were: "Let's just wait and see." Now they had waited and seen.

When Junior and Wyatt were out of earshot of the house, Wyatt turned on his son: "You damn, dumb, knot on a log! What did I tell you when that girl moved in here—huh? What did I *tell* you?" Wyatt's powerful hands grabbed his son by the lapels of his jacket and shook him. "You ain't got the brains God gave a jackass, boy. And what brains you do have are hanging between your legs!" Wyatt's face was deep red, verging on purple, and the veins were bulging. Junior didn't dare utter a word when his father got into this state. His head was hanging like a condemned man's. His eyes burned with dammed up tears and impotent rage. "Get in the truck," Wyatt ordered. Junior did as he was told, slumping down in the seat. Wyatt's fists banged the steering wheel. "Of all the girls you had to bang, it just had to be Colleen, didn't it? It was just too much to ask that you left that one girl alone, wasn't it?" Junior looked at his feet. "Say *something* you stupid son-of-a-bitch!"

"I—I thought…she was real pretty…I mean… I don't know what came over me…." Junior's words feebly trailed off when he saw the look in his father's eyes. Junior tried to swallow but it felt as though his Adam's apple would stick halfway through the motion. Hoarsely, he croaked "Where—ah, where are we goin', Daddy?"

"Well hell, son. As it's just such a *nice* day—and it being Saturday and all that—why I thought we'd go do us some fishing! Dumb-ass! Where do you *think* we're going? If you *can* think, that is. Going down to see Pastor Dugdale. He's got a wedding to plan, hasn't he?"

"Oh shit—" was all that managed to escape Junior's mouth before he stopped himself. Wyatt slapped the truck into low gear and floored the accelerator, the rear wheels spewing gravel as they spun out of the drive down to the road. Once on the tarmac, the tires squealed when he popped the clutch.

⧗

Rev. Matt Dugdale lived next to the First Presbyterian Church. In the pecking order of ministers, he saw himself as a cut above the many Baptists that inhabited the hills, hollows, towns and villages of this region. After all, he had been both to college *and* to seminary—a proper institution, not like those home-grown Bible 'colleges' that sprang up here and there throughout the South. And Dugdale saw himself as two or even *three* cuts above the Pentecostals and other holy-rollers that established chapels in run-down stores and warehouses. No, Matt had himself a proper brick church building, right on the main street in Bransford. The manse was a handsome, 1920s, two-storey house, with a fine front porch, from which the Dugdales could survey the town and greet the townsfolk as they passed by. Matt came from a long line of Presbyterian ministers. Most had either attained modest-to-large sized churches whose names began with 'First' or, occasionally, one became a seminary professor. Matt had aspired to the latter, but could never quite manage the rigors required of a doctoral student. No, Matt liked genial society, good food and drink—and golf. Thanks to the industrialists of the North Carolina's Piedmont region, golf courses had been built in and around the resort towns of the Blue Ridge Mountains. Bransford County just happened to have one, and—Presbyterians being seen as that bit more sophisticated than Baptists (and not averse to a drink—except in communion!)—two or three of the local business owners and the manager of the golf club himself, attended the First (and only) Presbyterian Church of Bransford. The rest of the town's elite were members of St. Paul's Episcopal Church—a source of constant irritation to the Rev. Dugdale. Episcopalians—especially in the South—saw themselves as the *established* Church, the Church of America's founding fathers—though without the legal status it enjoyed in England.

As it was mid-autumn, and there was still a chill in the late morning air, Matt wasn't in his rocking chair on the front porch. (He liked being seen to work on his sermon notes.) Wyatt parked the truck out front, waited for Junior to slink out of the passenger side, and then marched him up the concrete stairs that led from the sidewalk to the porch.

"You wait here." Wyatt pointed to the rocking chair.

Rev. Dugdale greeted Wyatt at the door. "Well, Sheriff. To what do I owe this honor?" Dugdale noticed Junior sitting in the rocker; but before he could make mention of it, Wyatt had firmly but gently escorted the minister back into his own house and into his study.

Sitting on the manse's front porch, Junior felt as exposed as if he had been placed in stocks on a medieval village green. He tried to wave nonchalantly as passersby acknowledged his presence on the porch. His father and the minister had been gone about fifteen minutes when Junior heard someone open the front door. It was Wyatt.

"Come on in, son. We've got some things to discuss."

Matt Dugdale liked to think of himself as a friend and wise counselor to the young couples he married; but mainly he coveted having his name in the society pages of the county newspaper and being invited into the homes of influential citizens. Only by sucking up to the rich and powerful could he ever hope to gain a larger congregation and better-paying position in cities like Charlotte, Winston-Salem or perhaps even Atlanta. So when the county sheriff presented him with a *fait accompli* regarding the *imminent* marriage of his son to the new English teacher at Bransford County High School, Matt was only too happy to turn necessity into a virtue.

As Junior entered the pastor's study, Matt greeted him warmly, taking Junior's limply outstretched hand into both of his and shaking it vigorously. "Congratulations, young man!" offered Matt, "I hear you're marrying that pretty young lady who's recently joined the high school faculty." Then in a more serious and avuncular tone, and still holding Junior's hand, Matt said, "Now, man to man, Junior, your father has told me that you've, ah, jumped the gun a little, heh-heh—but everything's going to be just fine, you hear? You and Colleen get over to the courthouse next week and get the license taken care of and I'll get on with wedding preparations for about a month from now." And then, to show that he too was a man and understood the world, he jibed Junior with: "We don't want to wait *too long* now, do we?" Nobody laughed. Matt coughed, quickly changed tack and offered his hand to Wyatt. "Sheriff, we'll get your boy fixed up right."

"Thank you, Pastor," responded Wyatt. They held each other's gaze for a moment. Then Matt extended his hand to Junior once again. Junior took it unenthusiastically. The strong grip that had served him well in high school sports was as dissipated as his free and easy days.

Matt offered a parting benediction: "I suspect you're a little shell-shocked by all this, son; but it's going to be all right. Believe me." Junior nodded weakly and forced a grim smile. Wyatt said they would see themselves out; and with that, the two McNairs left the minister in his study.

The wedding was a small affair—just family and a few close friends. "That's how *they* wanted it," Ginny told all enquirers, shaking her head as though she would have wished a more elaborate ceremony and celebration to follow. But almost anyone could see the makings of a typical 'shotgun' wedding. Colleen's mother and father had travelled up to Bransford for the wedding. For them, it was a difficult, somber occasion; not what they would have ever dreamt for their only daughter's wedding. Although Colleen was not through her first trimester of pregnancy, the suddenness of the announcement and the fact that the wedding would not take place in Colleen's home town and church, raised suspicions for her parents that would be answered the following June. Colleen's father, Martin, did what was expected of him and gave his daughter away in marriage; but his face and demeanor suggested he was handing her over to a firing squad. Her mother, Connie, dabbed her eyes with a lace handkerchief. As Rev. Dugdale asked the couple to repeat their vows, Junior had mumbled the words, as though hoping that—if they were inaudible—the Almighty wouldn't hold him to them. For her part, Colleen tried to make the best of the situation. Junior wasn't unintelligent and was far from ugly; perhaps he could be encouraged into making something of himself—both for his wife and the child they were soon to have. Colleen pledged her troth with boldness born of hope. So promises were made and half-made, rings exchanged and the groom kissed his bride—but without any of the fervor that had overtaken him *that* evening, some weeks before.

Following the wedding ceremony—and with the false bonhomie that was required of them—the party set out for the new Holiday Inn down on Highway 421. The McNairs had booked a room for Colleen's parents at the motel, as opposed to having them stay at their house, so that neither they nor the Watkinses would feel overly put upon or self-conscious. They had also taken the precaution of arranging a local trio (drums, bass and piano) to play in the small function room—something to liven the mood and perhaps drown out the uncomfortable silences. Rev. Dugdale and his wife, Dolores, joined the awkward party. He had been invited, no doubt, to lend an air of legitimacy—if not dignity—to the occasion. Although Matt was loquacious in the pulpit, he found himself at a loss for words in difficult pastoral settings. In fact, he preferred that his flock *didn't* call on him when life became morally complex. He clung tightly to his theology of 'it will all come out in the wash.' What else was God for except to be the cosmic 'fixer?' Try as he might, Matt couldn't think of an adequate excuse not to attend the dinner following the wedding. As Wyatt McNair was both the county sheriff *and* an elder in his church, Matt felt it would be impolitic to beg off. Thus he gave Dolores a brief resume of the union between the McNair and Watkins families and resigned himself to a Saturday of no golf.

Two hours of feigned festivity was about all the wedding party could stand. It was sufficient time for the families to exchange information about their backgrounds and lives. There were no speeches—there hadn't even been a best man. Matt did have an excuse to be the first to leave: a sermon to finish for tomorrow. He and Dolores thanked the McNairs for their hospitality, bade the couple and their parents farewell, and beat a hasty retreat to their car. Next it was the turn of Colleen's parents to leave. They excused themselves on the basis that it was now mid-afternoon and they had a very long drive back to the coast, where they had left their motel in the hands of a part-time member of staff; so it really was important that they get away—business called. Martin offered his hand to his new son-in-law, and with a breaking voice said, "Take care of her." Junior merely nodded.

Connie hugged her daughter and then stood on tiptoes and lightly kissed Junior's cheek. She turned to leave, stopped, started to speak, but said nothing. She simply smiled, took Martin's arm and walked away. As the Watkinses left the room, Wyatt turned to the remaining threesome and said, "Y'all go on out to the car. I'll settle the bill."

It had been decided that Colleen and Junior would start married life in the garage apartment—especially as a baby was due, and Colleen might need Ginny's help. It was also the case that Junior had no real earnings—not legal anyway—and Colleen had not had the chance to receive more than two months' teaching pay before Junior put her 'in a family way.' In 1956, pregnancy usually signaled the end of a woman's career—even in teaching. Colleen could just about see out the calendar year before her baby was due. However, the school board wouldn't be any too happy about her pregnancy once it began to show; thus she would probably be fired long before June. So what to do? Colleen shared her concerns with Ginny, who in turn discussed the options with Wyatt. Wyatt was a good friend of the high school principal. They would arrange it that Colleen would resign her position at the end of the autumn semester—with no recriminations.

That settled, it remained only to get Junior into gainful employment. Wyatt was calling in every favor and debt of gratitude owed to him. His second cousin, Merle Floyd, was about to open a new Sears hardware store down in Boone and said he could use a good floor manager. Although it was more than twenty-five miles away, and down winding mountain roads, it would have to do. As for Junior's whiskey business—Wyatt decided his son's moonshining days were over. It was too risky a venture with a new member of the family and would be one less encumbrance now that their family was about to expand even more. No, the still would be left to rust or—better—Wyatt could reveal its existence to the revenuers for a trophy. After all, it wasn't on his land. That would keep Wyatt in the ATF's good books and put Wyatt in even better standing with other whiskey distillers around the county, as there would be less competition. All-in-all, Wyatt reckoned he had sorted Junior's situation as best he could. Now it was up to his son and new wife to make the best they could for themselves.

As the end of the autumn semester drew near, Colleen's trim figure had begun to fill out ever so slightly. Her resignation was announced at a staff meeting, and, true to his agreement with Wyatt, the principal made little of it. Everyone knew that Colleen and Junior had been married and it hadn't taken many people very long to work out the reason behind it. Colleen finished the term with what was left of her dignity reasonably intact. On the last day, her students—with whom she had been popular—gave her a Christmas-cum-leaving present. Colleen cleaned out her desk, stifled her tears, took her possessions out to her car and left. It wasn't just the *job* she was leaving behind—it was her *dream* of being a teacher—an *inspiring teacher*—as well.

Colleen had hoped and dreamt of so much more. Her love of English literature, and especially romantic poetry, had planted within her the seedling of a vine that had desired to intertwine with a soul-mate. But rather than a fragrant wisteria or succulent grape vine, Colleen had found herself enveloped in *toxicodendron radicans,* that bane of wild and wooded areas in the American South: *poison ivy*—in the embodiment of Junior McNair. Whether stemming from simple denial or sprung of her optimism, Colleen nurtured the hope that, however badly their relationship had begun, it could be retrieved. This was her hope. But that hope was based on a relationship of *two* people, each of whom had very different views of their marriage. For Colleen, her marriage to Junior had come as a shock and disappointment—both of which she felt able and willing to overcome. For Junior, however, their marriage had come as a life of permanent probation, lived under the watchful eye of his sheriff father. From Junior's point of view, Colleen's pregnancy was just *bad luck.* Why should it have led to marriage, for God's sake? Why couldn't Colleen have gone home to her parents? As far as he was concerned, there was but one *real* victim in this situation: himself. His freedom and rampant, youthful manhood had been snatched from him—and unfairly—in his opinion. His life of carefree and casual enjoyment had gone from sixty to zero mph with one ejaculation and its aftermath.

Since the wedding, Ginny and Wyatt had invited the newlyweds over to the farmhouse for supper once or twice a week. Junior managed it for two or three weeks and then found himself making the excuse that he had to work late. This translated into his stopping at one or another of his favorite watering holes between work and home, such that, when he finally got back to the apartment, dinner was long over and Junior was 'well-oiled.' It was then that the rows between Junior and Colleen started in earnest. The shouting—mainly Junior's—could be heard next-door in the farmhouse. Whenever Wyatt and Ginny were in the same room and heard Junior's temper explode like a verbal volcano, their eyes would dart towards one another for an instant. Their silence was broken—more often than not—by Ginny, who murmured, "Sounds like Junior's been drinking," usually followed by: "Lord, he better not lay a hand on that child." By "that child" Ginny meant Colleen, but deep inside she also knew that it referred to her unborn grandchild.

At this point, the norm was for Wyatt to grunt and find a reason to leave the room. For both of them, Junior's explosions were a painful reminder of their early days as a married couple. Wyatt, too, had been overly fond of the moonshine distilled by his late uncle, from whom he had learned the art. It was only when an alcohol-fuelled punch cost Ginny and Wyatt their first-born child—a daughter—that Wyatt had sought help. Ginny had upheld Wyatt's plea that she tell the emergency room doctor that she had fallen foul of their milking cow. His part of the bargain was to go to their minister at the time, confess all, and stay away from liquor of any kind. Having been saved from an assault and battery charge by his young wife, Wyatt made good his on part of the bargain. And although he had continued to produce the illegal whiskey—they had come to depend on the added, undeclared income—Wyatt refrained from taking a drink. That was more than twenty-five years ago. Since that time, an uneasy truce had reigned over their relationship—enough so that they could produce two healthy sons; but there was little mutual affection between the two of them. Neither would have considered a divorce—not in those days. It was just accepted that that is the way it was between men and women. Neither really expected to be understood by the other. Marriage was a dutiful relationship, and both husband and wife knew their places. Their family secrets were probably not much different from others in rural America—or urban America for that matter—during that era. Nobody spoke about them—except perhaps in confession: either to a clergyman or a policeman. It all depended on how far things went.

In the days leading up to Christmas, Colleen tried her best to make it a festive occasion for both herself and Junior. That Christmas of 1956, before the baby was born, was still a season of hope for Colleen. Her life had not only changed outwardly, it was also changing inwardly. Thus Colleen used all the energy she found within her first trimester, and the added impetus of the Christmas spirit, to end 1956 on a positive and hopeful note. She did a lot of baking with Ginny, as well as collecting greenery from the mountainside to make wreathes and decorations. Such activities both kept her busy and kept her from thinking too hard about why she was spending her first Christmas ever away from her own family. For his part, Junior played the role of Scrooge. He deeply resented the way in which his 'wild oats' days had been curtailed, but hadn't the reflective ability to see his own hand in it. Instead he turned his resentment on his new wife and his parents. He reckoned someone had to pay for his unchosen domestic life. Thus Junior put the brakes on with all of Colleen's and Ginny's attempts to bring a Yuletide atmosphere to both households over Christmas. The day, which had betokened peace and goodwill for nearly two millennia, passed without evidence of either; the festive air was muted by Junior's brooding, sullen mood which kept Wyatt, Ginny and Colleen on edge.

Junior made it patently clear that he had started the marriage as he meant it to go on; and so began his and Colleen's long, slow, solo dance, each moving to their own private rhythms. The more she tried to reconcile both of them to their fate, the more Junior sabotaged their relationship. Yet Colleen could not let go of her desperate hope that the coming year held the promise of new life—both for her and Junior, as well as the child they were bringing into the world.

However, the promise of new life was broken—if not shattered— on New Year's Eve. Colleen and Ginny had thought it might be a pleasant break from their normal routine to invite some family and friends—including a few of Colleen's now former colleagues from the high school and Junior's new workmates—to a New Year's celebration. It would be a last blast for Junior and Colleen before her advancing pregnancy became too obvious. Once more Colleen, with Ginny's help, had tried to create a cheerful ambience. She had made paper chains, bought some party hats and poppers, prepared food and punch (allowing one bowl to be laced with moonshine), and generally set the stage to welcome in 1957.

This party was the first time that any of Colleen's former workmates—the few who were invited—had met with her and Junior as a married couple. She blushed whenever people referred to her as 'Mrs. McNair.' Junior dutifully, but glumly, shook people's hands, received their congratulations and—for those who had known Junior for some time—endured their nudges and surreptitious winks with regard to Colleen's condition. The gathering was enlivened by Nat King Cole 78s on the McNair phonograph, as well as some rockabilly music played on a record player that accommodated the newer 45s. People wore their silly hats, danced and laughed. Junior seethed.

A spring of holly adorned the non-alcoholic punch bowl. As the party was being held at the county sheriff's house, most of the party-goers availed themselves of this libation. However, some of the male attendees—and a few of the females—made at least two or three visits to the spiked punch.

Colleen steered clear of the intoxicating liquid—and not simply because she was pregnant. On the other hand, Junior made the most of the guests' presence to challenge the watchful eyes of his three family members and drink to excess. Each time he filled his glass he moved out of the reach of Wyatt, Ginny and Colleen. He let jovial members of the party speak to him at length and pretended to listen, all the while becoming drunker and drunker. As midnight drew near, Colleen and Ginny handed out the various party noise-makers. Everyone gleefully accepted them, except Junior. As the grandfather clock in the hallway struck the New Year, the gathered throng noisily shouted, rattled and buzzed. People began to clap each other on the back, shake each other's hands and wish one another a happy New Year.

When one of Colleen's former co-workers, Ray Wilkins, sought to include Junior in the celebration, Junior jerked his arm away and blurted, "Get your fuggin' han's off'a me!" Around the room, people turned to see what the commotion was all about. Their stares made Junior all the angrier: "Whadda fuck is ever'one lookin' at?"

Ray tried to calm the situation by saying to Junior, "Hey, Junior, take it easy. We just wanted you to join in the fun, that's all."

Getting right into Ray's face, Junior spat: "Well, you can just kiss my rosy red asshole, jerk-off! How'sat for some *fun?*"

"Now just a goddamn minute," started Ray, but a straight right from Junior connected with his jaw and sent him sprawling onto the floor.

"Want some more?" bawled Junior.

He was about to move in on Ray when he found his arms pinned behind his back by Wyatt, who had moved swiftly and unnoticed by the group of onlookers. Junior struggled for a moment, but then recognized the strong grip of his father. "That's enough, son. Just calm down."

"Piss ant," Junior threw at Ray as Wyatt pulled him from the room.

Two or three people helped Ray to his feet, while Colleen dipped a napkin in the punch and cleaned the blood from the corner of his mouth, all the while apologizing profusely both to Ray and anyone else within earshot. "Yeah, happy New Year," mumbled Ray.

As Wyatt marched Junior over to the garage apartment, people embarrassedly began to make their excuses to leave. The revelers offered looks of warm sympathy to Colleen as they kissed her cheek or shook her hand, and bade her good night and happy New Year. Colleen forced a smile and nodded.

"Y'all drive carefully, you hear?" called Ginny in a motherly tone as people got into their cars. "Mind them roads—they get awful icy." The drivers flashed their lights and honked their car horns as they drove away. A deathly white glow fell on the frosty ground outside the McNair home. Ginny shivered and quickly shut the door. She placed both of her hands on Colleen's shoulders: "Sugar, I'm so sorry. I don't know what to say... I—I had hoped...God, I'm just so sorry." They hugged one another and lingered in their mutual embrace.

After a moment or two Colleen leaned back, swept her hair away with her hand, and said "Guess I better go check on Jun—my husband." She took her overcoat from a peg in the hallway. As she buttoned it, with her back turned, she softly spoke to Ginny: "I know I'm not what he expected...or *wanted...*"

"Hush, child!" Ginny rushed to Colleen and put her arms around her once more. "Hush! Junior's drunk—that's all. Anyway, it's not *you*, Honey. It's *him*. It's...*us*...McNairs. You're a good woman and wife. Junior don't deserve the likes of you." Colleen wept silently in her mother-in-law's arms.

No more words passed between them until Colleen pulled back from Ginny's strong arms, dabbed her eyes with the cuffs of her overcoat and said, "Well, I better go. I'm sure Wyatt's got Junior settled down by now. Goodnight, Ginny."

"Sleep tight, young'un." They parted and Colleen stepped out into the crisp mountain air, her breath vaporizing in front of her.

Junior was still vomiting in the toilet when Colleen got into their apartment, his retching sounding something akin to a hog in a trough. The bathroom door stood open and Wyatt was standing by Junior with a pot of strong, black coffee. A mug dangled in the fingers of his other hand. "Hey," Colleen offered as she entered.

"Hey, Colleen," replied Wyatt. "Trying to replace the liquor with this stuff," Wyatt made a demonstrative motion with the coffee pot. Wyatt shifted uncomfortably from one foot to the other, bothered both by Colleen's presence and by the memories awakened within himself. "I think he's got most of it out of him," Wyatt stated, staring into the middle distance.

"Thanks, Wyatt. You want me to take over now?" Colleen was mustering a stoical smile. "Might as well, seeing as he's my husband." Junior groaned and spat into the toilet.

Wyatt looked over his shoulder at his son, then back at Colleen. He nodded without speaking, held out the coffee pot and mug for Colleen. As Colleen received them, Wyatt dropped his head to his chest, exhaling loudly. He breathed in deeply, looked again towards the middle distance, searching for words. "He—*Junior*—can be better than this. I know he can." He spoke more in hope than conviction and then strode quickly to the door, disappearing into the night.

Colleen listened to his footsteps on the wooden stairs. She then turned to her husband. She placed the coffee pot on the hand basin, laid her hand on his shoulder, and asked, "Shall we get you cleaned up?"

With a voice hoarse from his own bile, Junior croaked, "Fuck you."

Colleen swallowed her desire for a bitter response. "Honey, it's a new year. Can't we at least *try* to get off to a good start?"

"Don't 'Honey' me!" Junior growled as he pushed himself up from the toilet bowl.

"Let me help y—" Colleen never got to finish her sentence. Her solicitations were met with the same response as Ray Wilkins' earlier. Junior's fist caught her nose and left cheek, just below the eye. Colleen recoiled from the blow, her head hitting the tiled bathroom wall. Her unconscious body slipped to the floor, where Colleen was about to spend her second night—again following Junior's ministrations.

Junior snorted, "Stupid bitch," stepped over her, stumbled to the bedroom and collapsed across the bed.

Colleen came round sometime later. Her head and face ached; she tasted blood. The light was still on, so she slowly stretched her stiff limbs and pulled herself up by the rim of the hand basin. After blinking several times, she once more went through the process of assessing the damage in the mirror on the medicine cabinet: black eye, swollen cheek, and blood caked on her nose, lower face and lips. She lifted her hand and gingerly felt the lump on the back of her head. Colleen ran some water and patted it on her face. Wincing from pain, she cleaned the blood from her nostrils and lips. While leaning on the basin, she looked a long while at her face. Now Colleen understood the look in her mother-in-law's eyes, a look that was more than in the eyes alone; it was more what the term 'countenance' conjures up, for it expresses the person's *soul*. Colleen had been inducted into the guild of women whose countenances had been crafted by the men who possessed them, but did not know how to love them; men who also feared what they possessed: women, *womb*-men, creatures who bore both their brutish assaults and their children. Colleen put the bathmat by the small radiator, took her bathrobe from the hook on the back of the door, wrapped it around her, switched off the light and curled up on the mat to seek what sleep she could find.

New Year's morn dawned icy and clear. Wyatt had left before sunup as his deputies already had their hands full with car crashes and brawls brought on by too much booze. Ginny let the young couple sleep-in a respectable time before calling on them. Seeing the kitchen light was on, Ginny tapped lightly and tried the door knob. Finding it unlocked, she opened it and called softly "Are y'all up?" Snoring was coming from the bedroom, as Ginny rounded the corner into the small kitchen. Colleen was sitting with her back to the door, hovering over a cup of coffee. Her hair hung limply, obscuring her face. "Mornin', Colleen. Happy New Year." Ginny moved towards the table. Colleen didn't respond. "You okay, Hon?" No response. Ginny sat down opposite Colleen and then saw the state of her face. "Oh my God!" blurted Ginny. It all seemed a macabre replay of *that*

morning some four months before: same stage, same set, same actors. The difference this time was that Ginny was less tentative in her questioning. "Did Junior do this to you?" Colleen lifted her bruised face and looked at Ginny with impassive eyes. Elbows on the table, fingers interlaced, Colleen rested her head on the backs of her hands. Ginny got up from the table and charged into the bedroom where Junior was sprawled face down on the bed. She grabbed Junior by the ankle and shook him. "Wake up! Junior, get up!"

Junior, more drunk than hung-over, grunted and stirred. His mother called to him again. "What? Mama, what're you doin' here? What d'you want?"

"Get your lazy be-hind off that bed and get into the kitchen!" Ginny tugged at him again.

"Awright, awright—I'm coming!" slurred Junior. He shifted himself into a sitting position, looked blearily at his mother, tried to smile and said, "I gotta pee bad."

"Fine. Go pee," said Ginny, "but get right into the kitchen when you're done." Ginny went back to Colleen, whose head remained on her hands, her coffee undrunk. The two women heard the toilet flush, and then water running into the hand basin.

The bathroom door opened and Junior ambled towards the kitchen table with a towel in his hands, wiping his face and neck. Stony-faced, Ginny looked at Junior and asked mockingly, "Have you wished your wife a happy New Year?"

"Uh, no," grunted Junior. "Uh, hey Babe, happy New Year." Colleen neither replied nor moved.

"Join your wife and me at the table," ordered Ginny. Junior dragged himself to the table and slumped into a chair.

"Well. Here I am." Junior looked neither woman in the eye.

"You enjoy yourself last night, Junior? Have yourself a good time?" asked Ginny.

"It was all right, I *guess*," drawled Junior. "Hey, can I have some of that coffee?" inquired Junior, when he spied the mug in front of Colleen.

"In a minute, Junior," responded Ginny, adding: "Notice anything different about your wife?" Colleen had dropped her arms onto the table, but her face remained lowered. Ginny placed her hand under Colleen's chin and slowly raised her head, saying, "Honey, show Junior what a good time he had last night." Colleen started to weep.

Upon seeing her face, Junior's eyes quickly flicked back and forth; he shifted in his seat, while his head involuntarily jerked. "What're you saying, Mama? You saying *I* done that?"

"Are you saying you *didn't*?" fired back Ginny.

Junior gave a pained laugh and shook his head in disbelief. "Damn. You womenfolk." Junior again laughed. "What'd you do, Colleen? Drink too much punch and fall down the stairs? Mama, you seem to be forgetting that she also accused me of raping her, which is what got me into this god-awful situation in the first place." Junior again shook his head, muttering to himself, "Man, I just don't believe this."

"You knocked me out cold." This was the first time Colleen had spoken; both Ginny and Junior turned to look at her.

"Like hell I did!" retorted Junior. "Like hell I did. Shit, I was too drunk to do anything. Anyway, if you were knocked out, how'd you know it was me?" Looking pleased with himself, Junior folded his arms across his chest and looked out the window.

"I guess you didn't hit Ray Wilkins either?" offered Ginny.

"I don't know..." began Junior, but Ginny cut him off:

"He wished you happy New Year and you punched him in the face—we all saw it!"

Junior stood up so violently that his chair spilled over. Colleen instinctively withdrew, fearful of another attack. "I don't have to take this shit—from either of you. I'm outta here."

"Just where're you going, Junior?" demanded Ginny.

"Anywhere but here, Mama; anywhere but here." Junior grabbed his coat from the back of the apartment's one easy chair, fumbled around for his keys, and headed for the door, slamming it behind him on the way out. Colleen and Ginny heard the pickup door shut and then the engine being gunned. There was the sound of tires slipping on the frozen ground and gravel, and then a short squeal as the truck tires met the tarmac.

Ginny turned to Colleen. "Let's get some fresh coffee. Have you eaten anything?" Colleen shook her head. "I'll fix us some eggs. Then we'll get you cleaned up." Ginny set about finding the frying pan, eggs and butter. "Colleen, Honey? You know..." she paused, "it was like this for me and Wyatt...back before we had Junior..." she paused again, "...and Frank." Colleen's pregnancy prevented Ginny from saying anything about losing her first child. Ginny threw a large pat of butter into the hot frying pan. The resultant sizzling was a relief from the uncomfortable silence. She cracked the eggs and began frying them. "I think you need to come stay in the house with Wyatt and me...at least until the baby is born." Ginny's words came like a bolt out of the blue, but had the intended effect on Colleen.

"I—I think," Colleen croaked and then cleared her throat, "I think I'd like that."

"It's for the best," Ginny continued, "both for you and the baby. It'll give Junior time to get himself sorted out." Ginny turned the eggs, and grease from the butter spattered. "Junior can stay here in the apartment. We'll get your things out later today." Ginny nodded to herself in approval at her own words.

"I'd appreciate that," sniffed Colleen as she began to cry once more.

"Oh, Sugar! Don't cry—it's gonna be all right!" cooed Ginny from the stove. She put the eggs on the waiting plates and brought them to the table. "Come on, now. Get this into you—but wipe your nose first." She handed Colleen a tissue from her pocket. Colleen blew her nose, smiled weakly, and began to eat the fried egg. Ginny joined her. "We're going to look after you, Honey. We won't let Junior hurt you—or the baby."

Ginny was good to her word. Colleen was ensconced in the farm house by that afternoon. Junior got home at sunset to discover that his wife had moved out. He was torn between showing indignation that the 'womenfolk' had outflanked him and relief that he could go about his life without reference to Colleen. So ended New Year's Day 1957.

The young couple spent the next six months sleeping apart. Junior would join the family for most evening meals—Wyatt saw to this. Due to his being expected at supper, Junior had stopped his drinking on the return home from work. However, he either got plastered drinking beer or moonshine whilst watching TV in the apartment after dinner, or he drove to one of the bars in town. An uneasy quiet reigned over the evening meals which Colleen helped Ginny prepare. Along with the cooking, Colleen spent her days helping with the other chores that her growing belly allowed. Each woman welcomed the other's company for different reasons. Ginny warmly accepted her daughter-in-law's presence as a break from her own isolation. For her part, Colleen welcomed Ginny's motherly solicitude and wisdom—particularly her advice on how to survive men in this mountain region.

The baby was born in early June 1957. Colleen's water had broken while doing the breakfast dishes. She shouted for Ginny, who immediately rang Wyatt, who came and got them in his patrol car—that way Colleen could recline on the back seat if need be—and drove them down to the hospital in Boone. Colleen's labor was intense and Ginny remained with her throughout. Wyatt drove over to Sears to let Junior know that his wife was in the maternity ward and then went back to his office to await the news of his first grandchild.

Colleen found that her exhaustion from labor and giving birth was overcome by the joy of her tiny daughter suckling at her breast: Annabel Lee McNair. Prior to her becoming pregnant by Junior McNair—and even before she had moved to Bransford County—Colleen had already decided what names she would give to any children born to her. If a daughter: Annabel Lee. Through the joining of those four syllables, Annabel's mother had imparted both her romantic—and now melancholic—dispositions to her daughter, much as Junior McNair's sperm had set Annabel Lee on life's course by joining with Colleen's egg.

Junior stopped by the hospital after work to see his wife and newborn daughter. His parents were in the room with Colleen. When Junior appeared in the doorway, Ginny called him in, saying, "Junior, come see the beautiful little girl your Colleen's done brought into the world." Sheepishly, Junior approached the bedside. He looked at the tiny creature sleeping on Colleen's breast.

"Junior, meet Annabel—Annabel Lee," spoke Colleen. "I hope you like the name.... we've, ah, we've never really discussed names, have we?" Junior remained standing over mother and child.

"Well, sit *down*," ordered Ginny. Junior hastily perched on the side of the bed.

"Want to hold your new daughter?" inquired Colleen.

The moment before Junior reacted to the question seemed like an eternity to him. All in a flash, Junior reviewed his options. Part of him reacted as though all of this were a dream—*a nightmare*: "Me?—a *father?*" he thought. Part of him wanted to reject the whole situation as a charade—after all, he hadn't asked to play. And part of him was curious, even fascinated, by this tiny creature who had issued from his loins. Self-consciously, Junior reached out for the infant. Junior received Annabel Lee with both hands and held her stiffly in front of him. "She's uh—she's awful light," remarked Junior.

"She's not going to bite you," chided Ginny, "Put her in the crook of your arm, for heaven's sake!"

Junior did as he was told. Annabel Lee stirred and then sneezed.

"Here. Use this." Colleen offered Junior a tissue.

"Don't rub her face off!" goaded Ginny. Junior blushed and wiped Annabel Lee's nose. "You're gonna have to get used to these things," laughed Ginny.

"Yeah, well, I already got a job—if you ain't forgot," snapped Junior. "I reckon Colleen can handle the baby stuff. Here." He handed Annabel Lee back to Colleen. "I gotta go get me something to eat. See y'all later." And with that Junior left the room. He had made his point.

Once Colleen had left the hospital and returned home, discussion began about her and Junior's getting a place of their own—perhaps closer to Junior's work. Junior's boss, and relative, Merle Floyd, owned a couple of rental houses, and one was just off US 321, not far from Boone. Wyatt and Ginny both hoped that Junior's temper had settled and that he had resigned himself to married life, now that the baby was born. At least Junior's and Colleen's first child had been *born*—and was alive. This was more than could be said of Ginny and Wyatt's first child—of whom they both thought, but never spoke. They would only go so far as to say, "Well, we got through our rough patch of early married life," and that summarized their hope for Junior and Colleen.

It was almost on the anniversary of Annabel Lee's conception that Colleen and Junior moved into their new home. Wyatt and Ginny gave the couple a new television set as a house-warming gift. Colleen had no way of knowing at the time, but as with so many housewives, that electronic box would become more of a companion than she would have dared admit. But that was all to come.

⧗

Colleen's respite from Junior's brutality ended with their moving away from the McNair farm. The six months that she had spent in the house with Ginny and Wyatt, and the civil evening meals, had given everyone the false hope that Junior's temper was under control. Yet without the watchful eye of his parents, Junior lashed out at Colleen both verbally and physically whenever it suited his emotional state. At those times when Junior's assaults left visible marks, they both resorted to the typical lies of couples caught in the vicious cycle of domestic violence: tripping on the stairs, walking into a door, etc. Colleen wasn't the only woman in those parts to bear the stigmas of her man's visitations. She joined the conspiracy of silence that was emblematic of this stoical sorority.

As for Annabel Lee: she was growing into a strong and healthy child; she laughed easily and took delight in the world around her. She lost herself in the nursery rhymes, poems and stories her mother read to her. This set her apart from many of the nearby children whose parents were partly or wholly illiterate. It also put her outside her father's sphere of interests, as Junior's reading was limited to bills, newspaper comics and sports pages. So the child and her mother grew close. What Annabel Lee could neither know nor help was that, simply by *being*, she became a living reproach to Junior for his lust and unrestrained desire. To make matters worse, Annabel Lee daily came to resemble her mother—in both form and beauty. Even at five years of age, no one could mistake that she was other than Colleen's daughter. Yet rather than take delight in his lovely daughter—as some men might—Junior became intolerant of Annabel Lee's approach and childish demands. Being a delight to her mother, Annabel Lee wanted and expected the same from her father. She was unprepared for her father's angry rebuffs and acidic tone of voice. Annabel Lee loved hiding and springing out to surprise her father when he returned home from work. When she ran to throw her arms around him, Junior stiffened, shouting, "Colleen, would you get *your daughter* off'a me?" If Colleen did not respond quickly enough, Annabel Lee received a quick slap—on whatever part of her body Junior could reach. It wasn't long before Annabel Lee hid and stayed hidden when she knew her father was coming home. Mother and daughter became co-conspirators, moving stealthily about the house, to keep Annabel Lee out of her father's path—especially when he first came home from work or had been drinking.

However, a day arrived when Colleen had to leave town for a few days. Her father had had a heart attack, so Colleen arranged to take the bus down to Onslow County to see him and lend a hand to her mother. She went over Annabel Lee's daily routines with Junior. "It'll only be for a few days—'til Daddy gets out of the hospital." Colleen was almost apologetic in tone. Then pleadingly: "Honey, it could be good for you and Annabel Lee. She's such a fine little girl."

"Yeah, we'll see," was all that Junior could muster in response. "Just make sure you're back here in a *few* days. I got my own work to do, if you ain't noticed." Junior threw Colleen's suitcase into the back of the pickup and let himself into the driver's seat.

Colleen helped Annabel Lee into the truck and got in beside her. "Daddy's going to look after his good girl while mommy's away." Colleen patted Annabel Lee's leg. "So you show him just how good you can be, all right?"

"Okay, I will," responded Annabel Lee in a sing-song voice. She then looked expectantly at her father, who simply ignored her, started the truck and roared onto the road.

Once at the bus station, Junior chatted with one of the drivers while mother and daughter sat on a bench in the waiting room. When Colleen's bus was announced she called out to Junior, who responded, "Yeah, hold your horses; I heard it too." He hefted Colleen's bag and carried it to the bus. The two parents stood looking at one another uncomfortably.

As usual, Colleen broke the silence: "Y'all look after one another for me, okay?" Annabel Lee nodded, tears welling in her eyes. "Don't cry, Sweetie. Mommy'll be back soon."

She started to reach out to her daughter, but Junior barked, "Just get on the bus, Colleen; the kid'll be fine."

Colleen wheeled, mounted the steps into the bus and moved along the aisle to a window seat. Junior was already leading Annabel Lee back to the truck, but the child turned one last time to wave to her mother. Colleen blew her a kiss.

When Colleen arrived back home four days later, it was Ginny who picked her up at the bus station. Annabel Lee was with her grandmother. As soon as mother and daughter caught sight of one another, both ran to greet the other. Annabel Lee buried her face in her mother's thighs and squeezed her tightly. She was still clinging to her mother when Colleen tried to walk towards Ginny and the car. Annabel Lee finally responded to her mother's requests to let her move, but the child took hold of Colleen's hand and clutched it firmly. Colleen thought no more of the energetic greeting than that her daughter had truly missed her. All that changed at bath time.

Colleen was bent over the large, claw-footed tub, swishing the water as she poured in bubble bath, while Annabel Lee undressed herself behind her mother. When the child announced that she was ready to be helped over the high rim of the bath, Colleen turned to lift her. Just as she raised Annabel Lee, she noticed the bruising on her daughter's buttocks, thighs, upper arms and shoulders. She stopped in mid-motion, staring at the blackberry-colored blotches on Annabel Lee's milky skin. The child giggled and kicked her feet, chuckling, "Put me down!"

Colleen came to herself and placed Annabel Lee in the warm frothy water. "Sweetheart—how did mommy's darling girl get so many bruises?" Colleen tried to sound nonchalant.

Annabel Lee was gently blowing at bubbles she had in her cupped hands. Without looking at her mother, she said, "Don't know."

Now over her initial shock at the sight, Colleen's heart began to race. She tried to maintain a calm voice, but unsuccessfully, as her vocal chords were constricting: "Well, Sweetie, you've got quite a *lot* of bruises."

Annabel Lee was now rocking back and forth in the tub and starting to hum in a tuneless fashion. She broke her humming to say, "I think I fell down," and then went back to humming.

Colleen tried again: "But the bruises are *all over you*, Honey..." She paused. "Did daddy hit you?"

"Not sure," mumbled Annabel Lee through her bubbles; and then, softly, as though speaking to the bubbles: "I'm not supposed to say."

Colleen was swiftly on her feet. "Mommy'll be back in a minute, Sweetie."

Junior had arrived home while Colleen was preparing the bath, and was now drinking a beer and watching television as Colleen swept into the living room. "Where the hell's supper?" Junior fired at her.

Ignoring his question, Colleen returned his fire: "Junior, just what have you been doing to Annabel Lee? She's covered in bruises."

"Yeah, well, welcome back. Good to see you, too," he answered sarcastically.

"Why is your daughter covered in bruises? Answer me!" Risking one of Junior's backlashes, and within his arm's reach, Colleen hovered over him.

Without taking his eyes off the television, Junior breathed in slowly, exhaled and said, "Oh, so she's *my* daughter now? Well, let me put it this way: *Your* beloved daughter is a pain. The goddamn kid was in my way half the time. The other half, she didn't do *what* I told her *when* I told her. The kid's gotta learn some discipline. You're too soft on her, is the problem. Besides, nothing's broken."

"That's not the point, Junior. She's just *five*; she's a *child—your* child."

"So you keep tellin' me," interjected Junior.

"And if it was just a matter of 'discipline,' why'd you tell her not to say anything to me?" queried Colleen.

"Because I knew you'd shit yourself, just like you're doing now. So shut up and let me watch this program, unless you want some of what I gave your beloved Annabel Lee."

Colleen started to say something else, but checked herself when Junior shot her a glare that was a warning sign she knew too well. She backed away from him and returned to the bathroom.

Annabel Lee stood shivering with a towel wrapped around her. "Is Daddy going to hit me because I told you?" she whispered in childlike earnest.

"No, sweetheart, he's not," Colleen spoke more in hope than fact.

"Why doesn't Daddy like me?" sniffed Annabel Lee, holding onto her tears.

"Oh, Baby!" Colleen pulled Annabel Lee close to her. "He does like you… he just… Well, he… I don't know…" Colleen's voice trailed off. "But *I* love you—I don't just 'like' you; and I'm going to take care of you. I won't go away without you again. I promise." As Colleen knelt on the cold bathroom floor, the chill revived her memories of other nights spent lying on tiles and she shivered involuntarily. "Let's get your pajamas on. We'll both catch our death of cold in here!" Mother and daughter retreated to Annabel Lee's bedroom.

The sad fact was: that although mother and daughter could *retreat* to Annabel's room, they couldn't actually *escape*. Junior found both his wife and his daughter to be annoyances to him, but at the same time he needed them to be in his presence so that he could observe the impact he had on both. Like some potentate from ancient times, Junior reveled in the power of fear he held over his subjects. If Colleen and Annabel Lee spent 'too much' time in the bedroom reading stories or out in the backyard playing games, Junior concocted some reason to bring them back within his purview. He liked watching them lose their playful abandon and fall under his morose and menacing spell—particularly when he had been drinking heavily.

As the years went by, it almost seemed that Colleen's beauty drained from her face and body and into those of her daughter. As Annabel Lee entered into early adolescence, Colleen spent more time brushing her daughter's hair and helping her with her skin, than she spent on herself. Colleen's once lush auburn hair had become limp and stringy, to the point that she mainly kept it tied back in a bun—giving her a prematurely elderly look. Her eyes, which had been enhanced by her hair, had acquired the same impassive look that she had first seen in Ginny. And her face—once so attractive—now bore the scars of her time with Junior.

Conversely, Annabel Lee positively glowed—when she wasn't in her father's presence. Yet, despite the paucity of time spent around her father, she could hide neither her beauty nor her advancing womanhood. And Junior noticed both; and he was filled with mixed revulsion and lust. Annabel Lee was blissfully naïve and only interpreted her father's stares as the look of habitual anger and disdain. But Colleen saw what lay beneath the surface. As a woman who had known what it was like to be found attractive to men, Colleen could only hope and pray that her unease and sense of dread were unfounded.

Dying Time

I wasted time, and now doth time waste me.
Richard II

Even the strongest of home-made liquors those Appalachian Mountain hollows produced could not dent Junior's growing self-loathing. When he wasn't at work, he was drinking—at bars in town, road-houses outside of town (when he wanted to get laid), and at home (when he had no other option). Once in his house, taunting his wife and daughter became his main occupation.

Junior hated having any place in 'his' house inaccessible to him: including the bedroom of his pubescent daughter—as well as the bathroom, regardless of who was in it. Junior had long noticed Annabel Lee's budding breasts and increasingly shapely hips and legs. His daughter had also begun to experiment with make-up which—as with so many adolescent girls—added a year or two to her looks. Junior found more and more excuses to burst 'accidentally' into the bathroom when Annabel Lee was bathing; he found reasons to throw open the bedroom door and ask a question when she was dressing or getting ready for bed. He enjoyed her discomfort and self-consciousness, as well as the powerful and guilt-ridden stirring in his loins as he stared at her and smirked, "Sorry."

Colleen was painfully conscious of the dynamic that was developing in the household. She tried to get Junior to be more thoughtful about their daughter's dawning womanhood, to give her more consideration before barging into her bedroom or the bathroom. Junior's only response was, "I don't see either of you paying the rent. As the song goes, 'I'm paying the cost to be the boss.' You don't like my rules; y'all can find your own place." Junior had no idea how many times the thought had passed through Colleen's mind. But Colleen's work outside the home was unpaid—she mainly helped Ginny with various chores on the McNair farm, and was paid in kind with the fruits and vegetables they had canned. She often wondered whether she could go back to teaching. But in these parts, once a woman married—not to mention had a baby—her career was as good as over—even in 1969. She dreamt about leaving Bransford County and rejoining her parents in coastal North Carolina—perhaps she could help them run the motel? Yet at some level she knew that her will was broken: Junior had beaten and tongue-lashed it into meek and servile submission. The path out of her situation seemed a Sisyphean task and her dreams shattered, as against the huge boulder she would have to push up a forbidding hill. She was only thirty-five years old, but felt that—except for her daughter—her fruitful years were nearly over. Colleen's reason for living was to see Annabel Lee finish high school and leave the sphere of her father's influence. Yet that influence was far more than geographical; it was more so a contagion whose infection travelled with its host; and its outbreak was imminent.

For the most part, Annabel Lee was unaware of the tug of wills that was being waged by her parents. She went to school, got involved in a few extra-curricular activities, attended church on Sundays and a youth group on Sunday nights. Even as a young teen, she still delighted in having her mother read to her in the evening before going to sleep. It remained a special time—and refuge—for both mother and daughter. But, not unlike the unsuspecting Pompeians who lived beneath the shadow of Vesuvius in early 79 AD, their lives were about to change irrevocably.

The pressure within Junior McNair had been mounting for years. Giving his wife a good beating, administering the odd slap to his daughter, getting his rocks off with local hookers or old flames, only managed to postpone the volcanic eruption in Junior—but such diversions never altered the inevitable course of events.

One evening Colleen was later than usual getting back from the McNair place. Junior arrived home from work with the remainder of a six-pack in his hand. As Colleen was not home, he demanded that Annabel Lee make herself useful and fix him some dinner. His daughter complied in silence. Junior finished the six-pack with his meal, and then demanded that Annabel Lee go to the garage refrigerator and fetch him some more beer. Once more the girl obeyed.

Having brought the beer to her father, Annabel Lee said, "I'm going to have a bath now."

"Yeah, you do that," smiled Junior. Annabel Lee went to her room, collected her night clothes and went into the bathroom.

"Don't use all the hot water," shouted her father after her.

About a half-hour later, Annabel Lee emerged from the bathroom, wearing her pajamas and dressing gown, towel in hand and still drying her hair. "Come over here," called Junior. Sheepishly, Annabel Lee's bare feet softly padded across the floor to within a few paces of her father. Like a slave girl in a harem her eyes were fixed firmly on the floor. "Cat got your tongue?" asked Junior. Annabel Lee shook her head and kept her eyes subserviently on the floor. "Come over here, girl," coaxed Junior. Annabel Lee took a few tentative steps towards her father. "Come on, I ain't gonna bite." Junior motioned her closer. Annabel Lee was within an arm's reach of her father when she stopped. "Sit here," said Junior, patting his lap. His daughter didn't move. In an instant, Junior's arm shot out, grabbed Annabel Lee and pulled her onto his lap. "Now, ain't this cosy?" he taunted. Annabel Lee sat in mute terror on her father's lap. Junior patted his daughter on her backside: "You're growing up, ain't you, girl? You had any boys trying to get in your pants?" Junior laughed and his alcohol-laden breath and noxious comments caused Annabel Lee to turn her face away in panic and deep discomfort. "Whassa matter girl? You scared of your daddy?" Junior reached for the beer can on the side table. "Here, have some of this—it'll relax you." Still mute, Annabel Lee shook her head. "Your mama's not here to tell you off. Have a little drink with your old man." Annabel Lee started to get up, but Junior pulled her back onto his lap. "Whoa, little lady; not so fast! This is my party and you don't leave 'til I say so. Now have a drink with your daddy." Junior shoved the beer can into his daughter's face.

"No!" was all Annabel Lee could muster as she struggled to get off her father's lap. Junior was becoming aroused as she squirmed on his lap, trying to resist him.

"Well I say you're gonna have a beer with your daddy!" growled Junior as he grabbed her jaw and forced her mouth open. "Now drink it!" Annabel Lee coughed and spewed the beer from her lips, which only further enraged and excited her father. In a swift movement, Junior had her off his lap and onto the armchair, straddling her. "Open wide," he commanded as he squeezed her nose tightly thus forcing her to open her mouth. "Just a mouthful at a time—and be sure to swallow it!"

Annabel Lee gulped, swallowed and coughed as Junior poured in mouthful after mouthful of beer. She tried to utter the words: "Don't…like…it," but they were lost in the gurgling noises emanating from her throat.

"That's it," cooed Junior, "that's daddy's good girl."

When the can was finished, Annabel Lee caught her breath and shouted, "Let me go!"

"Now where would you wanna go?" teased her father. "This party's just getting started! We're gonna have us a lot of fun yet."

"I feel sick," groaned Annabel Lee, and she struggled again between her father's legs to get free. Junior was now fully aroused.

"Now look what you done," said Junior, with feigned surprise, as he pointed at the bulging erection in his trousers. "You do that to your daddy and now you just want to get up and leave? That just ain't gonna happen."

"Please let me go to my room," begged Annabel Lee, as she started to cry.

"Well, that's the first good idea you've had," quipped Junior. He stood up, snatched Annabel Lee off the chair and marched her into her bedroom. He slammed the door behind them and pushed his daughter onto the bed.

"Daddy...please..." Annabel Lee broke off her plea, as she didn't know what to ask or what to expect.

"'Daddy *please*,' you say? Well, that's a good girl. And daddy's gonna *please* you." Junior now exposed himself and approached the cowering Annabel Lee. She was openly bawling now and frantically shaking her head. "Why don't you show your daddy what you been parading around the house the last year or so?" As Junior reached for his daughter's dressing gown, her panic was released in a piercing shriek. With that, Junior slapped her hard across the face, saying, "Scream again young'un and there'll be worse." The next few minutes were a fetid mixture of sobs, blows, whisperings and groanings as Junior brutally violated his daughter.

Neither father nor daughter heard Colleen pull into the drive or come in the front door. Satiated with alcohol and lust, Junior had fallen into a stupor on his daughter's bed. Annabel Lee had passed out from the trauma. As Colleen called their names and walked through the house searching for father and daughter, nothing—no *thing*— could have prepared her for what she found. She found it curious that lights were on and the television was flickering, but beyond that there was silence. Colleen finally made her way to Annabel Lee's room and, after knocking lightly, opened the door. She stopped in mid-gait as though hitting a glass door. Junior lay across his daughter's lower torso, his trousers and underwear around his ankles. Annabel Lee's head, her face bruised and swollen, hung partially off the bed. Colleen, in stunned silence, took in the scene in mental slow-motion.

Annabel Lee's dressing gown was pulled open, her pajama top was pushed up to her neck and her breasts were exposed. Her initial shock gave way to a rush of adrenaline and Colleen virtually leapt across the threshold to the bedside. She rolled Junior off her daughter and frantically began patting Annabel Lee's face.

"Honey—what's happened? Are you all right?" Annabel Lee only groaned. This, at least, allayed Colleen's fears that her daughter was dead. She gently shook Annabel Lee, whose glazed eyes stared vacantly back at her mother's searching gaze. "Annabel Lee? Oh Baby—what's happened?" As Colleen helped her sit up, Annabel Lee caught sight of her father's body draped across her bed. She let out a shriek and threw her arms around her mother.

With this, Junior began to stir. He snorted, breathed deeply and exhaled. He then licked his lips, coughed and looked over at mother and daughter. "What's all the goddamn commotion?" Annabel Lee buried her face into her mother's midriff and wept hysterically. Junior rubbed his eyes and began to push himself up from the mattress. He then became conscious of the fact that his genitals were exposed. "Well, damn!" he said in a good-natured, still-far-from-sober way, tugging at his trousers. "Would you just look at me?" Junior smiled sheepishly at Colleen.

"You bastard!" growled Colleen, "You sick, sick bastard!"

"Now it seems I heard all that before...Lessee...Now when was that?"

Breaking free from Annabel Lee's clutch, Colleen began slapping and hitting Junior with all her might and fury: "Bastard! Bastard! Bastard!"

The blows quickened Junior's mind and reactions. His hands caught Colleen's arms by the wrists as she attempted to strike him again. "Bastard, huh? That what you think—*bitch*? Why don't you check my parents' marriage license, eh? I think you'll find that little ol' Junior McNair is as legitimate as they come in these parts." Colleen struggled against his tightening grip. "You wanna play a little rough with me? Is that what you want? You want to slap me again, do ya? I can play rough too. Let's see how you like a little slap." Junior gave Colleen a full swing, catching her face with his open right palm. The sound of the slap set Annabel Lee off with hysterical crying again. Colleen, stunned from the blow to her face, began instinctively to touch it with her hand when Junior's left caught the other side of her face. Her head recoiled from the impact. "See? Two can play your little game. Now, are you gonna calm down or would you like some more?"

Still dazed from the two blows, Colleen shielded her face and shook her head in disbelief: "How *could* you?"

"How could I *what?*" mocked Junior. "Just what do you think I've done?"

"You know full well what you've done," spat Colleen. "It wasn't enough that you had to rape me—now it's your own daughter!"

"Damn! This is one of them, whaddaya call 'em, *deja vus*? I swear! I remember hearing all this shit from you a few years ago! And just what makes you think it was rape? A girl can wiggle her ass around and shake her stuff all over the house—how do you know *she* didn't start it?"

"Just like *I* did, right Junior?"

"Damn straight, just like you did! As I remember, *you* invited *me* in that night and I didn't have to force no alcohol down your throat either! So don't tell me you didn't want it." Annabel Lee was still crying convulsively. Junior snapped at her: "Would you shut your mouth?! Goddamn, you're making some kind of racket!" Junior slapped Annabel Lee's thigh hard with his right hand while still restraining Colleen with a twist of her wrist: "Just stop it—now!" The girl flinched and curled into a ball. "Fucking women!" Junior pushed Colleen over onto the bed and got up. "I need me another drink." He pointed threateningly at Colleen and their daughter: "You two bitches had better just calm down if you know what's good for you." Junior gave them a menacing look for good measure as he finished hitching up his trousers. He then turned and closed the bedroom door firmly behind him as he left. Colleen heard the door from the kitchen to the garage being opened and then closed moments later. Next there was the spewing sound of a beer can being opened. Junior was talking to himself, cursing his women and swearing his disbelief.

Meanwhile Colleen cuddled her distraught daughter and considered their options. She stroked her daughter's sweat-matted hair: "Shssh, Sweetie, shssh. You've got to calm down. Daddy's not himself and we don't want to upset him any more, do we?" Colleen's mind raced: "What to do next? Could they get out of the house? What would Junior do? Could she take the pickup without Junior's stopping them?" Colleen sat there for what seemed an eternity. She heard Junior belch, followed quickly by the sound of a beer can being tossed across the living room. Then came the sound of yet another beer being opened. Colleen knew she had one chance: Junior would have to relieve himself eventually. As Annabel Lee was nearly catatonic, all Colleen could hope to do was get to the phone and ring Wyatt. Meanwhile she continued to comfort her battered and violated daughter. They remained imprisoned in Annabel Lee's room; held both by their disbelief and disgust at what had transpired there, as well as their fear of the man who would possibly repeat his deeds. Another loud belch came from the living room; followed by footsteps going towards the toilet.

When Colleen heard the door close, she slipped out of Annabel Lee's bedroom and tip-toed past the bathroom to her and Junior's bedroom. She could hear the sound of Junior's urine cascading into the toilet bowl. She quietly closed the door to their room and, hands shaking, dialed the number of Wyatt and Ginny. Colleen felt a silent prayer was answered when Wyatt picked up the phone. He had barely spoken when Colleen interrupted him: "Wyatt, it's Colleen. I don't have time to say much. You've got to get over here—fast! It's

Junior—he's out of control. He's attacked Annabel Lee and me...It's awful. Please hurry..."

At that moment the bedroom door burst open. Startled, Colleen slammed the receiver down. "What the fuck you doing? Who you talking to?"

"Noth—nobody," Colleen stammered. "I wasn't talking to anybody, I..."

"Like hell you weren't!" Junior charged into the room and grabbed Colleen by both arms. "Who was it? I heard you talking, woman—now who was it?!"

"Junior, I—you're *hurting* me, Junior. Please let me go!" Junior shook Colleen violently. "Tell me who you was callin', goddamnit!" Junior let go of Colleen with his right hand and slammed a fist into her face. There was a crack as the cartilage in her nose gave way and blood poured down her face. Slinging Colleen around like a rag-doll with his left hand, Junior slapped back and forth across her face. "Who'd you call? Tell me or you'll get more!" Still gripping her tightly, Junior whipped Colleen away from the bedside table. He jerked open the drawer and pulled out the .38 revolver that he kept there. He waved it in front of Colleen, saying, "I thought maybe you wanted *this*." Colleen only shook her head. "Naw? Well, guns ain't for nice little English teachers, now are they? And even if you did want it," Junior's voice took on a sing-song quality, "*I got it now*. And I think it might help me do some persuading—don't you?"

Colleen began to cry, sobbing, "Don't, Junior. Please don't!"

"Oh, you think I'm gonna shoot you, don't you? Naw, Baby, I tole you I'm just gonna use it to persuade you a little—like *this!*" Resembling the snap release of a football, Junior slammed the revolver into Colleen's face. And then again with a backhand. "This might help you remember who you called." Colleen tried to shield her face with her one free hand. This pathetic gesture only engendered more anger and disdain in Junior. With even greater force he struck the backs of her fingers with the weapon. Bones cracked. Colleen began to wail. This was echoed by the sound of their daughter who could hear the melee from her room. "Goddamn cry-babies!" raged Junior. In several quick movements he slapped Colleen's head with the .38. Her scalp was torn and bleeding. She sagged to the floor under the fury of his blows.

"Mama!" A bruised and dazed Annabel Lee stood in her parent's bedroom doorway. "Daddy, please don't hurt Mama!"

From her hands and knees on the floor, Colleen hoarsely whispered to her child, "Honey, please don't come in..."

"Listen to your mama, you whiney little piece 'a shit." Junior pointed the revolver at her. "We've had our party," snorted Junior. "This'un's just for adults." Junior looked at his daughter: the hollow eyes, bruised cheeks, lips and arms, the spots of blood below the waist of her white cotton nightgown. He pulled the hammer back on the .38 and aimed it at her forehead: "Now git!" Annabel Lee turned and fled to her bedroom.

Junior spurned his daughter like a modern-day Amnon—King David's son—who, having lusted over his sister for years, when he finally possessed her, came to hate her with the same intensity with which he had previously desired her. But in Junior's case, it was not his *sister* that he had raped—it was his *daughter*, the issue of his own flesh and blood.

With all of the shouting and crying, no one had heard Wyatt enter the house. Having been called to more than one case of domestic violence over the years, Wyatt moved steadily and quietly through the house. From the living room he could see Junior standing over Colleen, who was crumpled on the floor by their bed. Wyatt noted the revolver in Junior's hand and slowly removed his weapon from the holster. He flipped off the safety. Junior spoke to the inert form on the floor at his feet. "Now...where'd we get to? Oh, you were about to tell me who you called on the phone." He placed the heel of his shoe on her broken fingers and began slowly to grind them.

"She called *me*." Wyatt spoke in a firm, but calm voice.

Startled, Junior turned to the sound of the voice, and Colleen lifted her battered, bloody face as though towards the sun. "Daddy?" Junior blurted in puzzlement. He then turned back towards Colleen: "You called my daddy? You conniving bitch!"

Junior lifted the gun-hand as though about to strike her again, when Wyatt barked, "That's enough!"

At the sound of her grandfather's voice, Annabel Lee had come to her bedroom door and parted it slightly. Upon seeing Wyatt, she opened it fully. "Grandpa! Daddy's being mean to Mama and me!"

Wyatt was taken aback by the condition of his granddaughter. He turned towards Junior, motioned to both Colleen and Annabel Lee, and asked, "Son, just what in the hell have you been doing here?"

The bloody pulp, which had once been Colleen's face, let out a gut-wrenching bawl: "*He — fucked — his — own — daughter!*" Each word was spat out with blood and saliva, admixed with the poison with which Junior had infected her very being. Wyatt winced—as much from the sight of his daughter-in-law as from her words. His eyes moved from Colleen to his granddaughter. Annabel Lee stood in her bedroom doorway, eyes sunken in her face, glistening mucous running from her nose and down across her lips and chin. There was blood on her night-gown—below the waist; and there was blood running down the insides of her legs.

"Shit, Daddy. I didn't mean nothin' by it. I'm just a little drunk—that's all. L-let's, let's just forget the whole thing, awright?" Junior sighed heavily. "I mean, they'll be right as rain...in a few days." Junior was motioning drunkenly from Colleen to Annabel Lee with the revolver he still gripped in his hand. The revolver had clotted blood and hair on it—Colleen's.

"Junior, put the gun *down*. Now." The lack of hoped-for compassion in Wyatt's voice made its way through the testosterone and alcohol-induced haze in Junior's mind. It finally dawned on him that he was in trouble—serious trouble.

"You gon' arrest me, Daddy? Y'own boy? You gon' arrest *me*, put me in jail an' all that?" Junior's thumb slipped back the hammer. "Daddy...I mean, *Sher'ff*." Junior snorted. "I can't be lettin' you 'rest *me*. Shee-ut. It wasn't s'posed to happen this way. Unh-unh, no way. So I say *you* get out. This is my fuckin' house and my fuckin' women. So *you* get out! You ain't welcome here."

"Goddamnit, son. Put the gun *down*." The hand with the revolver slowly rose towards Wyatt. It was the last time Junior raised his hand against anyone. Wyatt squeezed the trigger and put a bullet through Junior's head. He dropped in a heap next to Colleen, knocking the lamp off the bedside table on his way down. After the report of the bullet exiting the barrel and Junior's collapse, all that could be heard was the gulping and low, convulsive groaning of Colleen, as she watched Junior's blood ooze onto the floor beside her. Annabel Lee stood transfixed, not uttering a sound. The various fluids emanating from her body said it all.

Frumpy Time

When in the chronicle of wasted time
I see descriptions of the fairest wights,
And beauty making beautiful old rime,
In praise of ladies dead and lovely knights.
                    Shakespeare, Sonnet 106

Colleen was released from the hospital ten days after the events of what, from thenceforth, was simply known as 'that night.' Her hand was in a cast and her face was stitched and still swollen. Annabel Lee had been treated in the hospital and released to the care of her grandparents. Neither mother nor daughter ever again set foot in the house they had shared with Junior. Now childless, and aged beyond their middle years, Ginny and Wyatt had collected all of Colleen's and Annabel Lee's things and brought them back to their house; Junior's they burned. His body they gave for medical research. There was never even a memorial service for his passing. Pastor Dugdale had come around and tried to talk Wyatt and Ginny into having a quiet service for their son, but, tight-lipped and ashen-faced, they had both shaken their heads 'no.' They thanked Rev. Dugdale for his concern and Wyatt ushered him to the door with only these words: "He's God's concern now."

As the days rolled on from that night, Wyatt took to working later and later—often missing meals. He lost weight and just chuckled softly at himself when he had to punch another hole in his belt to keep his trousers up. Whenever he was at home his reticence was engulfing. He seemed to be in a constant reverie and always took a while to return to the present moment when Ginny, or anyone else, spoke to him. Ginny was afraid that he would start drinking again, but the opposite happened. Wyatt took more interest in the work of the revenuers and helped them close one still after another. He became a figure of both fear and pity in the local community. Fear because of his relentless crusade against the moonshiners and pity because of...*that night.*

Colleen, with heightened self-consciousness due to the scars across her face, became a recluse. She hardly ever ventured to town and stopped going to church. She would occasionally drive Ginny to the store for weekly shopping, but even then stayed in the pickup—scarf around her head and tied under her chin, and wearing sunglasses. Neither Wyatt nor Ginny could interest her in doing much of anything beyond the bounds of their house and property. As Ginny put it to Wyatt one evening: "The light's done gone out in that girl."

As the three adults were ever enmeshed in their own mourning and introspection—over lives and ideals lost—none really had the time to notice that Annabel Lee was suffocating in the midst of it all. She, too, had been traumatized, but she didn't want to ruminate and dwell upon it. Annabel Lee wanted to forget. Her mother's and grandparents' main concern for Annabel Lee—that she might have been impregnated by her father—was relieved when her periods started again as the trauma following the attack began to fade. Gradually, the adults in the house began to give her the space and freedom from their over-concern, which she so craved. In the months following 'that night' Annabel Lee became a more fully-developed young woman. Her genetic code had fully conferred her mother's beauty upon her—and the high school boys took notice—even though she tended to 'dress down' and tried to look more plain, even 'frumpy.' Girls began to use the same adjective as a cruel nickname, as Annabel Lee—'Frumpy'—refused to conform to the hairstyles, make-up and short skirts that were all the fashion. Even boys picked up the nickname, feigning disinterest in her—although for untold dozens, her unadorned beauty was the subject of many a wet dream. For her part, Annabel Lee was both mystified and alarmed by her attractiveness to boys. She couldn't help but notice them dreamily looking at her in class, studying her face and breasts. Thus, in direct proportion to her physical development, she started to wear drab and shapeless clothes. Yet, in the same measure that her mother's light and looks faded, Annabel Lee's reached full bud and flowered; she could do nothing about that. At the same time, Colleen took less notice of her once-beloved daughter. They chatted a bit at meal times, but then Colleen would help with the dishes and go to her room. And for Ginny, who had borne only sons, the burgeoning womanhood of her granddaughter outstripped her ability to offer motherly advice.

It was also the case that Annabel Lee was something of a curiosity for both the boys and girls at her high school. All that was really known of 'that night' was that she had survived her father's drunken attack on both her mother and herself, and that she had sustained her injuries in trying to 'defend' her mother. They knew that Wyatt senior had killed Wyatt junior. No one knew of her rape except for her mother, Wyatt, Ginny and the doctor who had examined her in the hospital. Annabel Lee's bodily wounds were largely confined to bruising, which healed fairly quickly. The inner wounds were another matter entirely.

It wasn't much longer before boys started telephoning and asking Annabel Lee out on dates. On occasion, when Ginny answered the phone, she heard the caller ask for 'Frumpy.' As she told him that he had called the wrong number, the boy would nervously correct himself and ask for 'Annabel Lee.' Ginny, being a proud and protective grandmother, became curious as to why boys were calling her only grandchild 'Frumpy,' so she waited until an opportune time in order to pose the question. It came one evening when Wyatt was working late on a case and Colleen had taken herself to bed early. As often happened, Annabel Lee did her homework in front of the wood-burning stove in the living room. Having finished tidying the kitchen, Ginny came in to join Annabel Lee by the fire. Annabel Lee looked up from her books, smiled at her grandmother, and turned back to her work. They both sat quietly for a few minutes, and then Ginny—still wearing her apron—smoothed the fabric across her knees and finally broached the subject. "Annabel Lee?" The girl looked up from her schoolwork. "A couple of times, when…when I answer the phone, boys have…well…they've asked for 'Frumpy.' Why do they call you that?"

Annabel Lee smiled at her grandmother and shrugged, "It's just a nickname, I guess."

"Yes, Sugar, but 'Frumpy'? You're anything but *that*; you're a beautiful girl."

"Yeah, well, I guess it's the way I dress. I mean, I don't wear all the fashionable clothes and make-up that a lot of the girls wear." She paused for a moment: "They just took to calling me 'Frumpy.' I don't really mind."

Ginny sighed heavily. "Well, I wish they wouldn't—and they'd better not do it around me or your grandfather. That's all I got to say." Ginny turned her gaze to the flickering light from the woodstove; Frumpy returned to her school work.

Ginny tried to engage Colleen in discussions about Annabel Lee, boys and dating—especially with regard to what had happened on 'that night,' now more than a year past. Colleen would only look into the indeterminable distance and say, "Well, she's got to grow up sometime." Whenever Annabel Lee got dressed for a date, she would present herself in front of Colleen and Ginny for their approval. Colleen would smile weakly, pat her daughter's cheek, and say, "Just be careful."

By the time Annabel Lee was seventeen years old, and a senior in high school, one young buck had made his way to the top of the heap of suitors: a hothead named Carl Locklear. Carl was from down in the Sandhills of North Carolina. He had been a handful for his widowed mother, so she had sent him to live with her brother and his wife, Melvin and Dora Sanford. Her brother worked in construction and built houses in some of the mountain resorts. She had hoped that Carl might learn the trade from his uncle. Carl drove a souped up '65 ragtop Mustang—bought with some of the meager insurance money left by his father—and was never far from having his license taken away from him. Wyatt and his deputies knew Carl well; but apart from his driving exploits, he had never been on the wrong side of the law in Bransford County. Carl was 'so-so' as a student. He was of average intelligence, but smart enough to know that having an even smarter girlfriend could help ensure passing grades. In fact, Carl's only interest in high school—aside from the girls—was getting out of it. He liked having money and was always tinkering with his car and buying accessories: the obligatory fuzzy dice hanging from the rear view mirror, lake pipes (chrome), zebra-patterned seat covers, and the like. Thus Carl held two or three part-time jobs after school and on weekends, which gave him the appearance of a hard-working lad. His main job was pumping gas and stocking shelves at old man Whitlow's Country Store near Blowing Rock. The truth was that Carl worked only as hard as was required to achieve the bare minimum—and still get paid. He was what the older folks called a 'wild seed;' he had big plans and even bigger talk. Yet it was his smooth talk and fast driving that appealed to Annabel Lee—they made her forget. And Annabel Lee had a lot of forgetting to do. Carl's banter kept her amused, and his reckless driving exhilarated her; both provided a much-needed respite from the funereal atmosphere at the McNair place. At some level Annabel Lee knew that Carl was more interested in her looks and her body than in her brains. Yes, she helped him with homework and tutored him before big exams, but most of these sessions ended with his hand halfway up her skirt and her bra straps undone. Carl was shrewd enough to know that he'd better not go too far with Annabel Lee—at least while she was living under the same roof as the county sheriff—but he took it to the limit, which was as far as Annabel Lee let him go. So their relationship was largely one of mutual need; each providing something the other wanted.

As her senior year in high school progressed, Annabel Lee began to absent herself from the McNair home. She always had a plausible excuse: going to the library, helping other students after school, etc. Colleen would give her usual half-smile when her daughter said that she would be home late, tell her daughter to be careful and then retreat into herself. Ginny and Wyatt each suspected that Carl Locklear was lurking in the background and was the true reason behind Annabel Lee's absence. But the truth was that Wyatt and Ginny no longer voiced their thoughts to one another. Like Colleen, they were locked in their own desert places. All three adults were haunted by death and the ghosts of their memories. And so Annabel Lee slowly but surely made good her escape plans. It was set for graduation day—only a day before Annabel Lee's eighteenth birthday.

Like so many graduating seniors, a party had been planned to follow the commencement ceremony. Naturally Annabel Lee would be going to the party with Carl. Over the last two to three weeks before graduation, no one in the McNair home had noticed that Annabel Lee's dresser and closet had fewer clothes than normally. No one noticed that her gym bag was fuller than it had previously been. By the time graduation rolled around, Annabel Lee had a full week's clothing stashed in the trunk of Carl's car. Thus when Carl drove up to the McNair's house at half-past eight, after the graduation, none of the adults could begin to envisage the changes that lay in store between that night and when they would next see Annabel Lee. Before leaving her bedroom, Annabel Lee had written a letter to her mother, Wyatt and Ginny, telling them what she and Carl were planning—but without giving away the details. She placed the letter on her dresser. Downstairs, Carl was his usual, unctuous self: he 'sirred' and 'ma'amed' Annabel Lee's triumvirate of guardians, assured them that they would take care on this night of revelry for so many graduating teenagers, and then he and Annabel Lee disappeared into the night.

However, rather than heading towards a gathering of their classmates, Carl and Annabel Lee headed out on the circuitous mountain roads that finally connected them with Hwy 321, where they headed south. They were giddy with the cleverness of their plan and how easy it had been to fool Annabel Lee's mother and grandparents. After an hour and a half on the road their giddiness gave way to hunger, so they pulled into an all-night truck stop just outside of Hickory. They tanked up the Mustang and then fuelled themselves up on hamburgers and caffeine so they could stay awake for the rest of the journey.

The steep folds of the mountains gave way to the gently rolling Piedmont as they continued their southward journey towards the South Carolina state line. Their ultimate goal was a small town outside Rock Hill, where Carl had an older married cousin, named Darryl. Darryl and his wife Sherri lived in a trailer not far from the Catawba River. They were both twenty-two years of age and worked at a hosiery mill in Rock Hill. Carl often stayed with them and went fishing on the Catawba. It was also the case that South Carolina had long been the promised land for many an eloping young couple from North Carolina. Not unlike many of those who had preceded them on this journey; the planning, conniving and excitement vastly outweighed the future realities of married life—it could only be imagined as better than life lived up to that point in time.

It was well after midnight when the Mustang's headlights illuminated the mailbox that marked the end of the sandy drive leading to Darryl's trailer, which was set back in the pines. Barking dogs began to emerge from under the trailer as Carl and Annabel Lee pulled up. Darryl opened the screen door and stepped out onto the small wooden porch; behind him and just inside the door stood Sherri. A television flickered in the background. Darryl was in jeans and a white T-shirt and had a can of Budweiser in his hand. Sherri was bare-legged and wearing one of her husband's shirts, which hung halfway between her hips and knees. She ruffled up her long, streaked, peroxide-blond hair and took a drag on her cigarette.

Carl opened the door of the car, got out, stretched and yawned. "Hey, y'all," he said as the other door open and out came Annabel Lee. Carl motioned with his head towards his 'fiancée': "This here's Frumpy—uh, I mean her real name's Annabel Lee. Frumpy's just her nickname from school."

Darryl nodded and said, "Hey." He opened the screen door and offered the beer can to Sherri. "Hold this would ya, Babe, while I help them with their bags."

"Fine," said Sherri, as she took one last drag on her cigarette and flicked it through the open door. "Y'all come on in before the skeeters eat you up." The air was filled with the sounds of tree frogs, crickets, katydids and the hum of mosquitoes; the pungent aroma of the pines was as thick as the night creatures' songs were loud.

Carl and Darryl shook hands, and then Darryl slapped him on the back: "Well, you did it, cuz! Goddamn, if you didn't!" Darryl then offered his hand to Annabel Lee. "Heard a lot about you. Think you can handle this wild child?"

"Oh, he's not so bad," smiled Annabel Lee.

Carl opened the trunk of the car, which was full of an assortment of small bags, and handed two of the bags to Darryl. "Y'all ever hear of a *suitcase*?" wisecracked Darryl.

"Hey, man, we had to *sneak* these things out a little at a time! Didn't want her mama or sheriff grandpa asking questions and getting suspicious, now did we? Main thing is, we *did it* and we're here," retorted Carl.

"Yeah, cuz, you got that right," replied Darryl, ushering Carl and Annabel Lee to the trailer. "It ain't much, Frumpy—all right if I call you Frumpy?—but it's home," offered Darryl as they mounted the porch.

Sherri held the door open for them. "Darryl keeps promising to build us a nice cabin—big enough for us to make some babies." She gave Carl a peck on the cheek and hugged Annabel Lee, saying "Honey, it'll be nice to have you in the family."

"Thanks," said Annabel Lee, adding: "I hope we didn't keep you up. Y'all had to work today, didn't you?"

"Oh, don't worry," reassured Sherri. "Me and Darryl been watching the 'Fright Night' horror films in between dozing on the sofa."

"Let's take these things to your bedroom," suggested Darryl, "'cause there ain't much space in the living room—as you can see." Annabel Lee cast a questioning glance at Carl, who just smiled and shrugged. They were ushered to a small room with a modest double bed. "Here's the bridal suite," chuckled Darryl as he swept his hand in a wide arc. "Y'all want a beer," inquired Darryl, "or are you ready for some rack time? You've had a mighty long drive."

Carl was about to speak when Annabel Lee interjected: "We'd like to get unpacked, wouldn't we, Carl?"

"Uh—yeah, Sweetie. Whatever you say."

Standing in the hallway outside the door, Sherri yawned and said, "Speaking of rack time, Honey, let's leave these two lovebirds alone and get to bed ourselves. Oh—towels are on the chair here and the bathroom's just next door. Y'all sleep well, okay?"

Darryl and Sherri padded down the short hallway to their room, nudging and teasing each other. When Annabel Lee and Carl were alone, she closed the door and nervously fumbled for words: "You...have you told them? Or at least have you told Darryl, that we..."Annabel Lee puffed, "that...you and I haven't ever actually slept together?" Annabel Lee cast her eyes over the bed—which now looked smaller—and then looked upwards at Carl.

"We-ell," drawled Carl, "not exactly... I mean, *come on, Hon*—we're getting married in three days. Tomorrow you're eighteen anyway. What difference is a couple of days gonna make, huh?"

Annabel Lee blushed, cocked her head and considered Carl's words for a moment. "Okay," she said, "but under one condition."

"Yeah, sure, Frumpy—what is it?"

"I don't want to get pregnant right away. Remember, we've talked about my going to Appalachian next year to do teacher's training?"

"Well, uh, okay, um..." stammered Carl.

"You have brought something, *haven't you?*" pressed Annabel Lee.

Carl filled his lungs with air, his chest expanding; then he quickly exhaled: "Well...yeah...um... No."

"Yeah, no?" quizzed Annabel Lee. "Either you brought something or you haven't."

"Haven't," said a deflated Carl, "But I could ask Darryl—he's bound to have some."

"No you won't!" fired back Annabel Lee, "I don't want them to know what we're doing!"

"Well, for Christ's sake Honey, they're *married. They* do it."

"Let's wait then," offered Annabel Lee.

"Wait?! B-but, you've already said 'yes.' And we've waited for nearly a year." Carl began to sound pathetic.

"Well," sighed Annabel Lee, "if it's going to be that big of a deal for you, don't gas stations sell them?"

"Shit, Baby, you want me to drive God knows how many miles back up the road just to buy some rubbers?"

"Aren't I worth it?" coaxed Annabel Lee.

Carl didn't know whether to cry, laugh or scream. His brain was caught between his fatigue from hours of driving and a testosterone attack. He quickly paced back and forth. "Aw, all right then," he growled as he grabbed his car keys and fled the trailer. The Mustang spewed gravel as it shot out onto the highway, following the glow of its headlights towards what, in these parts, sufficed for the local birth control clinic: a filling station men's room.

Annabel Lee was sleeping soundly when Carl finally returned. Exhausted, and still fully dressed, Carl slipped onto the bed beside her and fell promptly asleep. It was just past midday when Carl and Annabel Lee awoke. They could hear the muffled voices of Darryl and Sherri in the kitchen, and could smell bacon frying. Annabel Lee had stirred first. She saw Carl lying next to her fully dressed and began to stroke his hair. Carl blinked, yawned and saw Annabel Lee's smiling face looking at him. "Were you successful?" grinned Annabel Lee.

"Uh…yeah, for all the good it did," Carl grumpily responded.

"Well, it's my birthday today…so perhaps you can use them tonight?"

Carl began to perk up at these words, "Why wait till tonight, birthday girl?"

"'Cause I'm *hungry*, that's why! And I'll bet you are too! Come on!"

Annabel Lee grabbed Carl by the hand and pulled him upright on the bed. He deftly snatched her back within kissing range and pressed his lips against hers. Annabel Lee kissed him passionately in return and let his hands explore her breasts and buttocks. Then she spun deftly out of his reach, and said, "Come on, Mr. Horny, let's get dressed and eat!" Carl pulled his jeans tightly around his erection and thrust his hips at Annabel Lee, who just smiled coyly and began to get dressed.

⌛

"It's about time you two got up," taunted Darryl as Carl and Annabel Lee shuffled into the small kitchen. The clock over the stove read twenty-past-one.

"Y'all sleep well?" asked Sherri as she stood over the stove cooking eggs and bacon.

"Y'all sleep *at all?*" teased Darryl over his cup of coffee. "And hey—did I hear you fire up the Pony and go somewhere after we'd gone to bed?" inquired Darryl with a twinkle in his eyes.

Annabel Lee smiled sheepishly at Carl who blushed and fumbled for words: "Uh, yeah, I…uh…forgot something."

"I'll bet you did!" interjected Darryl, "Had to go to the 'family planning clinic' at the Shell filling station, did you?"

"The *what?*" asked Sherri.

Darryl laughed at his own joke: "The rubber machine in the men's room at the Shell garage. They never lock it."

Now both Carl and Annabel Lee were blushing.

"Oh, leave them alone, Darryl." And then, more to herself than anyone in the room: "At least they show some common sense." Sherri shook her head but was smiling all the while, "Poor things." Sherri swung around with a skillet full of scrambled eggs and bacon. "Y'all better be hungry," she chided.

Annabel Lee and Carl were glad for the change of topic and tucked into the food set before them. "Worked up an appetite then?" fired Darryl.

"Oh Honey, stop it." Sherri made a fist and shook it at Darryl. "I'll tell some stories about you, if you don't." She made a mock grimace at Darryl, who threw up his hands in surrender.

Discussion of Carl's nocturnal ramble was put to rest. As added insurance, Carl piped up: "Hey, everybody—it's Frumpy's eighteenth birthday."

"Well then," drawled Darryl, "happy birthday, girl." Sherri joined in with well-wishes for Annabel Lee. "Now you can get *legally* drunk!"

quipped Darryl, who then added: "Hey Hon, maybe let's all go to The Pier tonight and celebrate."

"What's 'The Pier?'" asked Annabel Lee.

"It's a club built out onto the river," answered Sherri. "They play a lot of beach music and serve good drinks. They also got this sand-covered dance floor where you dance barefoot—just like being on the beach."

"I'm game!" said Carl. "Whaddaya say, Babe?"

"Sure," responded Annabel Lee, "guess I'm only eighteen once."

"Atta girl," came Carl's enthusiastic response.

That decided, the four of them finished their breakfast. Sherri spoke up first, as the last dregs of coffee were drunk: "Darryl and me will clean up in here. Carl, why don't you walk Frumpy down to the dock and show her the boat?"

"Hell, take her for a turn on the river if you like." chimed in Darryl, "It's a nice day, and she's gassed up."

"I might just do that," replied Carl. And then to Annabel Lee: "They got a nice outboard, Babe. Wanna go?"

"Sounds good," answered Annabel Lee, "maybe I can get a little tan for our wedding day."

"Y'all watch out for water moccasins as you go through them woods to the riverbank. They'll be out sunning themselves," warned Darryl. "Our neighbor down the road a piece stepped on one a few weeks ago. He'd been doing some night fishing and stepped on the damn thing as he came up from the river. He thought he'd got caught in some briars when it latched onto his leg, so he was kicking around trying to get free. But his wife, who was with him, felt the snake's tail whipping her legs as he jerked his leg around and knew what the problem was, so she grabbed it by the tail while her husband choked it to make it let go. Between 'em they finally got the damn thing off and she drove him to the county hospital. His leg swole up like a tree trunk and he was sick as shit for about a week. But he's okay now."

"Honey, don't scare 'em half to death," interjected Sherri.

"Yeah, it ain't like I've never been here before," replied Carl, "—and besides, we got timber rattlers up in the mountains. We can look after ourselves."

"Just mind that you do," said Darryl.

Carl and Annabel Lee returned to their bedroom to get their swimming things on before heading out in the boat. "Let me change first," demanded Annabel Lee. "Then you can come in and change."

"Do *what*?!" asked Carl. "I'll look stupid standing out here in the hall. Next you'll be saying we should sleep in different rooms tonight."

"Well," began Annabel Lee, "we aren't married *yet*."

Carl rolled his eyes and threw his head back. "Shit fire and save the matches!" he blurted in exasperation. "Is this about *them*," Carl indicated towards the door, "or about *us*? 'Cause if it's about *them*, then they think we're *already* sleeping together." Annabel Lee looked at the floor. "Hell, we already spent last night in here together—in case you forgot. You ain't getting cold feet, are you?— 'cause I can't take this shit if you are."

"No," she responded softly, "it's just that... Oh, never mind."

"All right then," said Carl, "It's settled. Let's get into our swimming suits." He began to strip down; Carl on one side of the bed and Annabel Lee on the other. Annabel Lee turned slightly to one side and began to undress—tentatively. However, she was fascinated enough to look at Carl in a sidelong glance. He caught her eye and asked: "Like what you see, Babe?" The last—and only—time she had seen a man even partially naked was *that night*—with her father. Annabel Lee shuddered involuntarily. Carl didn't notice: "Hurry up, Frumpy," he urged.

"Um, okay," was Annabel Lee's quiet reply. When she had got down to her under things, she sat on the edge of the bed.

"Want me to help you?" offered Carl, too eagerly.

"No, I do not. I can do it myself," came the firm reply.

"Well, come on then!" shot back Carl as he approached her from the end of the bed. Annabel Lee quickly slipped off her panties and bra and began to slip on her one-piece bathing suit.

Carl let out a whistle and then exhaled heavily, "Whoa, I've been waiting to see *that*! You are really *built*—like the proverbial brick shithouse!" He stood admiring her body with his hands on his hips.

"Carl!" sputtered Annabel Lee as blushed deeply and hurriedly pulled up the straps of her swimming suit. "Was that supposed to be a compliment?" Carl just shrugged.

Meanwhile Carl's penis had sprung to attention. He dropped his swimming trunks in front of Annabel Lee and said: "Look! This is what you do to me, Babe!"

"Don't! Not now!" chided Annabel Lee, keeping her voice low, "Put it away!"

"Man, this is driving me crazy," growled Carl. "How'm I supposed to walk through the trailer with a boner in my swimming suit?!"

"Well, *I* don't know," shrugged Annabel Lee, "maybe just carry a towel in front of you?" Carl harrumphed and grumpily did as he was told.

Already lethargic from the early summer day's heat, Darryl's and Sherri's dogs lazily looked up from their midday naps as Carl and Annabel Lee made their way down the sandy path to the riverbank, where the boat was tied to the mooring post of a small dock. They swished at mosquitoes as they went. "They won't bother us out on the river," Carl informed Annabel Lee.

Spanish moss hung off the live oaks and cypress trees which grew out into the marshy edges of the river. The pungent aroma of wisteria and honeysuckle hung heavily in the air. Carl helped Annabel Lee into the small boat and then slipped in beside her. He primed the outboard motor and then gave it a crank. It coughed, sputtered and then caught. A Kingfisher on the opposite bank was startled and took flight from its hunting perch. Carl revved the motor a few times until it began to purr and then cast off from the dock. They headed out onto the murky waters of the Catawba, the sun shimmering on the ripples and on the wake they left behind. "Man, this is the life," exclaimed Carl. He then let out what passed for a Rebel yell. Fishermen on the far bank looked up. Carl just gave them a lazy wave and sped down the middle of the river. "Wouldn't you just love to live on a river like this?" Carl asked more to himself than to Annabel Lee. "Love to have me a house on a river—*and* a house at Myrtle Beach. Now that would be the life." Carl was shaking his head with a wide grin as he imagined his ideal life. "What about you, Babe? Would you like that?"

Annabel Lee nodded, "I always liked it when Mama took me down to Onslow County to see my other grandparents. You know?— they got that motel outside Swansboro, near Bogue Inlet? It's pretty there. Maybe we can go see them sometime—after we're married."

Carl slowed the boat and cut the motor; they drifted along with the slow current. The only sounds were bird calls and the water lapping gently against the hull. Carl threw their towels in the bottom of the boat. He slipped off his seat and then reached up to Annabel Lee. "Let's get comfortable."

She let herself be drawn down next to him, saying, "Okay, but don't get too fresh—not out here in the middle of the river!" They kissed and cuddled until Carl's swimming trunks were bulging again. "There you go again," chided Annabel Lee.

"Can't help it, Babe. It's what you do to me," said Carl with blatant satisfaction as he looked at the miniature pup-tent over his loins. In one quick motion Annabel Lee threw her arm over the gunwale, scooped a handful of water and splashed it on Carl's groin. The cold water took Carl's breath away. It wasn't the only thing the water took away. "Shit! Hot a'mighty!" uttered Carl. "What'd you do that for?"

"Didn't want you getting over-excited," grinned Annabel Lee.

"Whoa," uttered Carl as he tried to pull the soaked bathing trunks away from his traumatized penis. "Damn, girl. You're something else, you really are!" Carl shook his head in disbelief and self-pity as he got back onto his seat and pulled the lanyard to restart the engine. Annabel Lee reflected upon Carl's desire for her and the shortening hours of her 'virginity'—as Carl knew it. She had heard girls back at the Bransford High locker room speaking in excited, hushed tones about who had lost her 'cherry' and to whom. Thankfully, Annabel Lee had never been the object of any of their chatter, but she did wonder exactly how the boys knew who was a virgin or not—and would Carl notice tonight? All she hoped for as the afternoon progressed was that the events of this night would somehow blot out the memories of *that night*. Her heart fluttering and her gut tightening, Annabel Lee felt herself to be a bundle of contradictions: excitement and anxiety, hope and fear.

Before she knew it, Carl was easing the motor boat up to the dock. He cut the motor and they coasted up to the wooden mooring post. "I'll jump out first," instructed Carl, "and then you throw me this line," holding it in front of Annabel Lee. She nodded, still coming out of her reverie. She tossed the line to Carl, who deftly tied the boat to the dock and then helped his soon-to-be bride out of the boat. Carl grabbed Annabel Lee and kissed her hard while letting his hands roam about her body. "I can't wait till tonight"—his words filled with urgency.

"Well, you'll *have to wait*," responded Annabel Lee as her hands chased his. "Let's try not to get too worked up out here in the open." This time she gave herself liberty to pat Carl's bulging trunks. "Look at you," she giggled; pulling free of his grasp and then adjusting the straps of her swimming suit, her erect nipples showing through the thin material. Carl stood gazing at her, his eyes once again full of lust. Annabel Lee modestly draped a towel around her neck and discreetly over her breasts. "Hmm," she uttered, while making a mock frown at Carl's manifest arousal. "Better carry your towel in front again," she instructed him, "just to be safe!"

They walked back up the path to the trailer—the sand fine, warm and comfortable beneath their bare feet. As they mounted the squeaky wooden stairs to the porch, they could both hear and smell chicken being fried through the screen door. Sherri was standing over the stove, her right hand holding a fork and her left on Darryl's waist, as they both swayed to the Drifters' "This Magic Moment," occasionally bumping bottoms and laughing. "Hey y'all!" they both shouted over the shoulders, never missing a beat to the music.

Darryl had a beer in his left hand; he lifted it over his head and said: "Y'all want a drink? There's plenty of beer in the refrigerator." As "This Magic Moment" reached its climax, Darryl took the fork from Sherri's hand, set it by the stove, and spun his wife around while singing with the Drifters, dipping her as the song came to an end. "Gonna have us some fun tonight," he sang before the next song began on the record.

Darryl and Sherri kissed, and then she said, "Save the dancing for tonight, Babe! I got to watch this chicken now or we won't have nothin' to eat."

Carl and Annabel Lee clapped for Sherri and Darryl and then began to make their way down the corridor to their bedroom. "I'll take you up on that beer in a minute, cuz." Carl was still holding the towel in front of him and trying not to look too conspicuous. "First let me get washed up and changed." Annabel Lee punched him gently on his arm: "Frumpy too," he hastily added. They scurried into their tiny bedroom and both began to giggle. Carl whisked the towel away from his still prominent erection, and they both laughed out loud.

"Make sure you have a *cold* shower," suggested Annabel Lee.

"You wish," taunted Carl, as he dropped his trunks for the second time that day. For Annabel Lee, Carl's regularly engorged penis couldn't have cast a bigger shadow over her if it had been a pine tree.

It was an object of both threat and wonder; threat: for everything that had happened with her father's penis *that night*; and wonder: because she was enough of a woman to experience desire and knowledgeable enough to know that it had the power to impregnate her. Suddenly, it all became too much for Annabel Lee. Feeling giddy, she sat promptly on the bed. True to form, Carl took no notice. He grabbed his things and headed for the shower. Annabel Lee was glad to have a moment of solitude in order to recompose herself.

Top down and radio blaring, the Mustang screeched into the parking lot at The Pier. Two lovers were standing by their car, laughing and pawing at one another. The lights from Carl's car did nothing to deter them. As Darryl and Sherri led their younger charges to the entrance, they could see couples—locked in tight embraces—swaying to the music, which poured out of the open windows like the golden light. "You two ready to boogie down?" asked Darryl as he shook his backside in a semi-stoop.

"Right on!" came Carl's reply. They all laughed again as the men got out their wallets to pay the cover charge, after which they went straight to the bar.

"Drinks tonight are on Sherri and me—our gift to the high school graduates and soon-to-be newlyweds." Carl started to order but Darryl silenced him with a slight push to his chest: "Hold on cuz, ladies first."

"Why, thank you," curtsied Annabel Lee. She looked at the bartender and then at the drinks behind him and hesitated.

"What you havin', young lady?" queried the bartender. Looking then at the gathering throng in front of him, he added, "I'm flying solo tonight, so try to make it snappy." Nervously, Annabel Lee asked, "What do you have?"

With a world-weary expression which said "I don't believe this" the bartender jerked his head over his shoulder at the range of bottles on the shelves behind him and then silently spread his hands in front of him, indicating the beers on tap. Realizing that she needed to order something soon, Annabel Lee blurted out: "I'll have a Molotov Cocktail!" People standing near the bar broke out in laughter. Annabel Lee failed to see what was funny, and her face displayed the entire red spectrum.

The bartender dropped his head and shook it, and then looked up at Annabel Lee saying, "Okay, funny girl, let's see some ID." Annabel Lee nervously started to fish through her purse for her driver's license. Meanwhile, to help her save face, Sherri told Darryl and Carl to order their drinks first. Although she had located her license, Annabel Lee pretended to keep looking for it in order to have time to fight back the tears that had welled up in her eyes.

Sherri leaned close to her and said, "It's all right, Hon; let's you and me have their special wine punch—how's that sound?" Annabel Lee quickly nodded, gulped back a sob, and smiled at Sherri. Sherri took the driver's license from Annabel Lee's fingers and shoved it at the bartender. "She's eighteen today, shit-for-brains, and we'll both have the wine punch."

Unfazed, the bartender looked at the license, handed it back with a shrug, saying, "Hey, I don't make the laws."

Sherri nudged Darryl and said, "Me and Frumpy're going to the ladies' room. Grab our drinks for us and we'll be back in a minute."

"Right," said Darryl, "We'll find a table."

Once in the ladies' room, Sherri looked at herself in the mirror, brushed her dirty blond hair with her fingers and then lit a cigarette. "Want one?" she proffered the pack to Annabel Lee while blowing blue smoke over her shoulder.

"No, thanks," said Annabel Lee, and then added, "But thanks—for...*in there*," she nodded her head in the direction of the bar.

"Hey, Sugar, no problem," replied Sherri. She took a drag on her cigarette and then studied Annabel Lee for a minute. "You ain't used to places like this, are you?" Sherri waved her cigarette in an arc around herself to indicate The Pier.

Annabel Lee looked at her feet and shook her head. "I—I don't really drink...alcohol, that is. The bartender made me nervous, so I just ordered the first drink that came into my mind. But what was so funny about it?"

Taking another long, slow drag on her cigarette and squinting through the smoke, Sherri reached over to Annabel Lee and stroked her long auburn hair. "Honey, a Molotov cocktail is a *gasoline bomb*." The younger woman smiled at her. They looked at each other for a moment and then both bent double in laughter. "That's the way, girl; shake it off! Think you're ready for some fun now?" queried Sherri.

Annabel lee shrugged, grinned and said, "Yeah—I think so."

"Good," snapped Sherri as she crushed out her cigarette and threw it into a waste bin. "Let's go give those men of ours a run for their money!" They both laughed and headed back into the crowded barroom.

The rest of the evening saw a mixture of dancing, laughing and drinking. The latter was being carefully calculated by Carl, as he wanted Annabel Lee to drink enough to be open to his advances, but not so much as to pass out. The foursome decided to leave at 11.30 p.m. As they made their way towards the parking lot, Darryl laid his hand on Carl's shoulder and said, "Take it easy going home, cuz. The cops often set speed traps near here. But it ain't the speeding they want to catch you for—they want to nail you for drunk driving. A machine like yours will attract them like flies on shit."

"Got it," replied Carl. The two men helped Sherri and Annabel Lee into the back.

As Darryl got in, he flopped into his seat and, with a wave of his hand, said, "Driver. Take me drunk... I'm home." He and Carl fell about laughing and then banged their heads together, each exclaiming with pain while continuing their guffawing.

"You okay to drive, Carl?" inquired Sherri.

"Yeah, I'm fine," Carl replied, rubbing his head.

"Well, y'all be careful up there, okay," remonstrated Sherri, "You got precious cargo back here."

"Indeed, ma'am," was all Carl said, tipping his imaginary chauffeur's cap. For once, Carl took his time. He was volubly telling Darryl about his big plans for his and Annabel Lee's future. Sherri and Annabel Lee chatted tipsily together, laughing at just about everything—most of which would be less than amusing when sober. For her part, Annabel Lee wanted to fill the space both within her and outside her with words—words which would somehow relieve her of the mounting pressure within her chest. She felt as though she were a child's rubber ring—used for swimming—just like the one she had when aged four or five. Her father had overfilled it with air and when she had jumped into the swimming pool, it had popped, letting all the pressure out at once. Throughout the evening, Carl's eyes had slowly, but surely, filled her with the pressure she now felt within herself: eyes that leered, winked and lusted for her. Eyes that had begun to remind her of her father's eyes. Eyes that peeled off her clothing. She now realized that she had been undressed dozens—maybe even hundreds—of times by men—not just by Carl and her father, but by boys at school, teachers, and shopkeepers. Something finally clicked for her and began to make sense. For years—since she had begun to develop as a woman—she had felt there was something *wrong* with *her*—and that this was why her father had looked at her the way he did; and that this was why he had hit her and her mother; that *they* had somehow been doing *something* wrong and needed to be punished, that *they* had broken rules which weren't written down and could only be discovered once they were broken. In her mildly inebriated state she began to feel elevated. She breathed deeply and now it seemed that the heavy pressure of air had been replaced by something lighter than air—perhaps helium—yes, that was it, she was a helium-filled balloon floating over her past and could clearly see the topography of her life-land below. But then she remembered that her father had hit her even when she was tiny—long before she reached adolescence, long before he began to look at her in *that way*, long before *that night*. At this realization, her balloon-self began a rapid descent, but before crashing into the terrain of her memory below, it was lifted aloft by the lighter-than-air truth of her realization that men's stares had nothing to do with something *in her*, but something *in them*. Secure in this revelation, she felt that perhaps she could figure out why her father had beaten her so often at another such 'elevated' time. She would hang on tightly to the truth that men looked at her *in that way* because of who they were, and not because of her. "Yes, that is true!" she suddenly said aloud.

"What is, Honey?" asked Sherri.

"Huh?" responded a startled Annabel Lee.

Sherri was smoking a cigarette, her other hand extended outside the car, floating up and down with the breeze. "You been silent as the grave for four or five minutes, just staring up at the sky, and then you blurted out: 'That's true!' I thought maybe you were talking to me, so I asked '*what* is true?' But, hey, forget it. You're just a little tipsy."

Annabel Lee was glad that people couldn't read her thoughts the way it happened with the cartoon characters she had loved when she was small—the way their thoughts and ideas appeared in bubbles over their heads. She laughed and said, "Yeah, it was nothing. And you're right about my being a bit tipsy."

And then they were home, back at the trailer. The dogs came out from under the trailer, stretching, shaking the sleep from their bodies, and giving a few languid barks. Their tails began wagging as soon as they heard the voices of their master and mistress. Sherri and Darryl were crooning The Platters' song: "With this ring I promise I'll always love you, al-ways lo-ove you." Propping up one another, they stroked their dogs, who were anxiously lapping at their hands. Carl and Annabel Lee followed them, making their way up the steps to the trailer door. Darryl fumbled with his keys, dropped them and then chuckled to himself, "I do believe..." he burped, "that I am under the alcofluence of inhol." Sherri, who was now on her hands and knees, feeling for the keys, bit him on the calf, while hissing like a snake. "Oh my God! I'm being bitten by a water moccasin. Wait—no, it's the *Reptile Woman*. The feared *Reptile Woman* of the Catawba!" Sherri bit him again, just above the knee. "Sto-op! Do-on't!" called out Darryl in mock terror. "Sto-op! Do-on't!" Sherri bit him higher on his thigh, which elicited a low growl and then: *"Don't stop!"*

Annabel Lee and Carl looked at each other. His eyes were alight; Annabel Lee's were nervous and darting. Once inside the door, Darryl scooped Sherri up and threw her across his shoulder in a fireman's carry. He then stormed down the narrow corridor with Sherri playfully screaming for help—which she hoped would not be forthcoming. Their bedroom door slammed. Carl turned to Annabel Lee. You don't mind if we just *walk* to our bedroom, do you Fru—" and after the briefest of pauses: *"Mrs. Locklear?"*

Darryl extended his hand to Annabel Lee. She took his hand, saying "Why no, *Mr. Locklear.*"

The next hour or so was spent in the ritual that has so obsessed mankind since fig leaves and animal skins (not to mention loin cloths, leggings and codpieces, and finally trousers) were first thrown off in fits of passion. It turned out that, for all his bravado, Carl had never actually had intercourse with anyone. He never admitted it, of course, but then he didn't need to: his fumbling awkwardness said it all. From the moment they closed the bedroom door behind them, Carl was all over Annabel Lee like a cat with a pigeon: clothes flew like feathers. And the scene wasn't without its pain. Stripped of their outer garments, Carl eagerly pulled Annabel Lee onto the bed. As he struggled with Annabel Lee's elasticized bra straps, they sprang from his fingers with a loud 'thwap,' stinging the object of his passion. "Ouch!" cried Annabel Lee, "Be careful!" Naked, except for his underpants, priapic Carl hovered excitedly over his prey as the cat would have done with the pigeon—had its quarry been willing to pluck itself. His erect penis was straining at the fabric of his underwear. With mild trepidation—based on the frenetic activity thus far, and which presaged more to come—Annabel Lee slowly finished removing her bra, like the pigeon who knows that, having plucked its last feather, dinner will begin.

Carl was all but slavering over her, his mouth partly open and eyes big as dinner plates. Annabel Lee's panties were only partway down her legs when Carl tucked in. While greedily kissing her and pawing at her breasts, Carl was also trying to position himself between her legs. The fact that Annabel Lee's legs were somewhat bound together by her panties had escaped his notice. She couldn't say anything as her mouth was filled with Carl's probing tongue. When Carl finally had to come up for air, he gasped "Baby, you got to open your legs wider."

Annabel Lee started to tell him the problem, but then was overcome by the absurdity of it all, and burst out laughing. Believing that she was laughing at him, Carl took offence. Lifting himself on extended arms, and trying to keep his voice low, he barked at her: "We gotta do this *right*!" Seeing that Carl still had his underwear on, Annabel Lee put her hand over her mouth to try to stifle her laughter, but it would not be contained. Like a boy being belittled on a playground, Carl punched Annabel Lee on the shoulder, "Stop it, I said!"

"Ouch, Carl. That hurt!" she whelped.

"Well then stop making fun of me! This ain't supposed to be *funny*."

Rubbing her shoulder, Annabel Lee, retorted, "But *look* at you. You still have your underpants *on* and I haven't got mine *off*—that's why we aren't getting anywhere. I just thought it was funny."

As though he were insensate, Carl looked down to verify her words. "Oh…uh, yeah." He dropped to his side and pulled down his underwear, his penis springing back and smacking against his bare belly.

This sound brought a slight smile to Annabel Lee's face as she continued to rub her arm. "Don't ever hit me again… *okay?* My daddy used to do that. I don't like it."

"No. No, Frumpy, I won't do it again…I'm sorry, Baby… I just thought you were laughing at me and all. It…it won't happen again." Carl then took stock of her nearly nude body. His eyes stopped at her panties, still bunched just below her knees. Trying now to sound the gentleman, Carl said, "Uh, let me help you with these." The last feather was plucked.

The next few minutes saw much groping around and prodding from Carl as he tried desperately to get his penis inside Annabel Lee. In the midst of it all, and somewhere deep inside herself, Annabel Lee was watching someone else trying to enter her…*that night.* Her father had known exactly what to do… and how. There wasn't all the uncertainty that surrounded Carl's untutored lovemaking. He hovered above Annabel Lee, supporting himself on his elbows, while trying to enter her without the use of hands—his or hers. However, all the excited pushing and thrusting set Carl off, and he prematurely ejaculated onto her pubis and halfway up her belly. Annabel Lee blinked in surprise as she felt the hot liquid spilling onto her. Carl groaned involuntarily with his orgasm, and then collapsed onto his side. He threw his arm across his eyes and swore softly: "Damn!"

Torn between asking Carl what the matter was and exploring the wetness on her body (had he *urinated?*), her right hand touched the sticky semen while the left touched Carl's shoulder. "What's wrong, Carl?" (Fascinated, the fingers of her right hand confirmed that it wasn't *urine* on her—"Ah," she thought with dawning realization. Annabel Lee had never seen or touched the semen deposited by her father. In her state of trauma, she had been rushed to hospital and then sedated, inspected and cleaned.)

"Can't you tell?" Carl's sulky response brought her back to the present moment. "Shit," he moaned.

Not knowing how to make Carl feel better, Annabel Lee simply said: "Wow. That—uh, that was a *lot*. You really did want me!" She stroked his shoulder and hoped that she had said the right thing.

"Yeah, well it wasn't supposed to happen like *that*."

"We can try again." Annabel Lee tried to sound cheerful; and then added tentatively: "It's probably better the way it happened, Carl. You, um…weren't wearing a prophylactic." (Annabel Lee didn't like using the colloquial 'rubber.')

The reassuring sound of Annabel Lee's voice was starting to help Carl come out of his embarrassment. "Hey—that's right. Listen, Babe, I'm really sorry… I mean…it was kind of an 'accident.'"

Annabel Lee turned towards him and they began to kiss again— this time with less urgency. "Ooh, hey!" gasped Carl. His semen had begun to cool down and he recoiled as the clammy viscous liquid was pressed against his lower torso. He instinctively reached down to clean it off but found his hand smothered in it from both of their bodies. "Yuck! Frumpy!?" He waved his hand about in search for something to wipe it on.

Annabel Lee giggled and handed him his underwear. Carl began to frown until she said: "Well, it's *yours*, so it might as well go on your undies!"

After he had cleaned his hand, Annabel Lee pointed to her belly and Carl dutifully wiped her as well. Carl was about to return to their lovemaking when Annabel Lee reminded him: "Sweetheart…before we get going again…hadn't you better find those condoms?"

Annabel Lee awoke with a start—dogs were barking and someone was snoring. She had been dreaming that she was back in her bed in Bransford County. Her mother had been reading her the melancholic poem which bore her name.

I was a child and she was a child,
In this kingdom by the sea;

But we loved with a love that was more than love—
I and my Annabel Lee;
With a love that the winged seraphs of heaven
Coveted her and me.

As a child, it had made no sense to her that *her* name had come from somewhere and someone else—after all, it was *her* name and that's the only way she knew herself. But *who* was she and *where* was she? As she came to consciousness, Annabel Lee felt someone's arm draped across her. As she lifted her head from the pillow, the sight of the inert male body shocked her into thinking—*fearing*—if only for a millisecond—that it was *that night* and that Carl's body was her father's. She dropped back onto the pillow; her head ached, and so did her loins. No, it wasn't *that night*—that night was long gone—and she was 'Frumpy,' and she was here in bed with Carl Locklear—soon to be her husband—in the trailer of his cousin near Rock Hill, S.C. And she had a hangover—her first. And she had to wee badly.

Annabel Lee gently removed Carl's deadweight arm from her chest and scooted to the edge of the bed. As she swung her legs to the floor and sat up, she felt a dull throb in her temples and behind her eyes. Carl grunted and snorted as she got off the bed and rummaged for clothes in order to make her way to the trailer's only toilet—she just hoped that no one else was already there as her bladder felt full-to-bursting. Annabel Lee put on one of Carl's shirts, which fell halfway to her knees, and modestly slipped on some panties. Against the eventuality that others might be up, she looked at her self in the mirror. Aghast at the pallor of her face and state of her hair, she began to go through her handbag to find her brush. Annabel Lee brushed the tangles from her hair and pinched her cheeks to bring some color to her unusually pale skin. Bolstered by these actions, Annabel Lee took her wash bag and ventured from the room.

The bathroom was free, but Annabel Lee could hear Sherri and Darryl in the kitchen. She could smell cooking, and the smoke from

Sherri's cigarette. Annabel Lee slipped quietly into the bathroom. After emptying her bladder, she lingered on the toilet seat. Urinating had stung a bit, so she took out her make-up mirror and inspected herself. She could never have imagined her mother doing something similar nearly nineteen years before—but for completely different reasons.

So it was done. She was 'officially' no longer a virgin—and, in any case, Carl had neither asked nor seemingly cared. As much as that was a relief to Annabel Lee, it then dawned on her that Carl's reticence about the possibility of Annabel Lee's being a virgin was because *he* was a virgin. She laughed to herself—Carl, with all his big talk and supposed worldliness! Nevertheless, Annabel Lee took comfort in the fact that she and Carl were both *lovers* for the first time. So many milestones had been passed in the last few days: Graduating high school, eloping, getting drunk, making love—and tomorrow: marrying. Lost in her thoughts, Annabel Lee hadn't noticed that she was still perched on the toilet. A loud knock on the door and Carl's voice brought her to her senses. "Hey! You gonna be in there all day?"

"Go out back!" teased Sherri from the kitchen, "Darryl does!"

"Very funny," grumbled Carl.

"Just a minute," called Annabel Lee, "I'll be out in a minute." She flushed the toilet to cover the fact that she had simply been sitting there (for how long?) reflecting on her life's recent changes.

When she opened the door, Annabel Lee smiled sweetly at Carl, saying "Good morning, sweetheart," and attempted to kiss him on the cheek.

But Carl merely grunted and pressed by her, mumbling, "I gotta go bad," and hastily closed the door. Flummoxed—and somewhat embarrassed—Annabel Lee hoped that neither Sherri nor Darryl had noticed. As she stepped along the tiny corridor to her room, she was relieved to see that her hosts were huddled over their morning coffee, talking quietly and listening to the radio. Annabel Lee went into the bedroom and waited for Carl. There was a flutter in the pit of her stomach. Why had Carl ignored her? Was Carl short with her just because he had to pee or was it something else? Annabel Lee remembered all the conversations she had overheard between her peers at high school: about boys only 'loving' a girl until they 'got it'—and all the variations on "will you still respect me in the morning?" She dared not let her thoughts race down that path.

A few minutes later Carl returned from the bathroom. "Okay, Honey?" Annabel Lee meekly inquired.

"Yeah, I guess," replied Carl. "I was about to burst; and my head's aching a bit—must have a hangover." And then, as an after thought: "How're you?"

Somewhat reassured, Annabel Lee averred that she too had a hangover: "That wine punch sure *packed a punch*." She giggled at her pun, but Carl just nodded and grunted acknowledgement.

"Man, I could use some coffee—how about you?"

"Sure. Let's get dressed." Annabel Lee was determined to remain cheerful. As they searched for their clothes amidst the jumble from the previous night, Annabel Lee ventured to ask Carl: "I hope... that is, I mean...well... Was everything okay for you last night?" Her question was asked more in hope than expectation.

Carl was standing with his back to her, buttoning up his shirt. "Uh, yeah, Babe. You were fine, uh, I mean *great*. Really, you were great! Um, how...did I...uh... Was it okay for you too?" Even from behind, Annabel Lee could see that Carl was blushing.

Instinctively, she sought to reassure him. "I didn't really know too much of what to do myself—it being, well, new and all—but you did just fine."

Carl turned halfway towards Annabel Lee, smiled sheepishly, and said, "Thanks, Frumpy." He blushed again.

"You don't have to *thank* me, silly." Annabel Lee reached out for his hand. "I wanted to—I really did. And with *you*. It was just fine. *You* were just fine."

They were both dressed now, so to save himself more embarrassment, Carl quickly changed the subject: "Coffee! And food! I'm starving." As they started out the bedroom door, Annabel Lee stopped Carl, took his face in her hands and kissed him. Carl froze for a moment and then returned her kiss. They smiled at one another and then joined Sherri and Darryl at the breakfast table.

The rest of the day was spent with lazy chatter and another boat ride on the river—this time with all four of them. They were all lethargic after their night out and the day was sultry. Darryl found a spot to tether the boat under some overhanging branches, shading them from the scorching afternoon sun. To cool off, the men dived into the river from time to time—making sure that they splashed their womenfolk in the process. Sherri and Annabel Lee responded with the requisite squeals to gratify their men's efforts. On and off, they discussed the coming day's wedding. Sherri and Darryl were acting both as witnesses as well as best man and maid of honor. When Carl and Darryl were in the river, Sherri noticed that Annabel Lee was trying to keep up her end of their conversation and eavesdrop on what the two men might be saying. "Everything okay, Hon? Y'all not getting cold feet are you?" Sherri nodded her head lazily towards Carl, now some fifty yards from the boat.

"No," replied Annabel Lee, "at least I don't think I am. Carl's been a little odd today—this morning in particular." Both women glanced towards where the men were swimming, ascertaining that they wouldn't be overheard.

"What do you mean?" asked Sherri.

Annabel Lee paused, watched Carl horsing around with Darryl, and then, without looking at Sherri, continued: "Did y'all, well... Did y'all sleep together before you were married?" Then she checked herself, saying, "I'm sorry, Sherri, I really shouldn't be asking such things..."

"Hush up!" laughed Sherri, "It's just 'girl talk,' and heaven knows I don't get much of that out here." She indicated the remoteness of the heavily forested river banks which surrounded their piece of land. "Don't get me wrong," she added, "I love Darryl, and I do love where we live… I'd love it even more if he'd ever get around to building me that house!" She laughed with a smoker's croak. "But I only get to talk with other women when we're at the mill. 'Course, half the time it's so damn noisy in there you can barely hear yourself think! So it's nice to have you here—and to talk. Lordy, listen to me: just rambling on when you were asking me something. What was it, Hon?"

"Sex," said Annabel Lee in a half-whisper while glancing furtively towards Carl.

"Oh, that's right! Did me and Darryl do it before we got married! Ha!— *did* we?! That boy was all over me like gravy on biscuits!" She laughed and looked affectionately at Darryl who was floating on his back, mid-river. "Can't say I exactly fought him off." She chuckled again. "But we can't make it too easy for them, now can we?" Turning to face Annabel Lee, she tilted her head to one side and asked gently: "Why do you want to know, Sugar?"

Annabel Lee was both feeling encouraged by Sherri's openness and wishing that she hadn't broached the subject. "Oh, I don't know… it's just that last night…" she gulped air into her lungs: "Last night was the *first time* Carl and I have done it and I'm not sure I—uh, we, um, did it…well, *right*, and Carl got it everywhere but *inside* me and then he got angry at me because I laughed at him, well, not at him exactly, but at us—oh, I don't know!"

"Whoa!" interjected Sherri. "Slow down and breathe, girl!" She took a slow look around to see where her husband and Carl were. Annabel Lee was now suffused with a crimson flush. Sherri reached over and patted her hand. "Honey, don't you worry your sweet little head about *that*. For goodness' sake, at least you were in a *bed*; Carl and me did it the first time in the back of his daddy's Chevrolet! It wasn't a pretty sight." Sherri lowered her voice and leaned her face close to Annabel Lee's. "Y'all did manage it, right?" Annabel Lee nodded. Sherri looked at her searchingly. "So, was there a problem? You said Carl was acting a bit odd this morning."

"Yes, but I'm not sure why…" Annabel Lee struggled with her thoughts and feelings. "The first time…," she began slowly, "The first time, Carl kinda… *missed.*" She looked at Sherri hoping she would understand.

"Missed?" inquired Sherri, shaking her head in bewilderment.

Annabel Lee pointed towards her pubic region and then drew circles in the air around her lower belly. "It all came out here," she whispered.

"Ooh, now I see," nodded Sherri, still holding onto Annabel Lee's hand. "Got a bit over-excited, did he?" Annabel Lee smiled and nodded. "Well, Honey, just take it as a compliment that his boiler was fired up for you." Then Sherri drawled: "I don't know *why* men think they are all supposed to be some kind of great lovers when they never done it before!" She shook her head and added, "We all got to learn sometime."

Annabel Lee's face and neck had now lightened in hue from burgundy to rosé. "Whew!" she said, "Guess I could use a dip in this river!" She took a handful of water and splashed it across her face. "Oh, that's better!"

Sherri looked at Annabel Lee thoughtfully. "So, y'all gave it a little rest and tried again?" Annabel Lee nodded. "And everything went where it was supposed to go?" Another nod. "Carl happy that time?" Once more her friend nodded. "What about you, Honey? *You* like it?"

Annabel Lee half gave a Gallic shrug, waggled her head from side to side and then lifted her hands upwards. "Well, sort of… I mean it was *oka-a-ay*, but it hurt…*some*—and still does." Annabel Lee involuntarily looked towards her pubis.

"Y'all didn't use no K-Y or Vaseline?"

Annabel Lee raised her eyes heavenwards, screwed up one side of her mouth and shook her head in the negative. Once more the older woman patted the younger one's hand. She laughed the laugh of experience and said, "Y'all will learn, believe you me." The two young men were now swimming back towards the boat. "Look, Honey. You and me will have to talk again sometime. I'll find out from Darryl whether Carl had the guts to ask him anything about last night or whether he just played the stud. Let's just get you two married and you'll have plenty of time to work on the rest."

Carl and Darryl swam to opposite sides of the small boat so as not to upset it when they climbed aboard. Once again they playfully flicked water on their respective partners. As Darryl clambered over the gunwales of the motorboat, Sherri popped him on the rump with her towel. "Yow!" he yelped in mock pain, but then he grabbed both the towel and Sherri, pulling her in close for a passionate kiss. "Now that's what I need to warm me up! How 'bout you, Carl?"

"Sure enough," responded Carl manfully; but he and Annabel Lee only looked at one another sheepishly. Darryl cranked up the motor and they sped back to the small dock. A Great Blue Heron, which had been enjoying the view and the late afternoon sun from the railing, gracefully mounted the air on its huge wings.

As evening approached, the two women prepared the meal while the men drank beer and watched a baseball game, voicing their dismay whenever the umpire's judgment differed from their own. Once they all sat down at the table together, the festive spirit which had imbued the last two days gave way to a more pensive atmosphere—despite the fact that the women had joined in on the beer. However, they were not as immoderate as the night before. "I just got over one hangover today," quipped Annabel Lee, "and I don't want another one—especially not on my wedding day." Still, as the dinner progressed—and bellies were sated and palates wet—their tongues were loosened, leading Darryl and Sherri to ask Carl and Annabel Lee about their future plans, where they might live, the reasons why Annabel Lee and her mother lived with her deceased father's parents—and a variety of things that Carl had never mentioned. The host couple then reminisced about their courtship and marriage: how one had flowed into the other, as they had gone to the same schools since first grade and started dating when they were fifteen.

About eleven o'clock the foursome decided to call it a night and get some sleep before the big day. Their appointment with the justice of the peace was scheduled for ten o'clock at the Rock Hill court house. And although Darryl and Sherri were an integral part of the wedding plans, tomorrow—Monday—was still a working day for them. They had only been given half a day off from their jobs at the hosiery mill so they could attend the ceremony. Following the wedding, Carl and Annabel Lee planned to remain with Sherri and Darryl for another three days before returning to Bransford County to 'face the music.'

Crime Time

O! call back yesterday, bid time return.

Richard II

It was towards evening when Carl eased the Mustang up the gravel drive to Wyatt and Ginny's house. He stopped while still thirty or more yards away. Neither he nor Annabel Lee was quite ready to face what might turn out to be a bad scene between them and Annabel Lee's mother and grandparents. Their mood was as subdued as it had been exuberant only a week before. Carl switched off the motor and they both stared at the house in silence, each caught fully in the gravity of their decision to elope. Neither said anything for a moment or two. Wyatt's patrol car was nowhere in sight. The pickup was sitting beside the house. Both Carl and Annabel Lee felt easier about seeing Colleen and Ginny first. Wyatt was another matter. In addition to being the county sheriff, he had become quieter—and somewhat broodier—with the passing of time. Although it had nothing to do with Carl, he nevertheless felt the weight of Wyatt's long silences and was threatened by them. What might Wyatt do when finally he had something to bring him out of himself? The two young people looked at one another. Carl nodded and they both opened their car doors. Carl reached for Annabel Lee's hand as they got to the front of the car. Sheepishly they began to walk towards the front door when Carl stopped. "What's that?" Carl nodded towards the front porch. A wreath hung on the door.

"I don't know…" Annabel Lee's voiced trailed off. And then: "Oh God!" She let go off Carl's hand and ran for the door. Carl hastened to join her. When he mounted the steps to the porch, the screen door was already slamming in front of him. He heard Annabel Lee calling "Mama!? Grandma!?"

As Carl entered the front room, he noticed cards and flowers on the tables and the mantel. Annabel Lee was in the kitchen, where her mother and grandmother sat at the table. Annabel Lee looked hastily from one to the other. Both women looked pale and worn. "What's happened? What's wrong?" pleaded Annabel Lee. Carl appeared behind her in the doorway. He nodded nervously at the women. Their eyes acknowledged his presence.

"It's your grandpa," began Colleen. "He's dea—," she began, and then looked quickly at Ginny, who looked away. "He had an accident," Colleen resumed, "…and he died."

Annabel Lee started to wobble on her feet, so Carl quickly whisked a chair from under the table and helped her into it. Annabel Lee's mouth fell open and she tried to speak, but only unintelligible noises came forth. Carl sat down in a chair next to Annabel Lee, took her hand and squeezed it. Colleen got out of her chair, went to the sink and poured a glass of water for her daughter. She brought it to the table and set it in front of Annabel Lee. "Here, Honey, have a drink." Her soft words seemed to have an impact on Annabel Lee, who looked up at her mother and began to cry. Carl looked from one woman to the other and continued to squeeze Annabel Lee's hand. Colleen stroked her daughter's long hair as she pulled the girl's face into her breast.

Unable to take the wordless grief, Carl looked up at Colleen and asked, "What happened?"

"Car wreck," answered Colleen.

"Car wreck?" responded Carl, as though incredulous. "Where—uh, I mean, *how?*"

Colleen shook her head. "Nobody knows for sure. They found his car upside down in the Watauga River. It had gone through a guard rail and down the mountainside. One of the deputies, Roy Exum, says Wyatt radioed in to say he was chasing somebody—a speeder or something—no one really knows. They got worried when they didn't hear anything again and he didn't respond on his radio. A local farmer saw the broken guard rail and stopped to have a look. He reported the accident."

Carl slowly exhaled through his teeth, "Whew."

"The funeral was yesterday," added Colleen. "We would have let you know, but, well... You know."

Annabel Lee cried harder and pressed her face against her mother. Through her sobs and muffled voice, she said, "Mama, I'm so sorry."

Ginny stood up slowly from her chair and wearily said, "I'm going upstairs now." She briefly patted Annabel Lee's head, looked blankly at Carl and then languorously walked from the kitchen towards the stairs.

Sensing Carl's discomfiture, Colleen said, "So, you two are married now. Mr. and Mrs. Locklear." Colleen spoke the words as though she were tasting them and deciding whether or not she liked their flavor.

Carl nodded: "Uh, yes ma'am. Four days ago... We're real sorry about...I mean, well—uh..." Even the smooth-talking Carl had no words for this current situation. Events—tragic beyond his limited imagination—had overtaken the script he had prepared for himself and Annabel Lee. Individually, and unbeknownst to the other, both young people were secretly feeling guilty—not just about their elopement, but about *everything.*

Colleen lifted her daughter's left hand and examined the simple gold band. "Carl's got one just like it," sniffed Annabel Lee. Carl numbly lifted his hand for Colleen's inspection.

"Well. My little girl's married," reflected Colleen aloud. And then: "Y'all want some coffee or anything?"

"Sure would," responded Carl. Annabel Lee just shook her head.

Colleen gently removed herself from her daughter and went to the cupboards for the coffee and a mug. "How do you like it, Carl?" she asked.

"Milk and two sugars, please." Carl was relieved to have a topic to talk about other than Wyatt's death, although he couldn't get it out of his head. None of them could. As so often happens, a person's death makes him somehow more present than when alive. While Colleen put water on to boil, Carl looked at Annabel Lee. She returned his gaze with red brimming eyes. Carl just shrugged helplessly.

"So where will y'all be staying?" asked Colleen.

"We'd planned to stay at my uncle's place for a while—'til we could find a house or apartment to rent," responded Carl. He continued, "As Frump—I mean, Annabel Lee is planning to attend Appalachian this fall, we'd kinda figured we'd look closer to Boone. I'll still be working at Whitlow's until I can get something full-time, so that'd be nearby."

"And what do you hope to do, Carl? What kind of work do you like?" Colleen spoke over her shoulder as she readied the coffee. She realized that she knew virtually nothing about her new son-in-law.

Encouraged to speak of anything but Wyatt's death, Carl jumped at the chance to share some of his big plans. "I think my uncle'll hire me when he gets some more house-building contracts. I'm pretty good with my hands. There's a lot of chalets and such going up near them ski resorts around Boone. My uncle hopes to land a few of those jobs. When he does, I think I'll join him." Carl made it sound as though he would be doing his uncle a favor.

"Just so long as you take care of my Annabel Lee." Colleen looked wistfully at her daughter.

"Don't worry," reassured Carl, "she'll be fine with me." A weak smile creased her tear-stained face as Annabel Lee looked at her new husband.

⏳

"Fired? Y-you *f-fired* me?" stammered Carl.

"Damn right, I did," retorted old man Whitlow. "How'm I s'posed to run a business when my help disappears for a week without even telling me?"

"But, I just got married…." Carl feebly offered up his left hand with the evidence on his ring finger.

"Married!?" snorted old man Whitlow, and then added, "Good luck to your new wife." He shook his head in disgust as he mumbled to himself foul epithets coined for Carl.

"Can't you just give me another chance?" pleaded Carl. His eyes were beginning to burn, but he was determined not to cry in front of Whitlow.

"Too late," quipped Whitlow, "I done hired me another boy to do your job. Good worker, too." Whitlow smiled with self-satisfaction.

"Well, you still owe me my last week's wages," fired back Carl.

"Come back tomorrow," replied Whitlow, "I got work to do."

"Fine," Carl said through gritted teeth, "I'll be back in the morning." He got into his Mustang, banged the steering wheel with his fists, and then let his head drop against the wheel. "Man, oh, man," he spoke to himself, "What am I going to tell Frumpy?" Carl uttered a diphthonged "Shee-ut." He threw the Mustang into gear and spun out firing gravel around the store's forecourt. The tires grabbed the tarmac with a loud screech and he was gone. "Bastard! Sombitchin' bastard!" he screamed at the top of his lungs as he careened down the mountain road. "What the fuck am I gonna do now?!" But even then, in the midst of his rage, the kernel of an idea was forming. He knew he had to get his story right for Annabel Lee.

☒

As Carl drove up the rutted track to his uncle's house, he saw Annabel Lee sitting on the front porch in a rocking chair, reading. "Hey, Babe," Carl said nonchalantly as he strode up the lawn to the porch. Annabel Lee shielded the sun from her eyes with her free hand and replied: "Hey. What's happening? Aren't you working today?"

"Naw," drawled Carl, "old man Whitlow's given me the day off—kind of a wedding present. He said to come around tomorrow to collect my wages from the week before last and he'd give me my hours for the coming weeks."

"Well, that's right kind of him," smiled Annabel Lee.

Carl yawned and stretched, "So…uh, anybody home?"

"No, your uncle's working over near Valle Crucis and your aunt's gone to town for shopping."

His plan for tomorrow now firmly in his mind, Carl cockily leaned over and tilted his young's wife's face towards his. He kissed her deeply. Carl then looked at the book on her lap. "Whatcha reading, Babe?"

"It's called *The Grapes of Wrath*, by John Steinbeck."

"The grapes of *what*?"

"Wrath, silly. It means anger."

"Didn't know grapes ever got angry," teased Carl, and then added: "Any sex in it?"

Annabel Lee feigned disgust: "It's not *that kind* of book, Carl Locklear."

"Well, I'm *that kind* of man, and you're my kind of wife. So why don't we just go upstairs for a little while and I'll show you just what kind of man you married."

Annabel Lee started to put Carl off, but sensing her hesitation, Carl added: "Frumpy, I know you been upset about your grandpa and all that, but we've been married just over a week, Babe, and we ain't done it but a couple of times."

Uncertain of how she really felt about sex—or was it sex *and Carl?*...or sex *with* Carl?—Annabel Lee had claimed (genuinely) that she was a bit sore 'down there' and implored Carl that they take it a bit easy, at least to begin with. At first Carl had sworn and sulked, but in the end he had complied with Annabel Lee's wish. Today, however, she caught the hopeful, lustful gleam in Carl's eye. "Okay," she finally replied, "But let's lock the front door—just to be safe."

"Safe from *what?*" asked Carl as they mounted the stairs—more to himself than to Annabel Lee.

As Annabel Lee got up from the bed and headed towards the bathroom, Carl yawned, stretched himself cat-like and called to his wife: "Whatcha think about going away for a couple of days? Maybe go see your grandparents down in Swansboro? Bet they'd let us have a room in their motel for a night or two."

Carl heard water running and then Annabel Lee's querulous voice: "What about work?"

Expecting this, Carl replied, "No problem, Babe. Whitlow don't need me this coming weekend and not again 'til next Wednesday. Just got to go by and collect my wages. Let's throw some clothes in a suitcase and have us another road trip! I've wanted to meet your Mom's parents since you first told me about them. Bet they'll be surprised to see their granddaughter!"

"They sure would, Carl...but why don't we call them first—just to make sure it's all right?"

"Naw, Babe! Let's surprise them. What do you say? C'mon!"

"We-ell..." mused Annabel Lee, "...all right then! Let's do it! I'll start getting my things together."

"Be sure to throw in your bathing suit," added Carl for a measure of credibility. "We want to catch some rays on the beach there."

"So far, so good," Carl thought to himself. He now had his pretext for getting away for a few days. Next he just had to replay for his aunt and uncle the same yarns he had spun for Annabel Lee, and his plans were set. At supper that night, the young couple talked excitedly about their plans to make the surprise trip to Swansboro. Carl played up the 'wedding present,' of a few days off, from old man Whitlow. Carl made light of the fact that he and Annabel Lee had only just got back from their elopement to South Carolina and were now talking about travelling even farther—to the coast of North Carolina, some 400 miles away. "You're plumb crazier than I thought," opined his uncle over supper. "You're gonna drive nigh on 800 miles *for a weekend*?" Melvin shook his head and mumbled to himself, "Wouldn't know shit from Shinola, if you ask me."

"Which no one did, dear," cut in Carl's aunt Dora, "And there's no need to swear. There are ladies present." She primly straightened herself as she said these words, and then turned to Annabel Lee: "Please excuse Melvin, Frumpy; his bark's worse than his bite."

"Well, I tell you one thing," continued Melvin, pointing at Carl with his fork, "If this young'un *ever* hopes to work with me, he sure as hell won't be gallivanting all over the state! No sir!"

"They're young, dear…and newlyweds," cooed Dora. "Just give them a little time."

"Nobody gave *me* any time—or *us*, come to think of it," growled Melvin. Carl stared at his plate and Dora smiled sweetly at Annabel Lee.

A mocking bird woke them at daybreak. It was on the branch of the pine tree that stood outside their open bedroom window. "What *time* is it?" groaned Carl.

"'Time all old dogs were dead,' is what my Mama would say," chirped Annabel Lee, "So aren't you glad you're a pup?!" Then she added: "It's 5:45."

"Frumpy, how can *anybody* be so cheerful this *early?*" whined Carl plaintively.

"Well, if you recall, Mr. Locklear; it was your plan that we drive to my grandparents' today. So we might as well get ourselves moving. What time does Whitlow's open?"

"He'll me 'ere at eigh'," Carl's words were muffled in the pillow.

"What?!"

Carl removed his faced from the pillow: "He'll be there at eight. Just like always."

"So," proposed Annabel Lee, "if we get started from here by 7:30, we should be there when he opens. Once he pays you, we could start driving and be at my grandparents' by late afternoon." Pleased with her logic, Annabel Lee threw her pillow at Carl. "So get up, sleepy head! I'll fix breakfast."

They pulled away from Melvin and Nora's house right on the half-hour. Annabel Lee noticed that Carl was unusually quiet and somewhat restive. "Anything wrong, Sweetie?" she asked in a voice that begged for a 'no.'

"Naw, Babe. Everything's fine. Just feeling a bit tired, is all…and hoping that old man Whitlow is on time today." Carl's jaw and neck twitched. "Don't want us to have to wait around. We got us a *lo-ong* drive!" Carl accentuated the drawled diphthong in 'long' and gave a marginally convincing smile and wink at Annabel Lee. Annabel Lee smiled, nodded, and then looked out the window. Carl's thoughts were speeding up now; he took a quick glance at Annabel Lee. "Listen, Babe. As we got such a long drive ahead of us; what would you think about driving the first hundred miles or so?"

Surprised—because Carl rarely let anyone drive his beloved Mustang, even his wife—Annabel Lee gave her head mock thumps with the heel of her hand, and teasingly queried: "Could you repeat that, Mr. Locklear? I don't think I heard you correctly."

"Oh, you heard me sure enough, Frumpy. As I said, I'm just a little tired this morning… Probably from all that good lovin' yesterday afternoon and last night."

"Carl Locklear!" gasped Annabel Lee, miming Vivian Leigh's Scarlett O'Hara, "I'm sure I don't know what you're talking about." She waved an imaginary fan in front of her face.

Carl chuckled and then repeated: "So what about it? Wanna drive for a while? After we've been to Whitlow's? We could swap over then."

"Well, sure!" Annabel Lee jumped at the chance.

A few minutes later they were in sight of Whitlow's Country Store. Annabel Lee took note of the tentativeness in Carl's driving as they approached. There was none of the usual bravado of screeching to a halt, with dust and gravel flying every which way. Instead, Carl eased the Mustang off the road, and rather than parking immediately in front of the store or near the pumps, Carl edged the car in front of the open door of the service bay. He slipped the gearshift into neutral, pulled the handbrake, and left the motor running. "Don't want to block the gas pumps." Carl had answered Annabel Lee's unasked question. He leaned over and kissed Annabel Lee on the cheek. "Jump in the driver's seat, Babe, and get everything adjusted. I'll only be a minute."

As Carl got out of the car he took a quick look around before heading into the store. There were no customers yet. As Annabel Lee was walking around the front of the car, Carl called back. "When you're ready, just pull the pony over yonder past the pumps." Carl pointed to an oily patch of ground near the road where Whitlow often left cars that were waiting to be worked on.

"Fine," called back Annabel Lee, as she was moving into the driver's seat.

Carl knew that it would take her two or three minutes to get the seat and mirrors adjusted the way she liked and that during such time she would pay no attention to him.

Once inside, Carl called out for Whitlow. The 'old man' (who was probably not much over fifty, but had a shuffle that belied his years) came out from the office at the back. "Oh, it's you. I didn't hear you pull in." Carl had avoided the rubber cables that tripped a bell which let the pump attendant know a customer had arrived. Whitlow looked at Carl quizzically and then leaned around Carl to see where he had parked. Then he smirked and shook his head. "Guess you're here for your money. And good riddance, too."

"Yeah, well I guess that goes for both of us," retorted Carl.

Whitlow snorted at the young man's insolence and said, "Got your pay in an envelope in the back. You stay right there while I go get it." And then gruffly: "And don't touch nothin'."

"Don't worry," Carl replied in a patronizing tone.

As Whitlow disappeared into the office, Carl heard Annabel Lee shifting the Mustang into first and saw her glide by the front door. The pump bell rang twice. "Sounds like you got a customer, old man! Looks like he drove straight into the service bay." Carl now beamed with a self-satisfied smile.

"Like you'd care," called Whitlow as he came from the office. "Here." He shoved a greasy envelope into Carl's waiting hand. "That finishes our business, so git."

Whitlow went out front to find his customer. As he moved beyond the door, Carl quickly opened the cash register. As always on a Saturday, there were plenty of tens, twenties and fifties—local folk would be heading to and from their weekly shopping and Whitlow would cash checks for his regular customers. Carl deftly scooped up the lot and closed the drawer. He shoved the wad of cash into the front of his jeans and pushed his hands into his pockets to conceal the bulge as he quickly walked to the waiting car. Throwing open the passenger door, Carl hastily jumped in and said, "Let's roll, Babe!" Annabel Lee missed first gear as she let out the clutch and the gearbox let her know, with its metallic grinding. "Goddamnit," blared Carl, "watch what you're doing!" He looked out his window at Whitlow who had come out of the garage and was scratching his head, while looking at Carl's Mustang.

Disconcerted and self-conscious after Carl's shouting at her, Annabel Lee fumbled again, and then finally got the car into gear. When they pulled out onto the highway, she turned towards Carl, with tears and anger in her eyes, and bawled, "I thought *you wanted* me to drive, Carl! You don't have to be so ugly about it! I hardly ever drive your stupid car, so how do you expect me to get it right?"

"Okay, okay," said Carl, "Just put your foot down, all right?"

"I'll drive us straight back to Melvin and Nora's place, if you don't change your tone and apologize to me. I thought we were going away on a nice trip—a sort of honeymoon."

"Yeah, well—we are. I'm sorry, *okay?* I told you already that I'm feeling a little tired…a little uptight today. So let's just both calm down," Carl gesticulated with a level hand, palm down, "and get this show on the road. What do you say?" Carl shot her a winning grin.

"Fine," said Annabel Lee, blinking away the tears, "but *I* wasn't the one who was upset."

Carl sighed heavily and tried to slump back into his seat. The movement was made difficult by all the cash he had stuffed into his jeans. He shifted in the seat, trying to get comfortable. Annabel Lee noticed Carl's predicament and asked, "What's the matter?" Then she saw the bulge in the front of Carl's trousers. "*Carl?*" she drawled, "What is *that?*"

"Just you keep your eyes on the road!" Carl grabbed the steering wheel just as the Mustang started the slip off the blacktop. A cloud of dust was thrown up and gravel clanked inside the wheel wells. "These roads ain't exactly *straight*, you know!"

Unlike her normal, timid self, Annabel Lee reached over and felt the protuberance below Carl's belt. Carl snatched her hand away. "Cut that out!" he shouted.

"Carl?—what is it?" she demanded.

"It's just my money—my back pay—in cash. Okay?" Carl rested his chin on his hand as he leaned on the arm-rest. He stared out the window and hoped that Annabel Lee would ask no further questions.

Carl's hope was dashed: "Why didn't he just put it in an envelope or why didn't you just put it in your pockets?"

Carl shifted in his seat—both from the discomfort of Annabel Lee's questions and the wadded notes in his trousers. "Just *drive*, would you?" Carl was desperately trying to keep his cool.

"Okay, but *where*? You haven't said which road we're taking and now we're almost in Boone."

Carl sat bolt upright and nearly came out of his seat. Annabel Lee was right: they weren't headed anywhere in particular, and they sure as hell weren't headed for the coast. "Turn around! Turn around!" Carl was panicking now. Unthinkingly, he tried to grab the steering wheel and turn the car. Annabel Lee shrieked as they nearly collided with an oncoming car. As she fought off Carl's grip on the right side of the wheel, Carl suddenly let go, leaving her pulling to the left. And that is where the car went. They shot across the road, and as Annabel Lee tried to swerve, the two left wheels left the pavement and dropped into the ditch. The right two wheels were screeching from the sideways torque; the hub caps flew off and the exhaust system was torn away on the ditch's side bank.

With the unmuffled roar of the engine and amidst a great cloud of dust, the car finally ground to a halt and stalled. They were both stunned for a few moments. Annabel Lee was shaking violently, but was unhurt—her seatbelt having held her in check. Carl's nose was bleeding from being thrown forward onto the dash board. As the car was leaning at an angle on the driver's side, Carl had landed half on top of Annabel Lee. He struggled to push himself up. After having been tossed about the front seat, Carl's trousers had popped open and the cash had spilled onto the seats and floor. Annabel Lee used the steering wheel to pull herself towards Carl.

"What in heaven's name did you think you were doing?!" Each word left Annabel Lee's mouth with greater force and volume. "You could have killed us!"

Carl's right hand now covered his face. He had assumed that the blood he saw on Annabel Lee was hers, but he could taste blood and felt the warmth on his lips and chin. As he pulled his hand away, Carl stared in disbelief at the blood—which was now streaming down his shirt and onto the greenbacks protruding from his jeans' waist. Annabel Lee followed the trail of blood to the large amount of blood-spattered cash. Carl slowly looked at her, then looked at his lap and then again at his blood-covered hand. Annabel Lee thought he was going to cry, but instead Carl fought back his tears with rage. "Goddamnit to fucking hell!" he shouted. He bashed both fists onto the dash board. "Just look at what you've done!" he screamed at Annabel Lee.

"*Me*!?!" she retorted. "What about *you*? Why did you grab the steering wheel? What were you thinking?"

Carl broke into a rage: "I'll tell you what I'm thinking now! I'm thinking I shouldn't have married such a stupid bitch!"

Equally powered by adrenalin Annabel Lee fired back: "And what is all this money?" She started to speak again, but was cut short as Carl started to punch and hit her. Still pinned down by her seat belt, and with Carl on the upward side of the car, the young woman made an easy target. Soon their blood was spread equally over both of them.

In the melee that had ensued following their crash, neither Carl nor Annabel Lee had noticed other motorists pulling over to come to their aid. Neither of them had heard the sirens—first from the ambulance and then from the sheriff's department. The first would-be Good Samaritan had thought the shouts emanating from the car were cries for help; but as he pulled Carl's door open, he was so shocked at the assault taking place inside the car that he immediately stepped back, letting the door slam shut again. The man's wife stood well back from the car and said, "Warren, maybe you should just wait for the sheriff."

A man who had come alongside Warren asked him: "What in the hell is going on in there?"

Warren shrugged and said, "Beats me. Looks like two people tearing the shit outta each other."

The other man shook his head, spat out some tobacco juice, stared thoughtfully at the pattern it left in the dust and then said, "You'd think just wrecking their car woulda been enough for 'em. Nice car too…or *was*."

Meanwhile the commotion within the car had ceased. Suddenly the passenger door creaked open and Carl Locklear's bloodied face appeared in the opening. From inside the car they heard a plaintive: "Ouch! You're *standing* on me!"

The man named Warren spoke first. "You okay, buddy?" he inquired tentatively—without stepping any closer to the car.

Like a ground hog appearing from its hole and checking the safety around him, Carl scanned the surrounding scene before responding: "Uh—yeah, I'll… uh…I'll be fine. But maybe…maybe y'all could help my wife outta the car, huh?"

Carl's gaze had settled upon the deputy sheriff's car across the road from him. Roy Exum was getting out and adjusting his holster and club while speaking to an approaching paramedic. Carl quickly hoisted himself up onto the side of the car, and then swung his legs to the ground. He held onto the car for a brief time to steady himself, all the while keeping his eyes on Roy Exum. Warren and the other bystander started towards the car to help Annabel Lee, when the tobacco chewer nudged Warren and nodded towards Carl. Not only did Carl still have dollar bills sticking out above his belt, but he had also hastily stashed the bloodied money into his shirt and trouser pockets. The two men eyed Carl up and down warily. "Well, y'all just gonna stand there or are y'all gonna help my wife?" demanded Carl. Neither man made a move.

By then both Roy Exum and the paramedic were crossing the road to the wrecked Mustang. Annabel Lee was starting to shout for someone to come help her out of the car. Looking between Warren and the other man, Roy saw Carl by the car. Knowing he was spotted, Carl thought about trying to make a run for it, but hesitated. The two men turned behind them to see what had fixed Carl's gaze, and saw Deputy Exum. They in turn looked back at Carl. They saw his face blanch and thus turned once more to see what the cause was. What met their eyes unnerved them: Roy Exum had unholstered his revolver and was pointing it *between them* at Carl Locklear. "Holy shit!" uttered Warren. His tobacco-chewing companion nearly swallowed his 'chaw' and was doubled over, choking and coughing.

"You stay right where you are," declaimed Exum. (This was his first real arrest and he was pleased as punch to have an audience.) "I'm taking you in on… on suspicion of robbing Whitlow's Country Store." Then eyeing all the money sticking out of Carl's jeans and pockets, Exum proudly crowed: "And I *believe* I can see all the evidence I'm gonna need!" Both Warren and the tobacco chewer (who had now cleared his windpipe) moved delicately out of the line of Exum's pointed revolver.

"Shit!" was all that a disgusted Carl could mutter.

"Turn around and put your hands behind you!" shouted Roy, a little too theatrically. He fumbled for his handcuffs while aiming his sidearm at Carl. Carl had obediently turned his back and proffered his wrists to Exum. Roy then realized that he couldn't both aim his weapon and cuff Carl. So he turned to Warren and motioned him over. By now Roy had the handcuffs dangling from his left hand. Not wanting to say anything, he waggled the gun at Warren and motioned him with facial gestures to take it and hold it. Warren started to wave him off—and his wife was anxiously beckoning to him from a safe distance away—but in silent command Roy jerked his head towards where he was standing and nodded towards a place for Warren to join him. Warren came over and gingerly took the revolver. This bit of pantomime over, Roy dramatically placed the handcuffs on Carl. While doing so he leaned forward and whispered in Carl's ear: "You done fucked the dog this time, Locklear. I got you, boy." Deputy Exum grinned at Carl like the Cheshire cat with a cornered canary.

Roy and Carl began walking towards the squad car. Meanwhile, in the background could be heard Annabel Lee's ever-plaintive cry: "Would somebody puh-*lease* get *me* out of here!?"

Slammer Time

Oh God! That one might read the book of fate,
And see the revolution of the times
Make mountains level, and the continent, —
Weary of solid firmness, —melt itself
Into the sea!

Henry IV

Frumpy opened her eyes. People were looking down at her. Someone was patting her face. She heard the commotion of other people within a large room and then began to remember that she was in a courtroom. The judge, from his bench, was asking whether she needed a doctor; but a woman in uniform was saying that she was all right, that the defendant had simply fainted. Frumpy was helped to a chair, and after gaining full awareness of her situation, was helped to her feet and taken through the court to a holding cell, where she would be joined by other women being sentenced that day to a term in the women's correctional institution. Frumpy was still stunned by the fact that she had been sentenced to *prison*. How could this have happened? She wasn't a criminal. "Damn that Carl Locklear," she said aloud.

"Your man get you in here too?" came a voice to her a side. Frumpy turned in the direction of the voice. She saw a middle-aged woman sitting with her back against the cell wall and staring thoughtfully at the opposite wall.

"Did you speak to me?" asked Frumpy.

"I sure did. I asked you if your man got you in here. You were damning some man or other."

"That was Carl—my husband," explained Frumpy.

"Ain't it *always?*" said the older woman phlegmatically.

"*I* shouldn't be here at all," explained Frumpy, "I didn't do anything wrong. It was *Carl*; he stole the money. I was just driving the car." Realizing how this must have sounded (and did sound in court), Frumpy quickly re-phrased her last statement: "I was just driving Carl—my husband—to the store where he worked, so he could pick up his wages... And, well, he...he picked up *more* than that." Her cell mate just sighed. "He didn't use a gun or anything— honest!" Frumpy sounded as though she were pleading her case again. She looked at her hands for a moment and began again: "Carl got sentenced yesterday... He's been sent to the prison down in Harnett County," adding faintly, "We'd only been married for a couple of weeks." Frumpy looked at the other woman and asked, "So, um... did your husband—or man—get you into trouble as well?"

The woman smiled at her inner thoughts and shook her head reflectively. "Yeah. Yeah, you could say that," she said.

Tentatively, and completely unaware of jailhouse protocol, Frumpy queried: "Well, what did *he* do?"

"He died. That's what he did." The woman slowly turned and looked Frumpy in the eye.

"He...died? I...I don't understand." Frumpy shook her head in confusion.

"I killed the son-of-a-bitch. Shoulda left him years ago...but I didn't... I killed him instead. He died." The woman shrugged.

"Oh," gulped Frumpy.

A bored-looking female deputy came to the barred door of the holding cell. "Your mama and grandma are here to see you. Y'all got five minutes," she said disinterestedly. She had seen it all before. Frumpy was led through to a private interview room. The deputy said, "I'll be right outside," as she let her in. Still in a state of shock, Frumpy took a chair. As her mother and grandmother approached, the female guard barked out: "Y'all can't take that in there!" She motioned to a shopping bag that Frumpy's mother held in her right hand.

"It's just a few things for my daughter—you can check them," pleaded Colleen.

"She ain't going to summer camp, miz. Let me have it." The guard extended her hand, took the bag and immediately began to sort through it.

"There's not a gun or a file in it, if that's what you're lookin' for," grumbled Ginny.

"I don't make the rules," snapped the guard, "I just follow 'em. Y'all got five minutes."

Both Ginny and Colleen had been weeping and, when they saw Annabel Lee, their tears flowed again. "Oh Sugar," wept Colleen as she collapsed onto her daughter, kissing her and stroking her hair. "What's going to happen to my baby?"

Ginny gently pulled Colleen away from her equally frightened daughter and sat her in a chair. "We just got to pray for her," said Ginny, "'cause God's got to look after her now." The women sat huddled together, holding one another's hands, snuffling, crying and wiping their eyes and noses.

After a few moments, there came a knock from outside the open door and then: "Y'all got one minute."

"Let's pray," urged Ginny, as she took her daughter-in-law and granddaughter into her arms. Ginny prayed that God's protection might surround Annabel Lee as well as for her speedy release. Then she took her granddaughter's head in her hands and kissed her forcefully on the forehead.

The frightened youngster looked up at both women with tear-flooded eyes. "Oh, Mama!" was all she could utter and then fell onto her mother. Their embrace was interrupted by the female officer's entrance. She took Frumpy by her arm and led her away to the waiting prison bus.

Frumpy and the older woman she had met in the holding cell were escorted out to the waiting bus. The older woman smiled at her sympathetically and asked "What's your name, Honey?"

"'Frumpy' is what they call me—but my real name's Annabel Lee."

The woman looked her up and down. "Well, I suspect you could look anything but 'frumpy' when your hair's done up and you're wearing the right clothes."

Frumpy smiled and asked in return, "What's your name?"

"Brenda," replied the older woman as the two were helped up the steps of the waiting bus. There were already three other women on board, also being transported to the state Correctional Center for Women. Each one eyed the others as they were escorted onto the bus and took their seats. Armed guards sat in the back and the front of the bus, separated by steel mesh.

Frumpy couldn't help but think that it felt like the first day of riding the bus to school—except that this bus was grey, the windows were caged, and they were headed towards an education at which Frumpy could only guess. She and Brenda sat next to one another. She was glad of the company—even if the other woman had murdered her husband. Then Frumpy thought of how her grandfather, Wyatt, had killed his own son—her father—to protect Frumpy and her mother. She cast a quick glance of appraisal at Brenda, who was staring out the window, and thought to herself, "She doesn't *look* so bad."

The bus jerked into motion and brought both women out of their thoughts. They looked at one another. "I wonder what it's going to be like?—prison," Frumpy asked Brenda in a half-whisper.

"It ain't home, that's for sure," replied Brenda.

"How do—I mean, have you...*been there*...before?" ventured Frumpy.

"Once. I served about nine months," came the response.

"Is...is it...*bad*?" inquired Frumpy, hoping for a negative reply or at least some consolation.

Brenda turned and stared at her for a moment. "Some days weren't *so* bad...others were *hell*." Frumpy's eyes began to brim with tears; her lower lip began to quiver. Brenda continued to study Frumpy. "You *really didn't* help your husband with that robbery, did you?" Brenda's words were more of a statement than a question. Frumpy could only shake her head. "I wish I could look out for you," said Brenda, "but I'm going to be in maximum security. After the first few days we ain't going to see much of each other."

Glancing about furtively to see whether anyone had noticed her tears, Frumpy wiped her eyes on her sleeves and queried Brenda again: "Why will you be in maximum security?" asked Frumpy naively.

Brenda dropped her head forward in an exasperated manner while keeping her eyes fixed on Frumpy's: "Now *why* do you think?"

"Ah...*oh*," responded Frumpy as the penny dropped. Then she continued: "But what can you tell me? What do I need to know—about prison?"

Brenda sighed heavily, started to speak and then remained silent as she shook her head. Just when Frumpy thought her companion was determined not to speak, Brenda opened up: "Prison is different for every woman in it. It all depends on what she's done, where they put her and such. They got different grades of security. They'll probably start you in medium security until they see how you behave; how you adjust to life inside."

Brenda started to warm to the exercise of teacher and pupil—it helped her to think less about her own fate. "How you feeling right now, darling?"

"Scared, I guess," came Frumpy's reply.

"Well now, that's probably how you'll feel for the first few days… or weeks—until you figure things out, learn the rules, make some friends and such."

Frumpy smiled and stifled a guffaw at the thought of making friends in prison—it all sounded so improbable. Her world had altered so radically. Frumpy told Brenda so. "Yeah, well a woman's got to have her some friends behind bars—just like on the outside. It helps make the time easier—you'll see." Frumpy was attentive to her mentor's words and experience. "A lot of it—prison—is inside your head." Brenda pointed towards her temple. "You gotta find a way to keep it out: work in the sewing center, the kitchen—whatever. Or get yourself some schoolin'—you sound quite an educated young lady. They got all kinds of extension courses in prison. Main thing is: don't let it get inside your head. Got that? That's when you become 'institutionalized.'"

Frumpy nodded dutifully and repeated aloud: "Institutionalized," as though she were back in school.

As the bus rolled across the Piedmont, it stopped at two other towns to collect women who had been recently sentenced to prison. Frumpy watched them get on the bus, and wondered whether she had looked as bewildered as some of them when she first stepped on board. The women chatted and dozed for the rest of the journey. Late in the afternoon they saw a sign announcing the city limits of Fairborn, at which Brenda said: "Won't be long now." Frumpy simply nodded. Soon the bus was twisting and turning along side streets of a run-down neighborhood. Dogs barked at the bus and children stopped their games and stared at the women as the bus slowly drove by. Frumpy had the urge to wave to them, but then remembered where she was and where she was going.

Soon the bus pulled up in front of a fenced area with red brick buildings. There were numerous tall pines and deciduous trees, as well as flowers, on the grounds. Had it not been for the razor ribbon curled on top of the chain link fences, it might have looked much like any institution other than a prison. The bus stopped in front of the gate and guard house. A guard came out and exchanged pleasantries with the driver. Then the gate swung open and the bus drove through onto the prison grounds. Frumpy could see women in plain, blue cotton blouses and skirts moving about the premises. Some stopped and looked at the newcomers, but most simply carried on about their business. The bus halted in front of a two-storey building. The guard at the front of the bus stood up and said, "Welcome to your new home—courtesy of the great state of North Carolina." No one laughed or acknowledged the comment. They all stood up and glumly made their way from one small cage to a larger one.

The women were led the few steps from the bus into a building bearing the sign "Diagnostic Center." Two or three female staff members greeted them as they entered a modest-sized room with comfortable seating around the walls.

"Please take a seat," beckoned a non-uniformed woman. "My name is Dr. Kate McIntyre, and I'm one of the staff psychologists. I tend to work mostly with new arrivals, although I know that not all of you are new to this facility." Dr. McIntyre nodded towards Brenda and another woman. Her acknowledgement of the two former inmates was neither condescending nor too familiar, but somehow it helped put Frumpy at ease. "Most of you—except those who aren't first time *visitors*," there were actually a few laughs, "will spend your first three to four weeks here. You'll eat and sleep here while we gather some information about you and while you get used to your new surroundings. We'll get to know you and you will get to know us. We'll want to find out about your physical and mental health, work history, educational background and criminal record. You'll be given some tests—" at this a few women looked at each other inquiringly. "Don't worry, ladies," reassured McIntyre, "we're not going to carry out cruel experiments on your brains…" Nervous laughter followed. "But we do need to see how you're going to cope with life here, find out your education levels and needs, etc., so that *you* can make the most of your time here. Remember, you've been sent to prison *as* punishment, not *for* punishment." The first time arrivals looked at one another with some measure of relief. Those with previous prison experience simply stared into the middle distance. "Over the next few days you will be meeting security staff, social workers and chaplains, as well as meeting your correctional case manager, who will help decide how you will use your time here—and we hope you will use it well, to ensure that we won't be seeing you back here again." At these words, those who were previous offenders shuffled in their seats uncomfortably. "Remember, as many an inmate will tell you: you can simply serve your time or you can make your time here serve you. It's in your hands."

Over the succeeding days Frumpy and the others were asked to complete a variety of psychological instruments and aptitude tests. They were interviewed by one of the two psychologists, Kate McIntyre or her male colleague, Benjamin Katz. McIntyre tended to handle diagnostics, both for new arrivals and long-timers, and Ben Katz worked more with individual and group therapy, as well as referrals to the visiting psychiatrist. But when they had a large number of 'first-timers' they teamed up together to help process them through the system.

Frumpy and her new compatriots also met with social workers and other staff who informed them about aspects of prison life to do with matters such as family, children and spouses they had left behind, visiting rights, educational and work possibilities. There was the obligatory orientation to the rules and policies governing their conduct while they remained in the custody of the Division of Prisons.

This was introduced by the officer in charge of security, Captain Bob Waller—an imposing figure at six-foot four-inches tall—and a much smaller, but very affable, Lieutenant Jimmy Jenkins. Having been such a good student in high school, Frumpy focused intently on all that was presented to her and required of her—if only for the tantalizing promise in her prison handbook, which stated that if she read and followed the rules, her prison time would be shortened and her chances of returning to her home increased. Frumpy clung tenaciously to this promise and determined that she would be a model inmate.

It wasn't long before the new arrivals were finished with their intake and orientation process at the diagnostic center. According to the seriousness of the crime committed and the risk to the general population, the women were all assigned to their 'dorms.' Brenda, convicted for first degree murder, had already been put in Dorm C—maximum security—where she would await automatic appeal against the death penalty that came with her conviction. Frumpy, and nearly all the other first-timers, were assigned to medium custody dormitories, designated B1 and B2. The women had little private space: just a bunk and a small wardrobe with a few drawers. Showers were open and even the toilets were open to view. This was often the biggest shock for those coming here for the first time—especially those from middle-class homes with modern conveniences. For other women, this was the first time they had ever experienced indoor plumbing in their living quarters. The fact that their bodily functions and hygiene would be carried out in 'open-plan' style was of no consequence to them.

Frumpy was taken aback by her new surroundings. One of the women in the next bunk saw her disconcerted countenance and spoke to her: "Wanna know what the real *hell* of this place is? I'll tell you, Honey: *no privacy*. That's what it is. You gotta do everything—and

I mean *everything*—in full view of somebody else. But…you'll get used to it—you got to."

Frumpy acknowledged her new dorm mate: "I don't really know what I was expecting—cells, maybe. What's your name?—mine's Frumpy."

"Frumpy, eh?" the woman frowned for a second and then said, "I'm Violet—Violet Dixon. And before you ask, Honey, yeah, I been here before. Two-timer. And if it's cells you want—and Sugar, believe me, you don't be wanting *no cells* in this prison—then you gots to be in Dorm C. And they's some damned crazy people in there, sho'nuff!"

"Ha-have *you* been there?"

"No way, girl. You gots to be plain nasty—or out-ta yo' *mind* to be in there. Unh-unh, you don't want to be in no Dorm C."

Both women organized their few possessions in silence. It was not long before they would have their first meal in the dining hall. Except for those in maximum security, meals were taken in a common dining hall. As they made their way with dozens of others, Violet turned to Frumpy and said, "What's a nice white girl like you doing in here? And don't tell me you cut somebody, 'cause I ain't believin' that." Violet laughed.

To her surprise, Frumpy joined in the laughter. "Common law robbery—that's what the judge called it. My husband did it, but I was driving the car, so we both got time for it."

"First time?" queried Violet.

"Mmh-hmm," nodded Frumpy.

"Lord have mercy—talk about some *ba-ad* luck! I be stealin' all the time, that's why I'm here. Shop-lifting mainly—you know, put on two or three blouses or two or three sweaters and go sashaying outta that sto'! Sell 'em when I get back to the neighborhood."

The women were now in the serving line. For Frumpy, it was reminiscent of every school cafeteria she had ever seen—same sorts of chairs and tables, same smells, same bland institutional food and the same complaining about the food. She and Violet took their trays and sat next to each other. Violet acknowledged another inmate further down the table from them. The other woman asked, "Girl, what you doin' in here again?"

"Same ol' shit," answered Violet.

"Ain't it the truth!?" laughed the woman, "Ain't it the *truth*?!"

Turning back to Frumpy, Violet explained, "That girl's my sister."

"Your *sister*?" asked a perplexed Frumpy, "Then, didn't she know you were coming here?" Frumpy shook her head in confusion.

"No chile, not *that* way; not my mama's daughter, like me."

"Oh—you mean 'sisters' because you're both black—"

"Now just you hang on a minute and let me explain," interrupted Violet. "In here," she motioned unobtrusively around the dining hall which stood for the whole prison, "you gots to have you a family. You gotta get yourself connected with a *family*," counseled Violet. "But I have a family, back at home," replied Frumpy.

"No Sweetie, I mean *here*—in the prison. Just about all the women are in one family or another. It gives you a place, and people you can count on, like... well, like in a *family*," explained Violet. "Me, I got grandparents here, sisters, a brother, aunts and uncles, a husband and six children."

Frumpy looked at her quizzically and with some concern: "But we're all *women*," she protested.

"No-o, chile—how can I put it? We *make* our *own* families here—we're the women *and the men*."

"Do you mean like make-believe?" interrupted Frumpy.

"Well...yes...*but no*. It's no kind of game. It's damned *real*, chile." Frumpy frowned and tilted her head as she listened. "Look," Violet started over, "you had a mama and a daddy on the outside, right?" Frumpy nodded. "And you be married outside, too?" Again the younger woman nodded. "Well, the same goes in here. It's just that

128

we women be everybody: fathers, mothers, brothers, sisters and the like. And we look out for one another, get it?"

"Well, sorta..." replied Frumpy, "except I'm behind bars on account of what my husband did."

Violet laughed, "Amen to that! That's true about a lot of us—maybe *most*, if you count what fathers, uncles, husbands did... and maybe what some of us did to our men..." Violet trailed off, then after a nearly imperceptible shudder said, "Where was I? Oh yeah, family groups. So look, chile, I suppose we tryin' to bring some kind of 'normal' to this place by getting into family groups. I don't know how it started; it was like this the first time I come here five years ago. And it works. I mean, our family groups prob'ly do more to keep this prison running than anything the warden and guards do, and that's the truth! In its own way, being in families kinda makes life here seem more natural-like. And I suppose some of us never even had much of a family outside—leastways, not ones we'd like to go back to. Look-a here, sometimes, when they's a lot of tension between some of the women here, a marriage between two of the younger women in the different families helps to smooth things over."

"Y'all get *married* to each other?!" Frumpy was screwing up her face and shaking her head in disbelief.

"Heavens, girl! You think we all lesbians or something? There're sure enough some here, but it's not like that for most of us—no, *noo*. It's just a way for us to look after each other—particularly a way for the older ones to look after the younger ones, like you. You'll just have to see for yourself."

"I guess so," said Frumpy.

During the meal, one of Frumpy's dorm-mates, Lillian Walker, had been listening to her conversation with Violet. Once they were back in the dorm, Lillian approached her. "Look, Sugar. There's one woman here you don't want to get tangled up with—and that's 'DD.'"

"D-D?" queried Frumpy.

"Yeah, 'DD'—it stands for the 'Death Dyke.' She's plain nasty—a real devil-bitch if ever there was one. Real name's Janet Whittle."

"What's she in for?" asked Frumpy.

"Murder. Word is she's a contract killer. Ice water in her veins, too."

"Gosh," was the only word that Frumpy could muster. She thought for a moment, screwed up her brow and then asked: "Why do they call her Death *Dyke?*"

"Honey, don't you know what a 'dyke' is?"

"Well, I've *heard* the word..." said Frumpy.

"It means she's a lesbian—she likes sex with *women*—and she specially likes *young* women. So you watch out, okay?"

"Whom did she kill?" asked a curious Frumpy.

"More like 'how many?'" replied Lillian. "The word is that she was convicted for killing her lover."

"Why'd she do that?" inquired Frumpy.

"Well, it seems her female lover also had a liking for men. Went both ways. So she followed them to a motel where they used to rendezvous and blew them both away."

"But I thought you said she was a contract killer or something," queried Frumpy.

"Yeah, well it seems that once they had caught her for murdering her lover...*and her lover's lover*, the police also investigated her for the murder of a businessman at a convention somewhere—a contract 'hit.' Turns out she used the same gun both times. That's how they got her for the hit."

"Ah," uttered Frumpy. "But that isn't all," continued Lillian, "DD's husband went missing some years before all this happened. He owned a fancy old mansion and a lot of farm land outside New Bern. He and DD had themselves a nice big motor boat—big cabin job. Seems his boat disappeared from its mooring; later it runs aground near Cherry Point. Also seems her husband had simply 'disappeared' off their boat. Anyway, after a year or two she inherited all his property and money. Coroner reckoned it was accidental death—since no one found a suicide note or anything—and the body was never found. Most of us here reckon that she blew him away and buried his body where no one would ever find it." Lillian paused momentarily before continuing: "I guess she took a liking to killing as it seems she made a living at it. It wasn't too long after she inherited her husband's money that she took the contract job. And the rest you know. Just steer clear of her, okay?"

"Fine," replied Frumpy, "But just point her out to me so I'll know who she is, okay?" Then she added: "But why isn't she in maximum security?—if she's that dangerous?"

"Fair question," answered Lillian. "DD did her time in Dorm C when she arrived. She's now on appeal—*and that can take years*—and I reckon she hasn't been deemed an escape risk. Anyway, they got her in a medium security dorm and she looks after work shifts in the sewing room."

Lillian nodded to herself, as though satisfied with her reasoning and then both women sat in silence for a while, lost in their own thoughts. Lillian broke the silence, leaning close towards Frumpy. In a low voice she said: "She's actually *raped* a few women here."

The word 'raped' brought Frumpy out of her reverie. "Raped? Who?"

"DD. She's raped some women here. That's why you need to watch out."

Frumpy sadly knew something about rape—so just hearing the word made her spine stiffen—but in the context of another woman, she shook her head with incredulity.

Lillian looked around to see whether anyone else was listening. "Look Honey. It isn't only men who can do the raping. I mean, it doesn't just require a dick." Frumpy still looked querulously at Lillian. "Girl, you're going to have to learn some things fast in this place. Listen, DD used anything she could shove inside these women's private parts—hairbrushes, shampoo bottles." Lillian saw the shock and disgust that registered on Frumpy's face. "I know. It doesn't bear thinking about. Just watch out, that's all." In mute fear, Frumpy could only nod her head.

Lillian studied Frumpy's frightened and confused countenance. "Look, Hon. It's probably as good a time as any to ask: You want to join my family? I'd have to ask the grandparents, but I'm sure they'd welcome you." Frumpy weakly raised her shoulders in uncertainty. "Look young'un, I saw how upset you were about DD. A family'd give you protection—people you can rely on."

"Lillian, I—" Frumpy's voice cracked. Again she shrugged her shoulders and lifted her arms in despair.

"Just think about it, okay? No big rush. We'll talk about it later." Lillian put her strong arm around Frumpy's shoulders and gave her a squeeze and a gentle shake. "You'll get it together."

Each morning, before they left their dorms, the women had to 'detail' their personal belongings: beds neatly made, slippers tidied at the end of each bed, etc. There were a variety of daily occupations for the women—again, depending on their level of custody. Frumpy noticed that each weekday, immediately after breakfast, a bus arrived to take many of the women off the grounds. Some were on work release: cleaning government buildings—including the governor's mansion; others were on study release—attending classes at the nearby community college and other institutions. Most of these women were housed in Dorm A. Those who lived in medium custody had educational and work opportunities within the confines of the prison. Those who had never finished high school could work on their GED (General Equivalency Diploma); there were some who needed education in basic literacy and numeracy skills. As for work opportunities: the biggest employer of inmate labor was the 'sewing room'—a euphemism for what was in fact a small factory that made prison garments, for men as well as women. It sat a short way from the main buildings and slightly down a hill, with a loading dock backing onto the rear gate. This was so state trucks could easily collect the prison garb for men incarcerated at the nearly one-hundred correctional facilities around North Carolina. One or two women had tried hiding amongst the boxes of clothing with the hope of making a break. Unfortunately for them, the trucks only stopped within the gates of yet another prison and they were soon back at the Correctional Center for Women, locked up in Dorm C and with all privileges withdrawn.

Frumpy began her first work duties in the sewing room. She did general chores such as cleaning scrap material from the floor, helping shift boxes of finished uniforms and bringing the seamstresses more bolts of cloth. It was hot work in a building not made for comfort; and for a bright young woman such as Frumpy, it was mind-numbingly boring. She kept herself going by remembering that by following the rules and making the most of a bad situation, she would shorten her time here. It became a silent mantra for her.

From time to time, the prison warden, Mrs. Betty Nifong, would stroll through the sewing room and talk to the women. Like most prison wardens, hers was a political appointment and she had little to no background in corrections. Frumpy was struck by the fact that the warden dressed like the headmistress of a girl's finishing school—prim and proper. Despite the intense summer's heat within the sewing room—mitigated only by a few ceiling fans and open doors—Mrs. Nifong insisted that the women keep their blouses tucked in, and with only one button open at the neck.

"There she is, ol' 'Pumps & Pearls,'" muttered one of Frumpy's co-workers.

"Who?" responded a distracted Frumpy.

"The warden—'Pumps & Pearls.' Just look at her strutting along, telling us grown women how we s'posed to wear our clothes. Shee-ut. As though we don't know we're hot!" With the mention of heat, Frumpy reflexively wiped her brow. Her long hair was tied back in a pony tail, and small beads of perspiration were joining one another at her hairline to form trickles running down to her collar.

"Warden Nifong doesn't look very hot, does she?" commented Frumpy.

"*Hot*? Woman's a damn iceberg, if you ax me. Just wait 'til she talk to you, you'll see. Snow queen. And don't seem to know shit about women. If it don't *pay* to be *white*, mmh-mmh!"

Unconsciously, Frumpy took note of the skin color on her arms and then mumbled, "Guess you're right."

"Hey Honey—I ain't talkin' 'bout *you*. You in *here* now, Baby; you one of us. Hell, it don't matter what color you are in here anyway." The inmate laughed: "One thing for sure: *you* just ain't the right *kind* of white—the kind that keeps your ass outta here, no matter what you done. What's your name, girl?"

"Frumpy."

"Ha! And white folks say us niggers got funny names! Who call you that?"

"It's a nickname, really," answered Frumpy, "They called me that at school. I just got used to it. My real name's Annabel Lee."

"Mine's Alfreda," said her co-worker. "Help me tape this box shut, Sugar." Frumpy helped seal the box of men's trousers and then move it along with others to the loading bay.

Frumpy looked through the small glass window of the loading bay door. "What's that?" she pointed to a group of shirtless men lifting weights in a grassy area down below the prison fence. Alfreda peeked through the filmy glass and saw the men.

"That's what you ain't gonna get *none of* while you in here! That's what *that* is!" Alfreda laughed again.

"No. I mean what *kind* of place is that?" There was a flat-roofed, brick building behind the weight lifters.

"Oh—that's the pre-release unit for mens. Mens that's been in for a long time go there before they released. Helps 'em get used to

being out again. And Lord don't they need it! Being inside can sho'
mess with yo' head, and don't I know it?!"

"Y'all can quit your gabbin' and get back to work anytime you
like." Alfreda and Frumpy turned quickly to see one of the inmate
supervisors staring at them. The woman had short, cropped hair,
thick bushy eyebrows which accentuated two glowering eyes, a heavy
square jaw, no neck, no breasts and no waist. Frumpy's first thought
was that she was a man in a woman's prison uniform.

"We just havin' a quick breather," fired back Alfreda. "Come on,
girl," she tugged at Frumpy's arm, "let's get them other boxes sealed
and ready for shippin'." As Alfreda pulled Frumpy along with her,
Frumpy felt a smack on her backside as they passed the supervisor.
At the audible blow, Alfreda's grip tightened around Frumpy's bicep,
and signaled what she knew intuitively: not to look over her shoulder.
"Jest keep movin'," whispered Alfreda.

Once they were clear of the supervisor, Frumpy started to ask:
"Was that—?"

"DD?" Alfreda finished her question. "Uh-huh," That's *her* all
right, an' the last thing fresh meat—*white* meat—like you needs is
her on your case. You hear?"

Nervously looking over her shoulder, Frumpy nodded, "I hear.
But what do I *do*?" she asked plaintively. They were now sealing
boxes again.

"You in a family yet?" Frumpy shook her head 'no.' "Well, girl,
that's the first thing. DD tend to stay clear of a girl that got backup."
She stopped herself and looked up: "I ain't sayin' it's a guarantee, you
understand? But it sho' do help. Anybody ax you about joining they
family yet?"

"Yes. Lillian." Alfreda nodded in approval to herself. "Two-timer.
She all right. What you say to her?"

Feeling foolish now, Frumpy replied, "Well, I guess I kinda put
her off… told her I didn't know…"

"Don't you fret none 'bout that—we all been through it." Alfreda huffed as she lifted the sealed box onto the tack. "I s'pect you'll have a different answer for her tonight, right?" Alfreda smiled.

"I *s'pect* you're right," said Frumpy, returning the smile.

That evening, true to her word to Alfreda, Frumpy sought out Lillian. After telling her about the encounter with DD, Frumpy asked what she needed to do to become part of Lillian's family. "Well, there's no initiation ritual or secret handshake, if that's what you're wondering. I need to run it past the grandparents, my husband and a few of the other parents. But don't you worry none, it'll be okay—I've already pointed you out to a few of the family's 'elders.'" Frumpy nodded, but in a way that indicated she was unconvinced of Lillian's assurances. Seeing the younger woman's insecurity, Lillian laid a hand on her shoulder and said: "Listen. There're twenty-eight of us in our family—and we get on well with most of the other families. At most, DD has five or six cronies who run with her—mostly loners. And they got to use the same showers and toilets as us—so they know what can happen if they mess with one of ours. You put DD out of your mind now and get yourself some sleep."

Frumpy tried to do as she was told, but her sleep was fitful, punctuated by anxiety dreams of grim-faced, human-sized hairbrushes pursuing her around the prison grounds.

Frumpy was ecstatic when, the following evening, Lillian told her that she was to be considered a part of the family. Furthermore, Lillian had 'adopted' her as one of her own children. For Frumpy, this hadn't come a moment too soon. At least twice during her shift in the sewing room, she had noticed Janet Whittle, "DD," staring at her—studying her through the blue cloud of cigarette smoke. DD was shorter than Frumpy; and between the effect of the smoke and her thick, bushy eyebrows, DD's eyes took on the look of a predator lurking in undergrowth. As she concentrated on her target, DD indulged in her nervous habit of chewing the inside of her mouth, which gave her the look of an over-sized rodent gnawing on a nut. Whenever DD noticed Frumpy anxiously looking her way, she just smiled a menacing smile; and then resumed her nervous mouth-chewing and hungry staring. Frumpy was glad of Alfreda's company whenever they could work alongside each other—which wasn't often. The sewing room was its usual sweltering temperature, so the unwanted attention from DD made Frumpy sweat all the more.

Frumpy's biggest scare came when she was leaving at the end of her shift. DD made as if to block her path out of the packing area. As Frumpy turned sideways in order to push past, Death Dyke ran her finger along her prey's neck. Frumpy froze in terror. DD rubbed the sweat between her thumb and forefinger and said: "You're going to need a nice wash. I could do your back." The sound of DD's voice broke Frumpy's immobility. Without answering, she turned and headed for her dorm.

"But what am I going to do?" pleaded Frumpy. She sat on her bed surrounded by some of her family's 'elders.' "What can *you* do?"

Lillian, along with the other older women considered their new, young charge. "You say she touched you?" asked Thelma Johnson, Lillian's father in the family. Frumpy nodded. "Said she was gonna 'scrub your back' or some such?" Frumpy nodded assent again. "But she didn't hurt you none?"

"No," replied Frumpy, adding quickly: "but she *scares* me."

The elders took counsel for only a few minutes before they reached their collective decision: "Chunky whirl," stated Thelma and the others nodded and laughed in agreement.

"*Chunky whirl?*" queried Frumpy.

"Don't spoil it for the child!" blurted one of Frumpy's aunts. "Let her see for herself!" The other women chuckled and agreed that would be best.

Lillian asked her fellow 'elders': "Tomorrow lunch-time?"

"Sounds right," replied Thelma, "Best to nip this thing in the bud." She then turned to Frumpy and said in a conspiratorial voice: "Young'un, just make sure you're in the cafeteria same time as DD." Thelma then winked and said: "I gotta get me some sleep."

Frumpy awoke the next morning with a sense of anticipation. She confessed to her family that she had 'butterflies' in her stomach due to a combination of curiosity and worry: What on earth was a 'chunky whirl'? And what if it didn't work? Or worse: what if it back-fired? Where would that leave Frumpy with regard to DD?

Over breakfast the women re-assured Frumpy. In the first place, there were more of them than Death Dyke had in her motley group of friends. Secondly, Frumpy's family worked in every area of the prison, so she would never be alone. Finally, after the shock they had planned for DD, she'd have to be completely insane to mess with Frumpy—or any of their family—again. "However," Lillian leaned close to Frumpy, "there is one thing we're going to need from you."

Frumpy looked up from her stodgy oatmeal with slight panic in her eyes. "What's that?"

"You gotta let DD come on to you a bit today." Frumpy's mouth dropped open. "No, now listen Hon: don't stiff arm her; just play hard to get. Make her think that she might have a chance. Then sit near her at lunch. And when you're finished—you listening?—get up—make sure DD sees you—and saunter over to the restrooms. I guarantee you, we'll do the rest!"

Frumpy took a long, deep breath and exhaled slowly: "O-kaay…I gu-eess," she sighed. "I just hope y'all got it under control."

"Don't you worry your head over this thing," interjected Thelma from down the table. "We've handled this sort of thing before." The others nodded in agreement.

They finished their breakfast of 'wall paper paste'—as they referred to the oatmeal—and prepared to go their separate ways. "See ya at lunch!" they grinned at one another as they left.

Frumpy joined Alfreda in their common tasks of shifting bolts of material to the sewing machines, sealing boxes of uniforms, etc. Alfreda hummed spirituals softly to herself while Frumpy remained lost in thought. It wasn't long before DD came around to check on them. They assured her their work was going well, but DD was in no hurry to leave. She reached into her breast pocket, pulled out a packet of Marlboroughs, shook one out for herself and then offered one to Frumpy. Remembering what Lillian had said to her at breakfast, Frumpy hesitated before thanking DD and declining the offer. DD lit her cigarette, her eyes drinking in Frumpy through the cloud of exhaled smoke. The excitement of having her quarry in close proximity had her mouth moving rapidly and clicking audibly. "Maybe later?" grinned DD.

"Yeah, maybe later," smiled Frumpy, adding: "See you at lunch?"

DD's hungry smile widened: "Yeah, see you at lunch." She blew a smoke ring, took one last look at Frumpy and moved off to her other supervisory duties.

When DD was out of sight, Alfreda, stood up straight, placed one hand on her hip, turned Frumpy to face her with her other hand and demanded: "Girl! Whass *wrong* with you? You done gone plumb outta yo' head? Has DD done got to you?"

Frumpy smiled, shook her head and said, "My family's got it all fixed—or so they tell me. They have some sort of surprise for DD today—at lunchtime."

Alfreda let go of Frumpy's arm, uttered a "Humph," and looked Frumpy over and said: "Well, that's all right then." She started to resume her work, but then asked with girlish curiosity: "What they got planned?"

"They called it a 'chunky whirl,'" replied Frumpy.

"Whoooo, yass!" whooped Alfreda. "Ha-ha! That's sho' gonna be something to see. Yass!" Alfreda kept laughing to herself: "A chunky whirl! Hee-hee! Mmh-mmh—I like it!"

Frumpy interrupted Alfreda's pleasant reverie: "Ah—Alfreda, what's a 'chunky whirl?'"

Alfreda cocked her head sideways and looked at Frumpy. "You don't know what it is?" Frumpy shook her head and shrugged. "What your family tell you?"

"They just said I should wait and see."

Alfreda laughed again. "Then I ain't sayin' nuthin'! You'll find out soon enough. It's only two hours 'til lunch."

The women started back to their work, but then an idea came to Alfreda and she once more took Frumpy by the arm: "Looka here—I'd sho' like to see this thing. Where it gonna happen—could I come?"

Frumpy thought for a moment and said: "Well, I don't see why not. It's after lunch—in the cafeteria restrooms. I'm supposed to lead DD there...I just hope she follows me."

"Ha!" spouted Alfreda, "They ain't *no* doubting that! She sho'nuff hot for you!" And then to herself, as she turned back to work: "Mmh-mmh, Lawd have mercy! She's some crazy woman!"

Frumpy was somewhat startled by the sound of the lunch bell. Both she and Alfreda had retreated to their own thoughts since their earlier conversation. Frumpy felt her heart start to pound as she considered what was soon to happen. "Look," she said to Alfreda who had turned to leave, "would you mind staying with me? You know, go with me to the cafeteria?"

"All right," replied Alfreda smiling gently at Frumpy, "but just so long as *I* ain't gotta talk to that DD."

They both went to the washroom to tidy up before going to lunch. As they came out, DD was about to enter. Her bushy eyebrows rose up like sentinels and a grim smile drew across her nicotine stained teeth. "Going to lunch, sweetheart?" inquired DD, ignoring Alfreda. "I'll be right out," added DD—her words sounding more like a threat than a promise.

"I'll see you over there," anticipated Frumpy, "Alfreda and I need to stop by the prison store first."

"Make mine Marlboroughs," rasped DD as she entered the washroom.

"Let's go!" whispered Frumpy to Alfreda and they marched towards the door double-time.

Once they went through the cafeteria line, Frumpy and Alfreda made sure they sat between other groups of inmates, so that DD would have to sit at least two chairs away. They were well into their meals when DD appeared with her tray. She looked perturbed that her 'prey' was out of reach. But as she plopped herself down in her seat, she said loudly: "Didja get my cigarettes, Sweetie?" smiling towards Frumpy. Like a rooster in a farmyard, she wanted everyone to know that this hen was hers.

Frumpy blushed as people turned towards her, but she managed to smile and say: "Not yet. Alfreda and I were famished, so we came here first. How about after lunch?"

"That'll do fine," grunted DD as she tucked into her food, her teeth fairly snatching the meat from the tines.

From the next table, Frumpy caught sight of Thelma who simply nodded her approval at proceedings thus far. Under her breath, Frumpy said to Alfreda: "I just hope I can pull this off."

Beneath the table, Alfreda gave Frumpy's thigh a comforting pat, while she smacked her lips and said: "Damn. This food ain't bad!... It's *terrible*!" All the women laughed and added their own estimations of their midday fare.

Frumpy quickly lost her appetite—but it had nothing to do with the food. She pushed her meat and vegetables around the plate, occasionally taking small bites, as she waited for DD to finish her meal. When DD had tossed back the dregs of her iced tea, Frumpy got to her feet and slowly stretched her arms high over her head, revealing the shape of her breasts, and tossing her hair back. With her heart beating a tattoo, she took a deep breath, looked over at DD and smiled. Then she said, to no one in particular, "Guess I better take this tray back and then go to the little girls' room." Like a trout on a damsel fly, DD took the bait and was on her feet following Frumpy to the hatch where they returned their trays and utensils. In the heat of her lust, DD hadn't noticed the fact that half a dozen women, including Alfreda, had all felt the call of nature at the same time.

As Frumpy deposited her things, she looked over her shoulder at DD and said: "See you in a minute?"

DD quickly shot back: "I'll be right there!" They made their way to the cafeteria toilets, Frumpy entering first, with DD hot on her heels. No sooner were they inside the restroom than the trap closed: two women blocked the doorway, two more had pinned DD's arms behind her and another was shoving wadded paper towels into her surprised mouth. DD gave up struggling as a bad idea when Thelma and Lillian stepped forward. Thelma put her thick forefinger in DD's face: "You don't never fuck with *my* family! Got that?"

In true terror, DD nodded furiously and tried to say something, but it was lost in her over-stuffed mouth. Thelma jerked her head towards one of the toilet bowls and before DD knew it, Lillian and three other women had whisked DD off her feet and had her torso and legs in the air. Thelma called to Frumpy: "Come on, child. You'll want to see this." Frumpy made her way to where Thelma was indicating. The toilet bowl had at least two bowels' worth of turds floating in it. As Frumpy stepped aside, the four women holding DD quickly set about their work. At this point DD let out a great groan of protest and tried to wriggle free. The women simply tightened their grips and shoved her head down the bowl. As though DD were a human toilet brush they pushed her head in and out several times, and then Thelma asked Frumpy to pull the flush. Still stunned by what she was witnessing, Frumpy did as she was told. The whooshing and sloshing of the flush were joined by the cacophony of DD's snorting and retching. Her captors, their work done, lifted their burden and dumped her in the corner of the restroom. Thelma stood over the now-submissive DD, her face and hair bespattered with feces: "This never happened—understand?" DD mutely nodded.

No one stopped to gloat; instead Lillian took Frumpy by the shoulder, quietly saying, "Let's go," and guided her to the now open door. Behind them, they could hear the spluttering and gagging of a much-diminished DD. All the women filed out, the smiles on their faces suggesting a satisfaction beyond what might be normally expected in their circumstances.

Once outside the building, Thelma simply ordered: "Everybody back to your work."

Frumpy remained in her state of dazed astonishment and had to be led by Alfreda, who, once they were some yards away from the cafeteria, could no longer contain herself. She raised one hand to her mouth and clasped her belly with the other as she bent over with laughter. "Lawd have mercy! I ain't never seen nothin' like it!" Alfreda almost choked from her previously suppressed laughter. "Oh he'p me, Jesus!" she cried as she howled again with laughter.

Frumpy now led Alfreda over to a bench outside Dorm B1 where Alfreda collapsed in a heap of hilarity. A female guard, crossing the yard, stopped to see what the commotion was, but Frumpy waved her off, saying, "She's just heard a funny joke."

"Oh Lawd, yes!" added Alfreda as she dissolved again in fits of laughter. And then to Frumpy: "Wasn't that some *shit*?" convulsing again at her own joke. "I guess *now* you know what a 'chunky whirl' is, huh?!"

Recovering from her state of mild nervous shock, Frumpy surprised herself by joining in Alfreda's laughter. "I guess I *do*," she croaked as her nervous tension released itself in belly-splitting guffaws. "D-do you think," asked Frumpy, "that sh-she'll come back to w-work?"

"Not 'fore she take a shower!" snorted Alfreda.

"Well, what do you think she'll tell the guards?" inquired Frumpy—and then becoming somewhat alarmed: "I mean, do you think she'll report us?"

Recovering now from her near-hysteria, Alfreda sat up and said, "Not if she know what's good for her. She'll pro'bly say she passed out and slipped—fell head-first down the toilet—or something. But she ain't about to say what *really* happened."

Frumpy quipped: "Maybe she could say she was practicing diving?"

"Oh you go ahead on, girl! You go ahead on! Don't get me started again." The two got up from the bench and headed back for the sewing room.

Sighing Time

But thought's the slave of life, and life time's fool;
And time, that takes survey of all the world,
Must have a stop.

Henry IV

A few weeks after DD's 'chunky whirl,' on a late summer's evening, some of the women were sitting out in the prison yard, between the B blocks and the front gate enjoying the slight breeze that stirred the air. The sun hung low in the horizon, behind the two-storied dorms. From the administration building came a lone figure—a man. Like meerkats on the savannah, the women all took note. It was the young assistant chaplain—Stephen Travis. He was working at the prison on an intern year from the nearby Methodist divinity school. As he crossed the yard an inmate said: "Like to have confession alone with him for ten minutes."

"Ten?" said another, "Give me the whole *eve*-nin' with a bottle of *co-mune-yon* wine!" Most of the women laughed. Some even shouted their suggestive thoughts at him as he walked across the grounds—but only when they couldn't be identified.

As he walked by, Travis could feel himself blushing. He didn't know whether to look at the women—laugh and share their joke (at his expense)—or stare straight ahead. The overpowering presence of the dozen or so pairs of eyes tracking his every move kept his eyes fixed forward. Travis tried to act and walk as though everything

145

was normal, but he could feel his legs starting to go rubbery. He felt sweat trickle past his ear and down his neck. His hands felt like lead weights and now swung out of step with his stride. Travis rounded the corner of the building that shielded him from the women's stares and made his way to the 'Control Center,' from where prison security was coordinated. He couldn't help but breathe a sigh of relief.

The women talked about him after he had passed. "A bit young— but ripe for pickin'!"

"I wonder is he married? I don't see no ring on his finger."

"Think he'd marry *you* girl?—and I bet that it ain't his *finger* you care about!"

Frumpy spoke up: "Isn't that a bit *mean*? After all, he *is* a *chaplain.*"

"What you say, girl? With a body like yours?—ain't you never walked past a construction site, with mens shouting all kinds of things at you?"

"Ain't that the truth!?" chimed in another.

Frumpy was blushing now. And she remembered all too well what some men's eyes had felt like. "Well, it's just that he seems so *nice*, that's all. He helped in my orientation here." Laughter.

"Ooh—he *nice* all right!" More laughter.

"Stay in here a few years young'un, and you'll be wanting more than *nice*. *Down* and *dirty* more like it." Other voices added agreement. Frumpy waited until conversations drifted on to other subjects and then made her way to the dorm. She thought about Chaplain Travis.

Frumpy liked the chaplain, although she wasn't exactly sure why. Travis was young and attractive—all the inmates saw that—but he was surprisingly shy. It was clear he didn't enjoy the verbal attention he received from the women. And he wasn't as voluble as most Southern ministers she had met. Just as they had done this evening, Frumpy's fellow inmates often talked about what they would like to do with him. This bothered her. They would sometimes request a visit to the chaplains' office just to spend some time around the young man. He had a slim, athletic frame, so some of the women would make up 'spiritual' problems just for some time to ogle him. He didn't seem the wiser. Why was that? Couldn't he see what they were up to? Whenever Frumpy would chide those who had shouted at Travis, they would taunt her about being sweet on him. But the truth was, nearly all the women found him respectful of them—almost deferential—and that was outside their usual experience of the men they had known. It wasn't so much that Travis was *holy*—although he was a minister; as a man, he was well… just *different*.

Chaplain Stephen Travis had begun his intern year only a few months earlier. The Methodist divinity school, where he studied, was itself an integral part of an august southern university, named for its founder. The founder had been one of the chief magnates in the tobacco industry during the early 20th century, and the limestone marvel of English gothic revival that made up the main campus was built with the proceeds of that addictive, carcinogenic substance that was rolled between thin pieces of paper, set alight and inhaled. So that no one might forget whose money had built the university, a bronze statue of the aforementioned founder stood facing the perpendicular cathedral-sized 'chapel' that bore his name. And, as a further reminder of where the money had come from, a well-smoked stogy was clinched between his fingers. European visitors to the university (of which there were many) were often struck—not only by a European 'gothic' cathedral in 20th century America—but also by how naked the chapel looked, as no medieval building of that size could have stood so tall without the external cosseting of flying buttresses. To them, it looked as odd as a tall pine tree would have looked to local town folk had it been stripped of its branches. But such idiosyncrasies were not to be questioned when a tobacco multi-millionaire wanted to erect a structure to the glory of God. And besides, his builders and architects had the advantage of 20th century steel to act as inner support—what need had they of flying buttresses? It would have been a waste of good limestone. No, both the founder and the chapel builders wanted people to follow the bell tower's clean lines upwards—heavenwards—much as the local proletariat had looked up to the cigar-smoking benefactor. Or so it was hoped.

Stephen Travis had bucked the trend of most of his fellow trainee ministers in that he opted for the year behind bars instead of in a comfortable middle-class parish—unusual for a twenty-five year old, himself from a white, middle-class home. In the three months he had been at the Correctional Center for Women, he had found himself going through many an unwritten *rite de passage*: beginning as an object of curiosity for the inmates, being patronized by some of the older guards and tolerated by the warden. Still, he had stuck it out and was making his way on the narrow path between the inmates and security staff. He had been quick to discern that his success as a chaplain depended on respecting and being there for both groups—not always the easiest of tasks. Without that critical insight, he would have been finished before he started.

Travis worked under the immediate supervision of Chaplain Marvin T. Goodman—senior chaplain and coordinator of all religious services, pastoral counseling, prison visitors, etc. Rev. Goodman—or "Marv"—as he liked to be called by his friends, was a little man—in every sense of the word: the kind that made other men pay for what he lacked in stature. In school, he had neither been tall enough for basketball nor big enough for football. He was tailor-made for short-stop in baseball, but refused this obvious —but spurious—honor. He didn't want to make a virtue of nature-given necessity. Marv spoke in a manner that suggested he had just awakened to an idea: a combination of surprise and dawning awareness—a "well whad-da-ya know?!" kind of voice. It ranged somewhere between Yogi Bear ("Hey Boo-boo!") and a comical Bing Crosby. He was a son of Appalachia, and did everything he could to lose the accent and colloquialisms that gave away his origins. Marv was one of those men who—being just clever enough—found that within the Church, they could create the empire or fiefdom that would have been denied them in the world of commerce or perhaps the military. To fill in the inches of stature that nature—or God?—had not given him, Goodman had recently completed his Doctor of Ministry degree—not a full-blown PhD (of which he wasn't academically capable). Nevertheless, filled with the pride of his new-found dignity, Marv insisted that people in the prison—apart from Warden Nifong—refer to him as "*Doctor* Goodman". In short, he was a martinet. Most of the time this was cloaked beneath layers of Southern etiquette, smooth talk and politesse. Stephen Travis found him affable enough and could deal with the martinet in Goodman—after all, the man was his supervisor. Yet despite the fact that he was somewhat shy and retiring, Travis was also an astute observer of people; and he had begun to have niggling questions—even doubts—about Goodman. There was much gossip about Goodman among staff and inmates: speculation about why his wife had left him and his peculiar 'fondness' for certain of the younger inmates. That took some sorting out. Still, until he had reasons to think otherwise, Stephen had decided to ignore the gossip and work with Goodman as best he could.

After first-timers to the prison had been there long enough to settle in and make the necessary adjustments to incarceration, they were allowed to have occasional family visits. At the women's correctional facility these took place on Sunday afternoons. Frumpy was both excited and nervous about seeing her mother and grandmother. They had exchanged letters, but Frumpy knew that the inmates' mail was read and censored, so she was overly cautious about what she wrote, but also didn't want to upset her two closest relatives with tales from 'inside.' She wondered whether she had begun to change, to 'look' like an inmate, a convict. Frumpy had been told by a long-timer that: "Anybody behind bars looks like a convict." And Frumpy had to admit that, fairly or not, she had indeed been convicted.

On the day of visitation, as the afternoon drew near, Frumpy grew more and more nervous. She talked with some of her new family who were lounging on their beds—the one day they were allowed to do so. Eileen Daltry, who was about ten years Frumpy's senior—and one of her 'aunts'—listened to her worries and then offered some advice. "So, don't 'look like a convict.' Fix yourself up a bit—put on some lip-stick and brush your hair. You've got lovely hair, so don't just tie it back. Fluff it up a bit. If you don't want your mama and grandma to worry about you, then don't look like *you're* worried, get it?" Frumpy smiled and said she would try. "Look, Hon. Most of our families think that all prisons are like Alcatraz—except for those who have done time. They only know what they've seen in films—you know: tough guys, like Bogart or Cagney, rattling tin cups against the bars of their cells." She waved her hands indicatively: "Hell, this looks more like a barrack than a prison. The real prison is in here," she pointed to her head. "So don't show *that* to your mama, okay? Most days, it's easy just to get on with life here; it only really comes home when you see folks from outside. I know we haven't exactly got it good, but it isn't easy for them either. And I suppose that's kinda what makes it prison."

Frumpy listened, taking in Eileen's words, and then nodded. "Thanks. You're right. They've been through a lot too—ever since my arrest and trial. I'll do my best."

Prison visitation was held in the auditorium. There were spot checks on the women going into the visiting area, but mandatory body searches—including internal searches—after the visit. If it were invasive and embarrassing for the inmates, it wasn't the most pleasant of tasks for the guards. Afterwards the guards often had a good laugh over what they had found secreted on or *inside* the women: "Damn! Can you believe she had *this* up her?" It was drugs mostly, but also blades, money and other contraband.

The auditorium was set out with several double rows of chairs, facing each other. Apart from the greeting, there was meant to be as little bodily contact as possible; but those inmates who had small children were often allowed to hold them during the visit. However, they, in turn, were subjected to more rigorous searches afterwards, as much contraband was smuggled into the prison inside infants' diapers.

Visiting times were usually limited to an hour on busy visitation days—but could be up to a maximum of two hours. Frumpy arrived at the auditorium door, announced her name and was pointed to where two women sat, anxiously scanning the room. Their eyes settled on Frumpy and they began to wave excitedly—and then Colleen began to cry. When her daughter came within reach, Colleen was nearly choking from a mixture of both tears and joyful laughter. Mother and daughter embraced; they stepped back from one another, still clasping the other's shoulders, and then embraced again. Frumpy's eyes had welled up with tears, but she fought the urge to let her emotions show—feeling inwardly chastised by her conversation with Eileen. Next, Frumpy turned to her grandmother: "Hey, Grandma. How are you?"

"Not bad for an old woman," croaked Ginny, also trying to keep her emotions in check.

As though becoming aware of their surroundings for the first time—and the various eyes fixed upon them, the three women sat down. They looked sheepishly at one another.

"Did y'all have a good drive down?" asked Frumpy.

"Yes, Honey," replied Ginny, "Your mama's a good driver. I ain't been down to this part of the state in umpteen years. It sure is some distance!"

"But you both got here okay," sighed Frumpy, "and it's just so good to see you!"

Colleen cast a motherly eye over her only child. "And you, Annabel Lee. We've missed you." Before she could cry again, Colleen quickly added: "Looks like they're feeding you well. I was afraid you'd...well...be all *thin*."

"No, Mama," assured Frumpy, "it's a lot like school food, believe it or not. The cooks here can't hold a candle to either of you, but it's good enough."

They fell silent for a few moments. Around them buzzed the noise of other women re-united with their loved ones—and especially their children—some of whom were crying. Ginny broke their silence by saying: "You'll never guess where your mama and I are going!"

Glad to have her curiosity piqued, Frumpy asked, "Where?"

Ginny continued, "Well, we're gonna stay overnight here in Fairborn—at a motel not too far away—and then tomorrow we're driving all the way down to the coast to see your other grandparents!"

"Really?!" responded Frumpy, and then, almost girlishly: "I wish I could go with you!" At those words, her mother and grandmother glanced once more at their surroundings, and the guards stationed throughout the auditorium. "Well, say 'hi' to Nanna and Gramps for me, okay?"

"We'll do that, Sugar. You can count on it." Colleen patted her daughter's knee. Then she took a deep breath, looked Frumpy in the eye, and asked: "Have you heard anything from Carl, down in Harnett prison?"

Frumpy dropped her head, looked at her hands, and then shook her head. Still looking at her hands, she said, "I...I wrote him once... but I got it back." She paused. "It seems he sent it back. I don't think he wants to hear from me." Frumpy looked up at her mother and grandmother, gave a weak smile and shrugged. "Guess it's all over between him and me."

"I never did like that boy none," interjected Ginny. "Thought he was a hot shot—and just look where it got him...*and you*."

Colleen bit her lip and then asked: "Have you talked to anybody? Have they got a minister here?"

"We have a chaplain," started Frumpy, "Well, two actually. That's one of them over there." Frumpy nodded towards Stephen Travis, who was deep in conversation with one of the guards, Lt. Jenkins.

"He looks too young to be a minister," opined Ginny.

"You say that about your new doctor, too, Mama," laughed Colleen. She had taken to calling Ginny 'Mama' since there were just the two of them back at the farm. So long removed from her own parents, Colleen felt closer to Ginny than to anyone else.

"Well, he looks real nice," offered Ginny. "What about the other chaplain?"

"His name is Chaplain Goodman—he's the *senior* chaplain here."

"Senior, huh? What's that make him?" Ginny snorted, "Thirty years old—*maybe?*" All three women laughed.

Colleen spoke up: "Well, I for one am glad that you have someone to talk to—about your spiritual needs. I'm sure you need it in a place like...well: *here.*"

Frumpy nodded and then confessed: "I haven't actually spoken to either of them since my orientation—but I will soon. I have gone to Sunday services—and sometimes to the mid-week services." Both older women nodded approval.

"You got to keep right with God, young'un," counseled Ginny, "especially now."

Across the auditorium, Travis and Jenkins were still chatting. Jenkins, who had kept a watchful eye on the young chaplain over his first few months, decided to test the aspiring minister's mettle: "So, what you hoping to do for these inmates, Chaplain?"

"I guess I hope to bring some measure of God's forgiveness to them. Society and the courts sure haven't offered them much." Lt. Jenkins and Chaplain Travis stood in thoughtful silence for a few moments.

Jenkins then broke their silence: "Well, I ain't convinced that the Lord's forgiveness is all that encompassing." Travis crinkled his face, but before he could respond, Jenkins continued, "No, listen. I nearly got myself saved once. Went to a tent revival meeting that was passing through our town. I had got fed up with sitting on the mourners' bench at the back of the church every Sunday while everybody else went forward during the altar call. So one night I heard this travellin' preacher holding forth in a big tent on some pasture land, just down the road from my family's house. We had no street lights in that part of town back then, so the glow from lighting within the tent showed me the way. As it was a warm evening, the big, opening flaps were drawn back, and on stage I seen this preacher dressed all in white. He cut quite a figure in his white suit and he had a nice head of shiny, black hair. So I sidled up to the tent and slipped in the back. He had finished his sermon and was callin' folk forward for repentance. 'Tell it all!' he was shoutin', 'Tell it all and Jesus'll forgive it!' So people was goin' forward and tellin' the most gawdawful stuff they'd done. 'Didn't matter,' they was told, 'be-cause Jesus'd fix it.' Well now, that sounded pretty good to me, as I ain't exactly lived a saintly life. But I still wasn't sure about gettin' in front of all them people and tellin' my bad deeds. So I sat and watched the others go forward. I gotta tell you, they looked mighty relieved once they had told all about their carryings on: drinking and honky-tonking, gambling, cheating on their wives or husbands, shop-lifting, stealing from the company funds—you know, all the kinds of things that get people locked-up in places like this." He cast a cheeky eye at Travis. "Anyway, about the time that I thought I'd like to feel better about myself and maybe get Jesus to help me, this fellow goes up front, and, starting from his childhood—I figure he was maybe thirty-five at the time—he lays it *all* on the line; and I mean *all*. There was all the stuff you'd expect: stealing change from his father's trouser pockets, smoking out behind the barn and lying to his mother about it. And after each confession the preacher lays his hand on the man's shoulder and says: 'Tell it all, brother, tell it all! Give it to Jesus and he'll forgive you!' Then he told about cheating on tests in school. 'Tell it all!' came the response. So the man continues: he'd slept with loads of different women—*lied* to them, saying he loved 'em, just to get 'em in bed. 'Tell it all!' shouts the preacher. He'd siphoned gas outta his neighbor's tractor to run his car—'Tell it all!' shouts the reverend. Then the man remembered that one of the gals he bedded had had a child—probably his. 'Tell it all, brother! Be brave in the power of God's forgiveness.' Then the fellow went silent; seems he'd covered just about every last thing he wanted Jesus to fix. So in a real quiet voice the preacher asks him: 'Brother, is there *anything* else?' The whole tent meeting was silent as they watched the fellow. Well sir, the man thinks for a moment—he looks down at the floor for a while—and then (and I can see it now, Chaplain), with his face full of the assurance of the forgiveness of the sweet Lord Jesus Christ, he lifts his face heavenward and says, 'I got so drunk once, that I accepted a crazy bet from my friends. They, uh, bet me ten dollars I'd never do…uh…*it*.' And in a very grave voice the preacher asked him: 'What was it, son? What did you do?' 'I… uh…I' 'Yes, son, go ahead,' says the preacher. 'I fucked a chicken…' The preacher has his arm raised above the fellow and says, 'Tell it all bro-…gawd-*damn* if I'd 'a told that!'" Travis burst out laughing. He realized that he was making a spectacle of himself for both inmates and visitors, but he couldn't contain it. Jenkins had lured him in.

"Well, Chaplain," continued Jenkins without cracking a smile, "half the place was laughing their heads off and the other half was plumb upset that the preacher had cussed. And that's still as close as I ever got to being saved. Truth to tell, it left me unsure as to just how far Mr. Jesus is willing to forgive us…" Jenkins was looking down at his feet, absorbed in his memories. Then he sniffed, allowed himself a big smile, shook his head and said: "Damn, that *was* funny! Well, gotta get back to work, Chaplain. See ya round."

"Sure thing." Chaplain Travis headed out of the auditorium towards his office. He was never quite sure how much of Jenkins' stories was to be believed.

Before Travis got through the door, he heard a commotion going on at the far end of the auditorium. He hovered just inside to see what the noise was all about. An inmate's visiting time with her family and child was coming to an end, but the woman had refused to let go of her little boy—a lad of no more than four years of age. The son was crying and clinging to his mother as tightly as she was to him. His distress had set her crying as well. One of the male guards, Fred Bain, was arguing with the mother and shouting at her to put the child down. Bain's aggressive tone set both mother and child to crying even harder. A female guard stood nearby but didn't interfere with Bain. Parting time was always difficult—particularly for inmates whose children were still quite young. However, this situation was becoming more extreme and was sending forth ripples across the hall—riots were made of lesser incidents. Conversations between family members began to trail off as the fracas between Bain and the mother with her child escalated.

As nearly everyone's eyes were fixed upon Bain and the inmate, no one had paid too much attention to Chaplain Travis' approach. "I've got this," Travis stated calmly, but firmly.

Bain was thrown off his tempestuous stride. "Wh-what do you mean, Chaplain?"

"Just what I said," replied Travis, "I've got it. They're all coming over to the office with me." Stephen motioned for the family to get up and follow him out of the auditorium, the mother and child still clinging tightly to each other. He knew the mother and son could more easily be uncoupled in quieter circumstances.

"Well, you're welcome to 'em!" Bain had to have the last word. Conversations in the visitation area began to return to normal.

Frumpy and her family once more turned their attention to one another. As Colleen and Ginny had another equally long journey the next day, they let Frumpy know that they needed to eat and rest. Chastened by the traumatic farewell they had witnessed between mother and son, Frumpy, Colleen and Ginny had tacitly decided to part quickly and without emotion. They all summoned forth their best smiles, hugged each other and quickly headed for their respective doors. Each secretly breathed a sigh of relief: that she had made the first connection between the worlds of freedom and incarceration, and that it had gone as well as could have been expected—perhaps better. Frumpy was even surprised to find that there was a certain lightness to her step that had not been present when she had entered the auditorium.

Officer Fred Bain was a 'graduate' of the US Marine Corps—not unusual for one who had grown up in the shadow of the Marines. His tiny hamlet in Jones County was sandwiched between the rumble of maneuvers from Camp Lejeune and the roar of aircraft from Cherry Point Marine Air Station. So it was natural that when, after one-too-many appearances before the local magistrate for drunken and disorderly behavior (largely consisting of bullying patrons half his size in the local watering hole), he was offered the following choice: to serve a custodial sentence or to join the US Marines and learn to fight properly. After all, in the mid-1960s the United States was involved in a little 'police action' in Southeast Asia which required hot-blooded young men who were spoiling for a fight. At first, Fred responded well to the Marines—they shouted, trained, re-shaped and engrained leatherneck discipline into this red-neck, bullying, bar-brawler.

By 1968 Fred had gained his sergeant's stripes and was soon aboard a transport to Danang airbase in South Vietnam. He was one of many replacements sent out in the wake of the Tet Offensive. However, apart from the odd rocket or mortar attack, Bain never saw any action—at least not the kind for which the Marines are best remembered. For the one thing that Bain—along with most bullies—had learned well, was how to suck up to people who have more power than they. With appropriate brown-nosing, Bain had got himself assigned to regimental supply. So began his career in organized and sanctioned chickenshit: barking orders to clerks and privates, trying to sound the seasoned veteran—but assiduously avoiding beer-drinking sessions with fellow non-coms who were 'grunts.' He bought 'trophies' from Lurps—the long-range reconnaissance patrollers—with which he decorated his 'hooch,' to give it that authentic touch. Nevertheless, it didn't take anyone long to detect the nature of chickenshit: that distinct combination of pettiness and imperiousness mixed with meaninglessness. Thus he became dubbed 'Sgt. Chickenshit.' Bain talked the talk of the Marine Corps, but his walk missed the spirit of *Semper Fi'*. Although he had intended to be a lifer, it wasn't to be. Even his relatively secure supply job had occasionally required getting shot at when he ventured from Danang, and this had become too much for him. Despite his eventual rotation back to the US and being safely ensconced in Camp Lejeune once more, Bain no longer saw eye-to-eye with the Marine Corps' ethos: the spit, polish and discipline were beginning to wear on him.

So by 1974 Bain had 'graduated' from the US Marine Corps and become a guard in the North Carolina Department of Correction. In sum: he'd 'volunteered' for military service in order to avoid jail time and put in enough years to build up the beginnings of a nice pension and leave with an honorable discharge. Like so many veterans before him, who had worked for Uncle Sam, Fred could continue to build his pension credits through state employment. But only like *some* veterans before him, Fred had enjoyed *not* having to decide what clothes to wear on a daily basis—and he had positively reveled in the authority endowed him by his three stripes. So why not join the prison system? The prison service gave him both a uniform *and* a chance to throw his weight around. The problem was that the Correctional Center for Women was *not* a Marine camp. And although the guards carried rank and followed a military-style chain of command, it *wasn't* the military and certainly not the Marine Corps. Thus it was not long before Officer Bain was again christened with a 'chickenshit' moniker: Officer Chickenshit or 'OC' for short. He was a pain to inmates and prison staff alike.

Although OC had grown up amongst the peanut, tobacco and soya bean fields of eastern North Carolina, he was possessed of a face that the sun would turn an angry red, but would never tan. As a relatively new member of the prison staff, Bain had, in addition to his security duties, the job of policing the grounds. With military precision he cautioned the women against throwing paper, candy wrappers and cigarette butts on the ground. Bain was known to have a short fuse to his temper, so the women went to great lengths to piss him off, just so that they could watch the display. He had unintentionally turned cussing into a performing art. Thus, when the women saw OC approaching, they would reach into the waste bins and throw refuse on the ground. Then they would pretend to be going about their business, all the while keeping an eye on Officer Bain. Upon seeing the offensive rubbish, Bain would first place his hands on his hips, then drop his head and shake it, followed closely by a string of good Southern expletives as he rolled his eyes heavenwards while still slowly shaking his head: "Kee-yus mah ice!" was usually the first to erupt, quickly trailed by "Hot a'mighty!," as he once more surveyed the infraction, and then: "Shee-ut far and save the matches" and other such colorful expressions born of the rural South. His head bobbed with each syllable. Add to this the blotchy, red patches adorning his face and neck, and Bain looked and sounded like a demented Howdy-Doody. At this point the women would no longer be able to contain themselves and would burst open with much-needed laughter. The entertainment value of OC's redneck soliloquy was worth the price of having to police the grounds under his aggrieved and watchful eye.

Staff psychologist Ben Katz had one word for Bain: "schmuck." Katz felt that OC was an unreasonably cruel and unusual punishment for all those incarcerated at the Correctional Center for Women. Bain had an opinion about everything: politics, justice, corrections, race, gender, psychology. One day he decided to argue with Katz over the 'value' of the therapy groups that were run by Katz and Kate McIntyre. "Hell, them women was born criminals and there's no changing that. Just put 'em to work until they've served out their time. You're wasting your time with all this *psycho*-logical thurpy, if you ask me."

"Which I didn't," fired back Katz, "but be sure to say 'hello' to Heinrich Himmler for me at your next book-burning, okay? I've got work to do." With that Ben Katz marched away in his usual quick step, rubbing his thinning pate as he went—something he did whenever he was agitated. Bain remained standing where their 'conversation' had ended, dumbfounded at Katz's response.

Travis was talking with some inmates who had been playing basketball and caught sight of Katz crossing the prison yard, grumbling to himself. Katz liked Travis—for several reasons. First, as the only Jewish member of staff, Ben felt somewhat isolated. Add to that the fact that most of the staff was Southern Baptists, and he felt even more isolated. Thus, in social terms, the fact that Travis was a Methodist almost made him as good as a Jew. In addition, Katz liked the fact that Travis could read Hebrew—not something many Christians took an interest in. In any event, Katz, along with the prison psychiatrist, Harold Deaton, provided several hours of clinical supervision every month for Travis—specifically for Travis' pastoral care with inmates who suffered from severe emotional and mental problems.

"Hey Ben!" called Travis. "Slow down! I need to ask you something."

Ben was still muttering angrily to himself: "That schmuck was born thirty years too late. Bain! Ha! He's the *bane* of everyone's existence."

"Pardon me?" said Travis.

"That schmuck, OC. He would've enjoyed working at Belsen the way most kids enjoy Disneyworld."

"Yeah, he's something else," agreed Travis.

But Katz was worked up: "No, I mean it—he's a first rate asshole. The schmuck requires industrial strength proctology!" Travis laughed at Ben's colorful turn of phrase. They stopped outside the diagnostics building. "So, what was it you wanted, Stephen?"

"It's about Clara May—Clara May Benson?—over in Dorm C?"

"Oh, yeah, right," nodded Ben, "The one who's *meshugganah*."

Travis chuckled. "Yep, she's the one."

"So what's the problem?"

"No problem really," said Travis, "I just don't understand some of the things she says."

"So if you did understand," chimed in Katz, "you'd be *meshugganah* too! What's to understand?"

"Well, for one—what is 'root-working'? She says her husband has 'root-worked her all the way from New York City' and has put 'Amazon animals' in her bed." Travis couldn't help but smile as he said it.

"Imaginary pets now, eh?" chuckled Katz. "I thought you were from the South, Stephen," smiled Ben as he put on his best imitation Southern accent: "Don't evuhbody 'round here indulge in a little down-home root-workin'?"

Travis laughed, "I might—if I knew what it was."

"Kate McIntyre knows more about it than I do," said Katz, "But it's some kind of voodoo—a mixture of African and Caribbean magic. Clara May believes her husband has put a spell on her—all the way from the Big Apple. She's crazy as a loon. Just make sure you see her when she's well dosed-up on Thorazine—after Deaton has seen her—she's a lot calmer then...but no less crazy."

"I'll keep that in mind," said Stephen.

Soured Time

How sour sweet music is,
When time is broke, and no proportion kept!
So it is in the music of men's lives.
Richard III

"Good *mawn*-in' Chaplain Travis!" beamed Charlene Walker, one of the prison's case workers. For a woman who had spent the best part of twenty years working behind the bars of the women's prison, Charlene had a remarkably cheery disposition.

"Charlene," replied Travis, "how is it you manage to be so upbeat in what could be considered a very depressing place?"

Charlene was quick to reply: "Well *you* ought to know, Stephen! It's faith in my Savior and the clear recognition that, for most of these women, life can *only get better*. That's what keeps me going. You can drown in all the sorrows of this place, or you can add one more plank to the ark that will hopefully get most—or at least *some*—of these ladies out of here—*for good*."

"I guess you're right, Charlene," said Travis. "I suppose right now I'm just seeing and hearing *the problems*. It takes some getting used to."

"Don't it *just*?!" smiled Charlene, "But you'll get there—if you plan to stick with this sort of ministry, that is."

"That's where I'm leaning," said Travis, feeling encouraged to talk about it. "The truth is... I don't feel *un*comfortable working here—not that I *enjoy* prison, mind you, but everything we do here seems...well...to *matter*—to the inmates *and* their families. Most of the people I'm studying with at the divinity school seem to want..." he paused, "Well, they seem to want nice, safe, middle-class churches—*white* churches. I don't know...but for me, that just seems like a cop-out *from* ministry—just a safe career path."

Charlene was from a largely Native American—but mixed— background. On the Native American side, she came from a tribal group largely referred to colloquially as 'Lumbee'—derived from the Lumber River whose banks and outlying regions they had inhabited for centuries. But over those same centuries had come colonists from Britain, continental Europe, and later, their African slaves. People being what they are, they did what human beings have done over the millennia: they had sex, married, 'interbred,' co-habited—whatever one wanted to call it—and they had offspring. The simple truth was that not even the most die-hard racist could claim to have 'pure blood'—whatever that was. This flesh and blood reality made all the more a sad joke out of the Ku Klux Klan billboards which still stood along I-95 and shocked Yankees driving between New York and Miami: "Help fight communism and integration. Join the United Klans of America." Travis knew that somewhere, not too many generations back, there was Cherokee blood in his family— something that had been spoken of only in whispers when he was a child in the 1950s, when 'white was right.'

Charlene had stood and looked at Travis thoughtfully after his admission regarding ministry. Her deep dark eyes looked into eyes that mirrored hers. "Church can be a funny old thing, Chaplain. But I believe, just as I stand here, that it is the one Lord God that made every single one of us. As the old saying goes: 'There but for the grace of God...' And if this is where you believe God has put you, then go with it. You've been here now, what?—four?—five months?" Stephen nodded. "Well, you seem to be settling in fine—and people like you. You're a little shy at first, I'll grant that, but your heart's in the right place, and you got a good head on your shoulders." Charlene's eyes darted, almost imperceptibly, towards the office that Travis shared with Goodman. "For a lot of us—inmates and staff—you're a welcome change. You stick with it, keep learning, and you'll do a heap of good."

Travis blushed a bit from the compliment. "Thanks, Charlene. I do appreciate that, but—uh, *you* stopped me. What is it you wanted?"

Charlene raised her eyes heavenwards, "Lordy, I'd forget my head if it weren't screwed on! I believe you had mentioned that you and Chaplain Goodman needed some more secretarial support—is that right?"

Travis' ear pricked up at the query. "Yes. Absolutely!" He glanced around and then added *sub voce*: "It's just that... uh... Marla Thompkins—who does some work for us a few hours a week?—well..." Travis halted.

"Out with it," prodded Charlene.

"Well, she never types out my handwritten letters the way *I wrote* them—the way I *want* them."

Charlene smiled. "Go on."

"You're really enjoying this, aren't you?!" chided Travis. He continued: "The letters always come out in a sort of...well... shall we say a *patois* of English *dialect*."

Charlene was laughing now. "I figured as much," she said.

In mock anger, Travis fired back at her: "Well, thanks for making me spell it out!"

"Forgive me," grinned Charlene, "we've all been through it. We try placing the girls who have at least a solid ninth-grade education in jobs where they can use reading and writing skills. As you know, so many women who come in here are totally, or functionally, illiterate. So we try to encourage them. Listen, let Goodman keep Marla on—I'll send you one of our newer arrivals, okay? But you'll have to share her with me on occasion."

"Okay," agreed Travis, "So what's her name?"

"Annabel Lee Locklear—but she goes by 'Frumpy.'"

Travis made a questioning face at the nickname, but quickly added: "When can she start?"

"Next week," said Charlene, "she's got to finish her job in the sewing room first. She's wasted there. The girl's bright—got her high school diploma. I think she'll do fine with y'all."

"Sounds great," replied Travis. "I'll look forward to her starting."

Frumpy began her first day as a chaplain's secretary on the Monday after Charlene and Stephen had talked. It was a fine, mid-autumn morning. There was a rich smell of decaying leaves and damp earth. And from nearby houses, whose occupants could not afford central heating, there was the smell of smoke from wood and coal fires. Goodman was in the administration building with the warden and Travis was sitting at his desk, writing notes and whistling softly to himself, when Frumpy reached the open door. She knocked softly as she peered around the doorframe. "Chaplain Travis?"

"Yes? Oh—hi! Are you Frum—um, Annabel Lee? The new secretary?"

"Yes, I am. I—I hope I'm not disturbing you." Travis lifted his arms and looked around as though to say: "What is there to disturb?" "Come on in and have a seat." Travis got up and pulled out the chair which sat in front of the electric typewriter on a nearby table. As Frumpy took her seat, Travis motioned towards the table. "Well, this is it! I'm afraid it's all we can offer as a work space."

"Oh, I'm sure it will be fine," smiled Frumpy.

"Now," began Travis, "first things first. What do you like to be called?" He noticed a slight color begin to appear in her cheeks.

She looked down as she shrugged and said, "Everybody calls me 'Frumpy.'"

Travis paused for a brief moment and asked: "But is that what *you* like to be called?"

Again Frumpy shrugged, blushed more, and said, "It will do. I'm used to it now."

Travis studied her for a moment and then said: "If you don't mind my asking—your given name is Annabel Lee, is it not?" At this, Frumpy looked up, smiled wistfully at Travis and nodded. "I had to memorize a poem in junior high school..." started Travis.

"By Edgar Allan Poe—I know," smiled Frumpy. "It was my mother's favorite poem. And Poe was her favorite author."

"Yes, I like it too," said Travis, "but it is a bit melancholic...*and tragic*." Realizing what he had just said, Travis started to apologize. "Oh—sorry! I'm sure that's not why your mother gave you that name."

Frumpy smiled and shook her head. "It's okay. I've sometimes wondered myself...especially now." She looked at her surroundings. "I mean...being *here* and all."

"Well, I seriously doubt that your name had anything to do with your ending up here."

"No, I have my husband to thank for that."

"Ah," was the only response her words elicited from Travis—he felt he had already 'put his foot in it' once; he'd just listen now.

"Do you need to know what I've done? I mean, why I'm in prison...in order to work here?" ventured Frumpy.

"No, only if you want to tell me. The job's already yours—if *you* want it, that is."

"So no one—my case worker or anyone—has told you what I've done?" asked Frumpy.

"No. It doesn't work like that. I can have access to inmates' files—if I should need them—but I rarely do. I'm just happy to hear what people want to share with me—where they are now." Frumpy nodded without saying anything. Her eyes moved about the room, but it was clear to Travis that she wasn't looking at anything—not outside herself anyway.

Frumpy let out a deep breath, cocked her head to one side and said, "I'd like to tell you about it—why I'm here. Is that okay?"

"Yes. Absolutely—but first let me close the door." Travis walked the few paces to the heavy wooden door.

After returning to his chair, Travis smiled at Frumpy. She returned his smile with a bashful curve of her closed lips, all the while wringing her hands on her lap. The chaplain dropped his head to one side, raising his eyebrows as he watched Frumpy. "You don't have to do this, you know," he offered.

Frumpy quickly nodded: "I know—but I want to…I think I need to tell you. And I promised Mama and Grandma that I would speak to you—a chaplain. They saw you on a visiting day—the first time they came here. I pointed you out when you were laughing so hard with Lt. Jenkins."

Travis blushed slightly: "Oh yeah—I remember. Jenkins told me the funniest story and caught me completely off guard. Lt. Jenkins is quite a character."

"My grandma thought you looked awfully young for a minister…" Travis blushed again. "But then she says that about nearly everybody these days: doctors, dentists, police… Anyway, I told them that I would speak to you…or Chaplain Goodman. I guess coming to work for you a couple of hours a day has finally helped me to do that." Frumpy gave a girlish giggle. Travis waited. Frumpy took a deep breath and let it out audibly. "Common law robbery—that's why I'm here." Still without looking at Travis, Frumpy smiled to herself and added: "It still sounds funny to hear myself say that—I've been *convicted* of common law robbery."

Frumpy then gave Travis an abridged version of the events that led to her arrest and conviction. Afterwards, she turned her eyes towards Travis: "Would *you* believe me if I said I never did it—that I didn't know that Carl was going to steal that money? I mean, I hear a lot of the girls say they don't deserve to be here—that it was their men that got them here and all that…"

"Frumpy, a lot of women *don't* deserve to be here. I'm afraid so much of our so-called 'justice' system depends upon color, money and background—perhaps money most of all. I'm coming to the opinion that justice yields to the biggest pocketbook. But you didn't come here to listen to my opinions, did you?" They both smiled. "Look, you asked me a question: whether I'd believe you weren't guilty of robbery; *if* you said you never did it. So, is *that* what you're saying?"

Frumpy nodded, "Yes. I am saying I never did it."

"I believe you."

Frumpy's brow furrowed as she searched Travis' face. "You *believe* me—*just like that?*"

"Yes: just like that. Listen Frumpy, I didn't ask you how you came to be in prison—it's actually none of my business. Your working in the chaplain's office wasn't contingent upon a 'confession.' I suspect you've had enough of that with the police, the court and such. You *chose* to tell me—so I honor and respect that. As for believing you: I give you the same courtesy that I would extend to anyone outside this prison. I will believe and trust you until you give me reason not to do so. Fair enough?"

"Fair enough," she replied. Frumpy sat and weighed his words on the scales of her heart and mind; the scales tipped in favor of trusting Travis.

It was nearly Thanksgiving before Frumpy saw her mother and grandmother again, although they had written to each other regularly. Frumpy had told Colleen and Ginny about her part-time secretarial work in the chaplains' office. Colleen had responded with both relief that Frumpy was out of the hot and monotonous work in the sewing room and joy that at least her daughter was able to use her education, if only in a small way. Colleen had then let on that she too had good news, but wanted to keep it a surprise until they next met. Thus there was anticipation on both sides when that November Sunday afternoon rolled around. Mother, daughter and grandmother all hugged, kissed and then hunched forward on their metal, folding chairs to hear one another's news and be as close to one another as possible. Frumpy noted that her mother looked somehow younger than when last they met—she wore just the slightest bit of make-up, to complement her peaches and cream skin, and her hair was brushed and shiny, pulled back into a loose pony-tail. "So Mama, what's the big secret?" implored Frumpy.

Colleen smiled impishly, but before she could speak Ginny broke in: "She's got a job! Your mama's teaching again!"

Colleen feigned anger at her mother-in-law: "Oh, hush your mouth, you spoil-sport!"

"Hush your own self," retorted Ginny good-naturedly, "You've kept this child waiting long enough. Somebody had to tell her!"

"Mama, that's wonderful!" exulted Frumpy. Her eyes brimmed with joyful tears as she grasped both of her mother's hands and squeezed them. "It's just so good for you—and so right. I...I had always hoped you would teach again."

Colleen reached out and stroked her daughter's hair. Then she quickly looked around and said: "I hope it's all right if I touch you? It's just so hard sitting here and looking at you like this. But listen—before you get too excited—I'm only a substitute teacher, at least for now. I just started back last month. I thought I'd take it gently to start with—."

At which point Ginny interrupted: "Yes, but you ought to see how often they call your mama to fill in as a substitute—two or three times every week." Ginny nodded as though to confirm the veracity of her statement.

"Well, I'm just so happy for you," Frumpy repeated, "at least we've all got some good news to share. Oh—and I have another bit of news…well, it's not news *yet*, but hopefully soon." Both Ginny and Colleen leaned forward and waited expectantly. "I told you they hope I'll soon be on minimum custody level, right? And that's part of how I got the job in the chaplains' office? Well, my case worker—Charlene Walker—is looking into my starting courses taught by the local community college—after Christmas. Isn't that great?" It was now Colleen's and Ginny's turn to congratulate Frumpy. Frumpy then dropped her head and lowered her tone as she said: "I know it's not like doing teacher's training at Appalachian State—or another university—not the way we had pictured anyhow; but it is a start."

Ginny spoke first: "Honey, none of our lives is what we had pictured, but we just got to keep moving on. With the help of the good Lord, we just got to keep moving on." These three lives, intertwined by bloodline and tragedy, were a collective witness to a dogged determination to survive—but not just a survival of biological functions—rather, theirs was a *willing* towards life itself; much as the germinated seed fights to break free of the suffocating earth. For this trinity of Carolina womanhood, it was a moment of Holy Communion.

They chatted on animatedly until Ginny pointed out that Colleen was teaching the next day and they had a long drive back up to the mountains. Before the older women got up to leave, Colleen hesitatingly inquired: "And Carl? Is there any news from him?"

Frumpy frowned and shook her head. Then she shrugged and said, "I guess it's Tammy Wynette time."

When her mother and grandmother looked puzzled, Frumpy said: "You know, her song: D-I-V-O-R-C-E?"

Colleen looked at her daughter longingly, but Ginny, ever practical, said: "At least when you get out of here, it will be a completely new start." With that said, they rose, kissed and bade each other farewell.

As Frumpy made her way to the room for her obligatory body search, Lillian Walker caught her eye. She was saying goodbye to a woman who looked much like Lillian (her sister?) and an old man, who was stooped over a walking stick. The two women joined up after they had been searched. Still buoyed by the visit with her mother and grandmother, Frumpy was the first to speak: "Was that your family? That woman looked a lot like you."

"My sister, Rita, and my father. He's lived with Rita since my mama... *died*...although it sometimes feels like I killed her."

"How so?" asked Frumpy.

"Coming in *here* this second time. Her heart was bad anyway, but when I came in here two years ago...well, she didn't last long." Despite her comparatively jubilant mood, Frumpy decided against offering any palliatives. "How old you think my father is?" queried Lillian.

"Gosh, I don't know," replied Frumpy.

"Well have a guess—I'm forty-one."

"Maybe seventy or seventy-five?" ventured Frumpy.

"He does look it, doesn't he?" sighed Lillian. "But he's sixty-two. Mama's death, and me coming back in here...well, it's made an old man out of him." This time it was Frumpy's turn to comfort her older companion. She placed her hand gently on Lillian's shoulder and they walked back to their dorm without saying another word.

Once inside, Lillian seemed to cheer up. "Say, did you tell your mother about joining our family here?"

"I did think about it," replied Frumpy, "but we had so much news to tell—*good* news—and I just didn't think there'd be time to explain it well...I mean, it does sound odd to people on the outside, doesn't it?"

"It sure does," nodded Lillian in agreement, "that it does."

Frumpy continued: "I guess I wondered whether my mother and grandmother might not feel a little...well, *jealous*... You know, like I'm replacing them or something—having a 'mother' and 'father' in here. What do you think?"

Lillian considered Frumpy's words for a moment and then said: "I suppose some might get jealous or get the wrong idea about things. It just makes a lot more sense once you've been inside for a while. You tell 'em—or not—in your own time."

☒

"Chaplain Travis? May I ax you a qwershun?" Janitta McCall's head was peering around the office door. Jannie, as she was known, was from rural, eastern North Carolina, where 'sk' became 'ks' or 'x,' 'questions' became 'qwershuns,' 'pencils' became 'pilncils,' 'elm trees' became 'ellums,' etc.

"Hi, Jannie. Sure, go ahead."

"Me and some of the sisters want to have us a Christmas pageant. We's wondering if you could he'p us out?"

Travis leaned back in his chair and put his hands behind his head. "Well, I guess it depends on what you need," he drawled.

"Well, sir, not all 'em can read. So we was wondering maybe you could help us with the Bible verses and such?"

"Okay, I'll give it a go—when are you planning to rehearse?"

"After supper, 'cause most of 'em work in the sewing room and others be doing they GED and such."

"Fine. I'll see you all at, say, 7:00 p.m. in the auditorium. I'll let the other staff know."

"Thanks, Chaplain Travis."

When Travis entered the prison hall that evening, the women were all present and had already started assigning parts for the pageant. "Hi ladies," Travis greeted them. The women made various acknowledgements to Travis.

"We gots a pro'lem already," stated Jannie.

"What's that?" asked Travis.

"Well, some girls want they to be mens in this pageant."

"Well, chile, it pretty clear that Gabriel and Joseph be mens," chimed in Yolanda Baker. She nodded knowingly to herself. Others joined her, mumbling in agreement. "Don't forget the Wise *Men*," said another woman.

"Well, I see your problem," averred Travis, "but the nature of a *women's* correctional institution does mean that men will be scarce."

"Yeah, but *you* a man," countered Yolanda, "an' we got other mens working here."

"That's true," said Travis, "but you'll have to ask them yourselves, if that's what you want. As for me, I'm no actor, so I'll stick with helping you get this pageant together. But just to be safe, why don't y'all practice *all* the parts?"

The pageant was, as many are, a conflation of Matthew's and Luke's Gospels. Yolanda Baker was playing Mary, and Marsha Ward was taking the part of the angel Gabriel. Chaplain Travis was press-ganged into the roles of assistant-director (alongside Janitta), speech coach and critic.

An off-stage narrator began reading: "Now the birth of Jesus Christ was on this wise." She paused: "*Wise?* What the hell that mean?"

"Don't you blaspheme!" shouted Jannie, "Girl, don't you blaspheme!"

The narrator apologized and said, "Jest don't know what they means by 'wise,' that's all."

"It means 'way,'" broke in Travis, "The birth of Jesus was in this *way*."

"Then why don't they jest say that?" queried the narrator. She began again: "Now the birth of Jesus was on this *wise*: When as his mother Mary was es-... es-pussied to Joseph..." The narrator giggled.

"Girl, *what you say*?!" exploded Jannie. "I done told you not to blaspheme! Don't you dare blaspheme! You gonna blaspheme in here then you just go ahead on, girl; you take yo'self outta here!"

"Well, it all right here in the Bible," retorted the narrator.

"You a lie and the truth ain't in you! They ain't *nothin'* about *pussy* in the Bible!" shouted Jannie—"Sorry, Chaplain Travis"— she quickly threw in. "You just go on and read what's written down. You said you could read, girl, so *read!*"

"The word is *espoused,*" corrected Travis, "It means to be engaged to be married."

On they faltered, with Marsha as Gabriel speaking to Joseph in a dream: "Joseph *though* son of David…"

"*Thou,*" blurted out Travis.

"*Now?*" asked a bewildered Gabriel, "Now *what?*"

"Not *now,*" replied an increasingly frustrated Travis: "*Thou.* As in 'you.'"

"*Me?* What about *me?*" asked a downcast Marsha.

Travis didn't know whether to laugh or cry. "Not *you,* Marsha. I mean the word you read: *thou*—t-h-o-u. It's pronounced *thou*—not 'though'—and it means 'you'.… or at least it used to…when the Bible was first translated into English."

There was a brief period of silence and then Jannie spoke up: "What you mean 'when the Bible first trans-*slated* into English,' Chaplain Travis?"

"Just *that,* Jannie. The Bible wasn't *always* in English. That only happened about four-hundred years ago. This King James Version that you're using, it's only been around for just over three-hundred-and-sixty years. Before that the English-speaking world used *Latin.*" Travis realized how crazy that must have sounded as he registered the puzzlement in the faces that confronted him. He stumbled on: "And before that, the Bible was in Hebrew, Aramaic and Greek." Travis saw the many baffled and skeptical stares surrounding him. Trying to be helpful he added: "Look, why don't y'all use some of the *Good News* Bibles I have back in the office? I have dozens of them. They'd be a lot easier to read—and they're in *modern* English, not this outdated stuff."

"Say *what?*" came a voice from one of the shepherds. "You saying the *Bible* is outdated?" Wanda Aitkins approached Chaplain Travis, her hands curled in fists, pressed against her hips. Aitkins was serving an indeterminate sentence for assault and battery, so Travis was mildly alarmed.

"No. *No.*" protested Travis. "I didn't say the *Bible* is outdated, I said the King James *Version* is outdated."

Wanda now removed her right hand from her hip and was shaking a finger at Travis, "Well, you listen here, Chaplain Travis, I'm a Bible-believing Christian, and if the King James Bible was good enough for Jesus—and *all of his disciples*," she added for good measure as she looked at her audience, "then it's good enough for any Christian. And that oughta include a man like you." She nodded in agreement with herself. Everyone now turned her attention to Chaplain Travis, and he knew that the floor was his—but that he didn't have a thing to say. He started to blurt out a few words, hoping some plausible excuse would come to him, to rescue him from this linguistic fray.

At that very moment a chirpy voice came from the rear of the auditorium: "How're y'all getting on with your pageant?" This was followed by the noisy crunch of an apple. Lt. Jenkins smiled at everyone. Travis raised his eyes heavenwards and then surreptitiously made a distressed face at Jenkins while pointing at himself. Jenkins immediately took the hint, saying, "Ladies, y'all don't mind if I borrow the good Chaplain, do you? I need to take him to Dorm C."

Travis turned back towards all the expectant faces and lifted his hands in a "Well, what're you going to do?" manner and went to join Jenkins. As an afterthought, he quickly said to Janitta. "Hey, Jannie, I'm really sorry, but maybe you'd better direct this pageant yourself, eh? Just remember those *Good News* Bibles, if you want them," he added as he quickly ducked around the door.

Jenkins and Travis exited the building and into the crisp night air. "Whew, Jenkins. Man, was I glad to see you! Oh—we're not really going to Dorm C, are we?"

"Naw, Chaplain," laughed Jenkins as he continued to munch his apple. "So you were having a little difficulty with our ladies?" Jenkins chuckled, wiping his lips on his uniform sleeve.

"You could say that," Travis shook his head. "And I'm not even going *to try* to explain."

"Good, good, 'cause I ain't asking." They were standing next to the basketball court now. Their breath was crystallizing in the chill air. Jenkins looked up at the night sky. Thin wisps of cloud were illuminated by the nearby town of Fairborn. "Gonna be a heavy frost tonight," offered Jenkins. Still looking at the sky he continued, "You know. You can sure learn a lot in a place like this—don't you think?"

"That's for sure," replied Travis. "They can't teach you about any of *this* in divinity school." Travis waved his arm in indication of the entire prison.

Jenkins suddenly turned his gaze upon the young chaplain: "Man, you're going to freeze out here—not even got a coat on! Let's go and get some coffee and warm up," invited Jenkins.

"Great!" accepted Travis, "just make my coffee *tea*, okay?"

"You got it!" Jenkins clapped Travis on the shoulder and they made their way to the administration building.

The spirit of the Christmas season within the women's prison was as dreary as the weather. Inmates often awaited cards, letters and parcels which never came. Those who received cards, photographs of children, or gifts of food, shared them with others who keenly felt their separation from life on the outside. Suicide watch was doubled and there were a couple of vain escape attempts. The few decorations that were allowed in the dormitories helped neither to transform the reality of incarceration nor to convey peace and good will. There were several more chapel services than normal, and those few inmates who had converted to The Nation of Islam—usually from Pentecostal, Apostolic and AME Zion backgrounds—watched wistfully as their sisters exchanged homemade Christmas cards and attended the various carol services offered by the chaplains and visiting church groups.

Jannie McCall's Christmas pageant was scheduled for the afternoon of December 23rd. Having no good excuse not to attend, Chaplain Travis was roped into a front row seat. Goodman had begged off, as he had Christmas Eve chapel services to prepare. It was also the case that he would be taking a week off from the afternoon of Christmas Day to New Year's Day. Goodman felt that it would be "good experience" for his young assistant to have a week on his own. For Travis, the pageant involved the first degree murder of the language of Shakespeare—as the women had steadfastly refused to use a modern English version. Travis did his best not to wince, and smiled woodenly throughout the whole production. In fact, his jaws ached after the performance—to the point that he could barely do the honor of thanking all the women for their "fascinating" performance and offering a closing prayer.

Travis wasted no time in heading back to his office. He nearly ran headlong into Ben Katz who was flipping through a sheaf of papers as he ambled through the corridor. Katz looked up and said: "Hey, Travis, how do you know when a Jewish American princess reaches orgasm?"

"Haven't a clue," responded Stephen.

"She drops her nail file. Happy Hanukkah!" grinned Katz, and he was gone.

Glad to be out of the tortured production he had just witnessed, Travis was about to open his office door when he heard a sharp 'whap' and then a woman's voice through clenched teeth: *"Just stop it!"*

At that moment, the door was flung open and Chaplain Goodman shot out of the office, nearly bowling over Stephen in the process. Without stopping, Marv pointed to several large boxes of Bibles, books and tracts from the American Bible Society, as well as cards for the inmates to use, and told Stephen to "help *your* secretary go through them and make sure each dormitory has some." As Goodman exited the building, Travis noted that he was rubbing his jaw.

Once inside the office, Stephen saw Frumpy, with her back towards him and breathing heavily as she leaned on her desk with both hands. "Need any help?" he asked tentatively. Frumpy just nodded, but didn't turn around. "Um, is everything okay?"

Frumpy reached up with her right hand and brushed her hair back. Stephen thought she might be crying, but when she turned to face him, he could see that her face was flushed with anger. Flummoxed, Stephen bridged their mutual discomfort by saying: "I didn't think you were on duty this afternoon."

"I'm not," Frumpy smiled with lips so tight they nearly lost their color, "but I don't have classes either as it's Christmas week. So I collected my mail and thought I'd come over here to offer my help."

Travis noticed that Frumpy had an opened letter in her hand, but made no mention of it. Instead he decided to discover the nature of the tension that filled the office. "Frumpy? Ah...something has obviously happened here—just before I came in." Frumpy continued to look at him. "But if you, uh, don't want to—."

"Talk about it?" Frumpy finished his sentence for him. "*Yes.* I *will* talk about it. Close the door." Frumpy was immediately taken aback by her own forthrightness, but Travis did as he was told. As he turned back to her, Frumpy pointed towards where she had last glimpsed Goodman and said, "I just smacked your boss."

Travis' back straightened with surprise. "Gosh" was the only word to leave his lips.

Frumpy took his silence as her cue to continue. "The *Reverend Good*-man, put his hand on my…" Now it was her turn to stumble for words: "…on my *ass*." She emphasized her choice of word and jutted her jaw forward for good measure.

Travis raised his eyebrows and let out a soft whistle through his teeth. He motioned towards Frumpy's chair and said, "Let's both sit down." Once settled Stephen's brow wrinkled as he sought for the right words. "How did it happen?"

Frumpy took a deep breath and exhaled quickly. As though it exhausted her to do it, she raised her arm and pointed towards the boxes of Bibles and cards on the table beside her. "Chaplain Goodman said you were attending the Christmas pageant and asked if I would help him organize all these materials from the American Bible Society." Frumpy paused for a moment and began again. "I said that is why I had come. So I placed my letter on top of the box next to the one I was emptying—so I could read it while I worked, and…" She drew out her next word and leaned forward for emphasis: "So-o-o, as I began to sort through the material, the *good* Chaplain *Good*man sidled up behind me—as though he were studying what was in the boxes—and put his…" Frumpy took another determined breath, "*crotch* right against my backside and then gave me a grope. When I started to move away he patted my ass and said"—and here she mocked Goodman's Yogi Bear voice—'Ooh, nice and firm.' So I smacked him." Frumpy took her lower lip between her teeth and bit it thoughtfully as she looked at the floor. Then she shook her head and said: "Men." She then looked up at Travis who was quietly observing her. "Present company excepted," she nodded towards Travis and smiled.

"Whew, thanks!" Travis returned her smile. He became more serious and said: "But what are you going to do?—report him?"

Frumpy shrugged wearily. "What's the point? There were no witnesses, so it's my word against his. And guess what: *I'm a convict.*"

Stephen was leaning forward, elbows on his knees. He let his head drop and shook it in a defeated manner. "I'm really sorry, Frumpy."

"I know, Chaplain Travis—*but hey*—it really would have been something if you'd walked in thirty seconds earlier!"

"Yeah, I guess so…" Stephen's voice trailed off as he contemplated that possibility.

"That would have put *you* in a pickle, wouldn't it?"

Frumpy's words were more rhetorical than query, but Travis chose to respond. "You're right about that. And I suspect my word would have had only slightly more weight than a convict's." He looked searchingly at Frumpy: "But are you okay now? Do you want to go back to your dorm?"

"No." Frumpy suddenly got to her feet. "There's no more escaping from the shit life deals out than there is escaping from this place. Let's get to work."

Frumpy was still clutching the opened letter in her hand. It was even more rumpled now. Stephen took it as an invitation to ask about it: "News from home?"

"Unh-unh," Frumpy shook her head as she glanced at the crumpled piece of paper. "It's from Carl—he wants a divorce…for a Christmas present, I guess," she added bitterly.

"Want to talk about it?" queried Travis.

"No…*and* yes," shrugged Frumpy. "I've been expecting it. He's never answered any of my letters—in fact, he's sent them all back. Merry Christmas, eh?"

"Yep," replied Travis, "Merry Christmas."

Frumpy stood up straight and placed her hands on her hips: "We haven't even been married a year. I guess prison has been our honeymoon…" She looked directly at Travis: "Some hotel, huh?" Then Frumpy laughed, as she wadded both letter and envelope into a ball and threw them into the waste paper basket. "The crap-ass bastard!"

Travis laughed out loud. Frumpy, in mock shame, threw her hand over her mouth—still laughing. "Oops! There I go again! Sorry, Chaplain Travis—I don't usually talk like that."

"Well, Frumpy," drawled Stephen, "sometimes it *do* help."

They began opening boxes and apportioning materials for each dorm in different piles around the office. "Do you still love him?— your husband—Carl?" asked Stephen.

Sighing heavily, Frumpy's eyes found a place in the middle-distance while she searched inside herself. "I don't know… I *thought* I did, but the truth is: I don't know." Frumpy looked at Travis almost pleadingly: "Is that awful?"

Now it was Travis' turn to sigh deeply. His brow furrowed and his lips pursed before speaking: "Maybe it would be awful—in other circumstances. But as you've said: he did get you put up in this honeymoon hotel—all expenses paid. That's not something that would warm the cockles of most women's hearts."

"Guess not," replied Frumpy, "but you know…*now*…after all this time… I'm not sure I ever loved him. I mean, I cared for him…and he was fun…he made me think about things other than myself… but I'm not sure it was love. It certainly doesn't feel like it now—*not here.*"

Travis quietly nodded his head. "So, what are you going to do?"

"I guess it's like my grandma said. I'll let him have his divorce— and I'll have me a new start when I get out of here." Frumpy nodded as though to put the final point on their discussion and they got back to work.

After ten minutes' silence, Frumpy piped up: "By the way, what did you think of the Christmas pageant?"

Stephen hesitated. "Ah, well…yes…it was…um…*interesting.*"

Frumpy laughed at Travis' response. She hadn't meant to put him in a predicament, but knew he would try to be kind. Frumpy eyed Travis with feigned suspicion. "Well, *I saw* the dress rehearsal and I've typed enough letters for you to know how precise you are with language!" Stephen blushed as Frumpy continued: "But you're right," she laughed, "it *was* interesting."

Once Travis and Frumpy had finished with the Bibles, books and cards, they turned their attention to the internal mail and inmates' notes and letters. Official intra-office mail was in manila envelopes, but most of what the inmates sent to the chaplains was simply on folded sheets of paper. Frumpy and Travis were both sitting at their desks, with their backs towards one another. Travis had asked Frumpy to help him sort through the requests for visits in order of urgency, as there were dozens of them—not unusual at this time of year. Frumpy made a slight gasping noise and uttered: "Oh my!" Stephen swiveled his chair round to see what the matter was. Blushing and looking perplexed, Frumpy handed a sheet of paper to the chaplain. It read:

Dear Chaplin Travis,

You mother-fucking son of a bitch. I am going to kill you you bastard but you wont know the day or time. But I am going to get you and you can count on it. Be prepared to die.

Love,

Lola Rogers Dorm C

"Ah—I see," replied Travis. "Guess you're a bit puzzled by this letter. So was I, the first time I got one from Lola." Travis smiled at Frumpy: "This is how she asks for a pastoral visit. Lola spends most of her time here in Dorm C."

"But...I...I don't understand," stammered Frumpy. "If she wants to see you, why does she have to be so *ugly* about it? I mean, if she wants to see you—*a chaplain*—shouldn't she be a little more respectful?" Frumpy thought about what she had just said in light of the earlier episode with Goodman. "Well, maybe she *could* address *Chaplain Goodman* that way, but she could have been nicer to you."

"I guess so," chuckled Travis, "but have you seen how she ends her letters?"

Frumpy quickly shook her head: "I—I didn't read that far..."

"Well, have a look!" motioned Travis. "See? Having threatened to kill me—and at a date and time unknown—she ends the letter: 'Love, Lola'! Can you believe it?!" Travis laughed again. "Evidently this is how Lola contacts anyone she wants to see: case worker, social worker, *me*—anybody. Poor thing's had a rotten life—outside of prison, anyway. Her glass eye is testimony to that. But I suppose I had better not say too much."

"I hear from some of the inmates that Lola drops her glass eye down the toilet sometimes and blocks it up," Frumpy giggled.

"That's true," drawled Travis. "I suppose the inmates can thank Lola that the plumbing in this institution is in such good shape— they often have to cut the pipes in order to fish out her glass eye!" Stephen paused, thought for a moment, and then said: "She tends to do it just about the time she's due to be released—or if something upsets her. And if they do release her, she always breaks her parole. Seems she likes it here; and the infractions help keep her safely locked up."

"She's been out and back in since I've been here," offered Frumpy.

Travis nodded, "Yeah, I know. And I suspect she'll do that a few more times yet."

Frumpy looked up from Lola's letter. "But *why*, Chaplain Travis? I can't imagine *wanting* to come back to prison. Isn't once enough?"

"You'd think so..." Travis had been looking down at his mail, but then stopped and looked up at Frumpy. "But what I have come to understand, Frumpy, is that for many women here, prison is the safest, most comfortable life they have ever known. A lot of them come back just to be with their prison 'families'—I'm sure you've heard the stories many of the women here have to tell."

"Not just the *other* women..." Frumpy's words were barely audible.

"I'm sorry, Frumpy. And I wasn't meaning to suggest that *only* other women have stories to tell about hard times on the outside."

"No, don't worry," Frumpy gave a painful smile. "I know you didn't mean it that way. It's just...*this place*...not to mention some of the *staff*."

"Yeah, I know." Travis checked his watch. "Hey. It's getting on time for supper. Shouldn't you be moseying along?"

"I suppose so," answered Frumpy as she looked at the clock on the wall.

Frumpy picked up her coat and prepared to leave. As she got to the door, Stephen said: "And Frumpy? Sorry about...well, you know: Goodman."

"Yeah, it's all right. I'll talk to some of the other girls about him and see what they suggest."

"Good idea," responded Travis. "Oh, and one other thing—this business about Carl—and the divorce? After what you've told me: he might actually be doing you a favor." Frumpy smiled, and then nodded. She buttoned up her coat against the cold and left.

Travis sat for a few moments and considered Lola's menacing missive. He laughed to himself when he considered how such a letter might be received by many ministers 'on the outside.' He dropped the note onto the pile of inmate requests. "Time to pay Lola a visit," he said, getting to his feet and removing his coat from the back of the chair.

Travis was buffeted by a fierce west wind as he made his way towards Dorm C, maximum security. There was a mixture of precipitation: rain, sleet and perhaps the odd flake of snow. Dorm C was a small, but formidable, single-storey, brick building. It was surrounded by its own chain-link fence, topped with razor ribbon. However, its single storey concealed the fact that it was actually two structures in one. The brick façade was merely the superstructure over a set of steel cells which housed those inmates considered to be the greatest risk—to others as well as to themselves. The women who inhabited these cells were serious offenders or seriously deranged—if not both. Dorm C also housed the majority of the prison's death row inmates. However, because Dorm C was nearly always full, and because the death penalty had an automatic appeal process which could drag on for years, those inmates who were sentenced to death and considered at low risk within the general population, were allowed to live in medium custody and work within the grounds.

Travis' visit to Dorm C had already been cleared from the Control Center. As he waited for the guard to open the heavy steel door, he shuddered involuntarily at the cold and wondered at the wisdom of fitting in one last visit before going home. He didn't fancy getting iced or snowed in at the prison—especially as he had a date tonight. Nevertheless, Lola's curiously-styled plea for a visit had pricked his conscience and so he had stayed. Once inside, he found Dorm C overheated as usual. This was partly due to the fact that there were several padded cells for those deemed a danger to themselves; and it was not uncommon for the women who were placed in them to be totally naked. This was a precaution against their ripping their clothes to shreds and garroting or hanging themselves.

Travis remembered how he had once been asked by Goodman to report the death of a family member to a woman in such a case of self-protective lock-up. As the woman was nude, he had been accompanied by a female guard who stood a few paces away. Travis had had to stand with his back to the small grilled window and tell the woman of the death of her loved one. Her tortured howling still haunted his dreams from time to time.

As Travis was escorted to see Lola, he was asked to make his visit from outside the cell, as Lola was on punishment for yet another infraction. The guard was too preoccupied to tell Travis the nature of the infraction, but when he rounded the corner to Lola's cell he could guess for himself. The place where her glass eye would have been was a crater—accentuated all the more by her pale skin—the eyelid almost winking macabrely at the chaplain. "Hey, Lola," began Travis, "I got your letter."

Although Lola was older than Travis by several years—a fact masked by her huge weight and baby pink skin—she grinned like a small child caught with her hand in the cookie jar: both guiltily and sheepishly. She sat with her hands folded together and pressed between her fleshy thighs. She shifted in her seat girlishly and occasionally peeped up at the chaplain with her one good eye.

"Officer Bradford says you're on punishment. Has there been a problem?"

Lola nodded and half-whispered: "Yes."

"Want to tell me about it?"

Lola looked up and smiled as she nodded assent. She rolled her head timidly—almost ducking between her shoulders—as though searching for the courage to speak, and then said: "Flushed my eye again."

"Yeah, well. I had kinda guessed," smiled Travis, but with compassion. "Do you want to tell me why?"

"They been talking about moving me out of here...want to put me back in medium custody."

"Is that such a bad thing, Lola? It's nearly Christmas—you could take part in some of the festivities." Lola dug her clasped hands deeper between her thighs, dropped her head and shook it 'no.' "They find your eye yet?" Again: a head shake 'no.' "You know, Lola, you could see me, Chaplain Goodman, your caseworker—and just about anybody else—a lot easier if you moved out to medium—or even minimum—custody." Lola remained silent. "You wouldn't have to send us letters—ever think about that?" Lola giggled—ostensibly at the thought of her letters' contents. The fact was that Lola rarely had anything to say. Her letters had their intended effect of bringing people to see her—but it was more like a wacky zoo visit, such that no one could be quite sure who was the one being observed. Stephen stood leaning on the bars for another few minutes. "Lola—would you like for me to have a prayer with you?" Lola looked up and smiled as if she had been offered a trip to the county fair. Travis prayed and offered her words of comfort—particularly with Christmas being so near.

As he made his way to the guard room and front door, Stephen could hear the moaning wind and the sleet slapping against the window. The weather, plus his visit to Lola—for whom this prison, and maximum security in particular, provided such sanctuary—caused him to reflect on the words a Catholic priest friend had said to him, but with reference to the Church: "The Church is like Noah's ark: if it weren't for the storm being so bad outside, you couldn't stand the stench inside." Then he thought of Frumpy's encounter with Chaplain Goodman. "Perhaps prison—and the Church—have a lot in common," he said to himself as he stepped out the front door.

It was nearly 4:00 p.m. on Christmas day and Travis had retreated to the relative calm of the staff room in the administration building. He had had to escape the heavy atmosphere which pervaded the auditorium during visitation time. The light outside was beginning to fade and a light rain was falling. He made himself a cup of tea and stood looking out the window across the parking lot and thinking to himself. "Could even a 'white Christmas' have brightened the spirits of those spending time behind bars?" It was doubtful. Perched on the border between the higher elevations of the Piedmont and the low-lying coastal plain which stretched for scores of miles to the Atlantic Ocean, Fairborn, North Carolina could usually count on being cold, cloud-covered and damp at Christmastide. Hardly conducive to a lightening of spirits.

For those who worked in the caring professions, it was axiomatic that with the approach of Christmas came the yearly high tide of depression, as well as suicide attempts—and successes. Thanks to

Coca-Cola-drinking Santas gracing the billboards visible from the prison's lower fence, Bing Crosby and Perry Como singing nostalgic Christmas songs on the record player in the prison auditorium, and Christmas greetings arriving in the prison post by the hundreds—the women serving time in the correctional facility were virtually bombarded with reminders that they were cut off—utterly isolated from their loved ones—at this supposedly warm, fuzzy time of year. And this feeling wasn't limited to the inmates. Like their counterparts in the health and emergency services, the prison guards and staff had to treat Christmas just like any other day on the job—only it was treated as a Sunday and the inmates were allowed to receive their maximum of three visitors. The correctional staff wasn't particularly happy about being away from their families any more than the inmates. Thus nerves became raw and tempers flared—especially as there were more strip searches than usual: this indignity usually following an emotional and painful parting only minutes beforehand. Contrary to what many of the inmates believed, it wasn't calculated to make their lives more miserable and spoil what little Christmas spirit that they might have; rather it was due to the fact that their visitors were wearing more layers of clothing than at warmer, dryer times of the year—thus increasing the risk of contraband being smuggled into the prison.

Travis' breath was beginning to condense onto the window pane. He began to trace out the form of a Christmas tree on the glass, as his mind tracked the course of the last twenty-four hours. This time yesterday—Christmas Eve—he had been conducting a carol service. Never in his life had he heard such lackluster singing—despite the fact that the women were allowed to choose the hymns and carols they wanted to sing. It might as well have been a funeral as opposed to being a celebration of the birth of the Prince of Peace. Women were gathered in their family groups and provided one another support as they inevitably broke into tears. It made no difference that Travis had tried to put everything he had into his strong tenor voice—or even the fact that a number of the supervising guards had joined in. An invisible vacuum of pain seemed to draw the notes and syllables from the women's voices. Travis left the prison as soon as practicable following the service—under the pretext that he still had Christmas morning's service to prepare. The simple fact was that he too had succumbed to the powerful downward pull of the collective emotional vacuum and was exhausted. As he had driven back to his little house on the far side of Fairborn he had had to resist the urge to dissolve into tears. Now, doubting any good he might have been able to do, Travis yielded to the temptation to review the morning's service through negative lenses. What joy had the service brought to anyone? "Joy to the world? Who's kidding whom?" he muttered to himself.

"Talking to yourself—mmh-mmh. That's a bad sign!" Lt. Jenkins sidled up to Travis holding a steaming cup of coffee. "S'matter, Chaplain?—Santy not bring you anything for Christmas?"

Travis let go a deep sigh that came close to being a sob. He gave an unconvincing smile and shrugged: "Oh, I don't know, Jimmy. It's this place…. Christmas…*me*." Jenkins took a long drink of his coffee and studied Travis through the steam.

After a moment he placed his hand on Travis' shoulder and gave it a squeeze. "Goodman's left you holding the fort, hasn't he? Well, go easy there, Stephen. It's your first Christmas here. And it's probably—and I'm taking a guess here—your first Christmas away from home and family, right?" Travis nodded. Jenkins continued: "Well, from what you've told me of your background, I reckon this place couldn't be much more different than where you grew up and the way your folks raised you."

"You can say that again!" chimed in Travis.

Jenkins swallowed another gulp of his coffee. "You going to see your folks before the New Year?"

"Nah, Goodman isn't back 'til New Year's Day, so I'm driving home as soon as he relieves me. I'll have a few days off before I need to be back here."

Jenkins nodded thoughtfully, "That's good. That's good." Staring out the window with Stephen, he added: "Spent my first Christmas away from my family back in '67, when I was in Vietnam. If that wasn't bad enough, we got the Tet offensive as a New Year's present from Charlie." Jenkins shook his head at the memory. "Man! After just over a year in Nam, I was never so glad to get home. Swore I was never going to leave again." Jenkins snorted a short laugh: "Working behind bars has helped me keep that promise!" He looked Travis in the eye: "You gotta let this one slide, Stephen—in this kind of work you have to take the long view. Hell, the average sentence here has got to be eight or ten years. You gotta take the long view."

The two men finished their drinks in silence. They turned away from the window to go rinse their mugs. Before they parted, Jenkins said, "You know, Stephen, it's a good thing Christmas here has got to you."

"How's that?" asked Stephen.

"Well, if it *didn't* bother you, then you'd need to worry. That'd be a sure sign this place had got under your skin."

Jenkins' words seemed to nudge a burden off Stephen's shoulders. He took a deep breath, straightened up and said, "Thanks, Jimmy. And Merry Christmas."

"You too," smiled Jimmy, "and have a good evening."

Crying Time

Time's glory is to calm contending kings,
To unmask falsehood, and bring truth to light.
The Rape of Lucrece

Marv Goodman was a minister who had—somewhere along the
line—ceased to believe anything that most Christians would hold
dear. Thus prison was as good a place as any for him to hide out.
After all, none of this minister's 'parishoners' could ever see him
outside of the role he played behind bars. For that matter, the role
Goodman played behind bars left a lot to be desired with regard to
the kingdom of heaven. The word on the street was that Goodman
owned several sub-standard rental properties. Whenever it neared
time for an inmate to be released, and if that inmate had no other
place to go, Goodman—all the while playing the honest, helpful man
of God—would offer the woman one of his houses or apartments.
It was a guaranteed 'residence plan' which was part of their parole
requirements. "First month free of rent!" he would beam sincerely.
Then, in an earnest and avuncular manner, he would lay his hand
tenderly upon the woman's shoulder and add: "Save yourself a little
money before you have to start paying rent. It will help you adjust
to inflation and other changes on the outside. Don't want to have
to worry about money, now do you?" Despite his reputation, some
women were still taken in by his offer; but most who accepted his
charity, also dolefully accepted that there would be a day of reckoning

for a 'free' first month's rent. He wasn't the first man to use them, and probably wouldn't be the last. The gossip regarding Goodman was so plentiful that it had even come to the ears of his young assistant, Stephen Travis. Much of the gossip was fuelled by stories from women who had had their parole revoked and had to serve out the remainder of their sentences behind bars.

When women were released on parole and found themselves in Goodman's 'care,' those who were young, healthy and attractive found that there was a price to pay for his type of mercy. This usually happened once they had received their first three or four pay checks. Their former chaplain, now landlord, would come to them, displaying concern, rubbing the back of his neck with a handkerchief, looking down and shaking his head, seemingly searching for the right words to say. He would explain that due to this blasted recession he "was going to *have to*"… not that *he wanted to*, mind you, but well…he "was going to have to raise the rent."

Having just begun the adjustment to earning some money, paying bills, and the like, the women would naturally be shocked. "How much?" would be their normal response.

Marv would once again rub the back of his neck with his handkerchief—as though this helped him think. Next he would 'hem' and 'haw' as though making calculations in his head and trying to find the fairest rent increase. This left his victims in suspense which nearly gave way to blackout when he finally replied that it might have to be as much as twenty-five or thirty percent. Panic-stricken, the women would ask, beg—*plead*—for his clemency. Parole was contingent on keeping both employment and a home-place. Most were doing menial jobs that paid very little: waitressing, office cleaning, etc. Couldn't the rent increase be postponed, they would beg—if only a little while? Wasn't there something that could be done? Goodman, would hang his head in feigned despair, shake his head 'no' and tell them that he had his mortgages and taxes to pay on all these properties. Then dramatically, an idea would flash across his eyes and his demeanor would lighten. "You know, I do have an old family place—my great aunt's house— which I'm keeping for my retirement. It's not far from the state capitol building. Been doing it up for years—it's one of those large old, Victorian houses. It's shared by some other parolees—but only those I trust, mind you. The good thing is: I'll not have to increase your rent; that will fall to whoever comes here next." The former inmate would almost collapse with relief. Goodman would help steady her—and perhaps even receive a grateful hug.

After the mood had settled they would discuss when the woman could make the move and whether she needed any help with transporting her things. Everything agreed, Marv would start to leave and then stop at the door, as if something had just dawned on him. "Oh, by the way, the ladies at my dear departed aunt's house do a little extra paid work—for me and some friends—private, you understand. And you get to keep what you earn. It's just some parties and entertaining—serving food and drinks and the like—you do like parties, don't you?" By this stage in the conversation—and with Goodman halfway out the door—the woman would usually just smile and nod, unaware just what Goodman's 'parties' entailed. "Fine!" Marv would beam, "Things'll work out just fine. You'll see. Got to run now. You take care." In time, those women who refused to play 'hostesses' for Goodman's party guests—conventioneers, legislators and businessmen—found that they had somehow violated their parole and were soon back inside the women's correctional center.

"Chaplain *Good*man?" snorted Sally Wilkins, "Now there's a misnomer if ever there was one!" She gave a sardonic laugh and shook her head. It was late winter and Sally was on her knees, working on the flower beds in the main yard of the prison. Sally taught horticulture to any interested parties in the prison. Travis clung to the sunshine that found its way through the still barren branches of the over-arching trees. He had decided to ask a long-timer why there were so many stories flying around about his supervisor. "I'll tell you one thing though…" Sally thoughtfully picked some tobacco from her Camel non-filter off the tip of her tongue. "That man has put a whole new meaning into giving *lip*-service when he gets the girls to pray with him."

"Umm… What exactly do you mean, Sally?" ventured the young chaplain. Travis was loath to confess that he had both heard the rumors and knew of Frumpy's experience. He had also wondered on more than one occasion why he was effectively banned from the office for short periods and sent on visiting rounds in the sewing room, classrooms, etc. One thing that Travis couldn't miss was the way that Goodman seemed to look through or past the inmates whenever they went on rounds together. He just wasn't *there*; he wasn't *present* for his flock.

Sally shielded her eyes from the sun with her garden trowel as she looked up at Travis and continued: "Well, think about it, Sugar. He has a girl go into his office for some 'pastoral counseling' and prayer. (Sally mimicked the black inmates' way of saying this, with one hand on her hip and her head keeping beat with each syllable.) And he gets her lips moving all right: around the head of his prick!" Sally paused and took a drag on her Camel; then she laughed: "Some of the girls call him 'Quickshot'—'cause he no sooner draws than he shoots!" She hooted and took another puff.

Travis only managed a pitiful "Oh" as he blushed and then drew a long, deep breath. "Damn!" was the next word to leave his mouth.

"Now don't go and lose your religion, Chaplain!" Sally guffawed, blowing smoke from her nostrils, "One rogue minister is enough!"

"But, Sally…d-do you know this to be true? I mean, has he asked you to—oh… gosh, no offence!" Travis was now turning shades of purple. Knowing that Sally was a lesbian, he was mortified that he had over-stepped the bounds and offended her.

"Chaplain, I'm too old and have been through too much shit in my life to be offended by something like that. I know you mean well—for all of us here. So let me just answer you straight: yeah, 'Reverend Doc-tor' *Bad*-man tried it on with me."

"Even knowing that, ah, you're not that way...*inclined*?" queried Travis.

"Of course," tossed back Sally with a wide grin. She took a last drag on her Camel. "I was a challenge to him. He asked me outright if I'd ever had sex with a man. I told him I had, but that it wasn't to my liking. He said maybe it all depends on the man. Told him I *doubt* it. But then he says how about I suck him off? He could donate a few cartons of Camels to the 'cause.' I told him to bend double and blow himself." Travis laughed. Sally shook her head and broke into a wry smile at her memory. "Know what that son-of-a-bitch did next?" Travis just shook his head. "Jerked himself off in front of me, that's what he did."

"Damn!"

"There you go again, Chaplain. You're gonna get your mouth washed out with soap!" laughed Sally.

"It wouldn't be the first time, Sally," chuckled Travis. "I can still taste Ivory soap if I put my mind to it! My mother used it on me regularly!—whenever I cussed."

"And you seem like such a nice boy," teased Sally.

"But look, Sally. Now that you've told me this...I mean, *good Lord*. Something should be done. Something *has* to be done. But then we'd need proof..." Travis' words trailed away to deep thought.

"Chaplain, not one of the young ladies in this institution is going to risk accusing Chaplain *Bad*man of asking her for a blowjob. They're all afraid they'll end up with some sort of infraction and get their time extended. No, in cases like this you have to fight fire with fire. Don't you fret yourself about it, okay? My sisters and me have an idea—best you don't know anything about it, understood? Ol' Quickshot will get his—all in good time. And we have plenty of that."

"Well, if you're sure…"

"Never been surer!" Sally smiled. "Feel good when you go home tonight, Chaplain. Talking to you has made me feel better."

"Thanks, Sally. Bye."

One unseasonably warm February afternoon, as Travis was rounding the corner of Dorm B and heading back towards the Control Center and then Dorm C, he nearly ran smack into an exasperated Lt. Jenkins. Jenkins had been storming along, mumbling to himself, while at the same time mopping his brow with his handkerchief. As he was holding his uniform hat slightly in front of him, he had not noticed Travis heading towards him. "Whoa, Lieutenant!" Travis called out in a friendly manner. "What's the matter?"

"Howdy Chaplain—it's that damn—'scuse me—OC…*a-gain*! Heard him chewing out one of the other officers because something or other wasn't done *just right*—by the book—and that doesn't half piss me off. 'Scuse me again, Chaplain."

"Not to worry, Jimmy." Travis and Jenkins always started off on a formal—but still friendly—basis, and then would change to the familiarity of first names.

"OC just can't get it through his thick head that this ain't the Marine Corps, and that he is no longer a sergeant, but a 'virgin'—a 'cherry'—especially in this line of work. He's the new guy. In this chain of command, *he's* at the *bottom*."

Jenkins, too, had served in Vietnam, but in the army. And unlike Bain, he had seen combat. And also unlike Bain, he had left the military *behind* him with his discharge. Following his stint in the army, Jenkins had joined the Department of Correction and excelled as a prison officer—thus his rank.

Jenkins was calming down now. He wiped the back of his neck with his now damp handkerchief and smiled to himself, shaking his head in silent amusement in a way that Travis liked to see. "What is it, Jimmy?" prodded Travis. "Come on, share it!"

Jenkins looked up at Travis and with a wide grin said, "Know what that *stew*-pid SOB said?"

"Nope."

"He was hollering and screaming at Officer Mitchell and came out with this." Mimicking Bain, Jenkins put his hands on his hips, rolled his head upwards and said, "'Yew can kee-yus my ice and go to hell and I'm just the man to do it!' I mean—*what* is that supposed to *mean*, I ask you? 'I'm just the man to *do it*'—Do *what*, pray tell?"

Travis was laughing now, "I guess he was saying that he was 'greatly peeved.'"

"Ha!" burst out Jenkins, "I like that! 'Greatly peeved,'" he repeated in a mock English accent. "You're a good 'un, chaplain."

"You too, Jimmy. Catch you later."

Stephen arrived at the front door of Dorm C. He was on his way to discuss the casework he had under the supervision of the prison's psychiatrist, Harold Deaton. Harold was a laconic man, who had perhaps once aspired to great things in his chosen field of medicine, but was now resigned to spreading himself around the prison system, mainly keeping severely disturbed inmates sedated with Thorazine. Deaton was in the interview room, by the front office of Dorm C.

"Good afternoon, Dr. Deaton," began Travis.

"Afternoon," smiled Deaton as he motioned Stephen to a waiting chair. "So how are our patients?" inquired Harold, "Crazy as ever?"

"So it would seem," replied Travis. "In particular, it's Clara May Benson."

"Ah," sighed Deaton, raising his eyebrows.

"I suppose I keep trying to make some sense out of the things she tells me."

"And is it working?" asked Deaton.

"Well...I *hear* her words, but I often haven't got a clue what she's talking about. For instance, yesterday, when I saw her, she was saying how she's the 'onliest' child in her family because her younger sister 'done got the *smiling mighty Jesus* and died when she was three.'" Deaton was grinning broadly now. "So *what*—if anything—is the 'smiling mighty Jesus?'"

Almost laughing now, Deaton asked Travis: "Ever hear of *spinal meningitis?*" Now Travis was laughing as well. "I never ceased to be entertained by our ladies' renditions of medical terminology," chuckled Deaton, "What else does dear Clara May have to say?" Deaton now seemed to be warming to his supervision session with the aspiring chaplain. It provided a break in the monotony of Thorazine injections for patients who rarely got better.

"More Jesus, actually—in fact, a belly full!"

"How's that?" replied Deaton, his curiosity piqued.

"Well, again yesterday—when I was visiting her here in Dorm C—she told me that she wanted to talk about Jesus."

"Well, you're the chaplain, *Chaplain*," interjected Deaton, smiling.

"Then she told me that she 'had Jesus in her tummy.'"

"Must've caused her some bad indigestion!" Harold was now on a roll.

"So, I asked her how Jesus had come to be in her tummy—"

"This I gotta hear!" broke in Deaton.

"And she said that Jesus had come to her, and that when she had opened her mouth, he jumped in and 'just slid right on down.'" Travis paused for a moment and then added: "Oh, I did ask her how that felt—having Jesus in her tummy—and she just smiled and said: 'It feels *real good.*'"

Deaton just laughed and shook his head in disbelief. He spun his chair around and faced the afternoon sunlight, streaming in the window—having first been strained through chain-link fencing and barbed-wire. He put his hands behind his head and slowly repeated: "Smiling mighty Jesus…Jesus in her tummy… Mmh-mmh, she's a case." Without turning back to Stephen, Harold inquired: "So then, *Chap-lain* Travis, what have you learned in working with our Clara May?" Deaton was slowly swiveling back and forth, and seemed to be studying something far in the distance.

"I don't know," started Travis, "maybe the border between where *your work* begins and mine ends?"

"My work," started Deaton. A small laugh snuffled its way out of his nose and throat as he turned his chair back towards Stephen. "My work is to stick her with a needle backed up by a large dose of Thorazine. That's as far as my work takes me with Clara May and dozens like her—across the prison system. I see them for maybe five—ten—minutes each, every couple of weeks. That poor creature is schizophrenic. According to her files and crime records, without anti-psychotic medication, she's as likely to slice you up with a kitchen knife as look at you. Apart from pharmacological intervention and offering psychiatric taxonomy, I probably cannot do much more than you."

"Is there anything else I could do?" inquired Stephen.

Deaton had begun to gather up patients' notes. "Yeah, Stephen, there is. Take her out for walks—outside this building sometime. Do a few circuits inside the perimeter fence. God knows this place is enough to make anybody crazy."

Both men stood and shook hands. Deaton looked warmly at Travis and winked. Deaton took up his briefcase and headed for the door and Travis went to make his rounds in the cell block.

The sun was low in the horizon when Stephen notified the guard that he was ready to be let out from the cell block. However, just as she turned the key they heard alarm bells sounding. The officer hurriedly let Travis out and then both of them went to Dorm C's front office where they looked out the windows to see what the cause of the alarm was. Stephen saw two officers—with firearms—running from the Control Center towards the front gate. The telephone rang on the office desk and the guard answered it. "Yes. Yes. I understand." She turned and looked at Travis and then said, "Yes, he's here. I will. Understood. Got it." The guard put the phone down, looked at Travis and said: "Major breakout. Captain Waller and Warden Nifong want you up by the front gate. I got to lock this place down." She escorted Travis to the front door and let him out.

Lt. Jenkins was waiting by the gate to the Dorm C compound—an armed officer was watching his back. Jenkins motioned for Travis to hurry, so he ran to the gate, while asking: "What's going on?" Jenkins just motioned towards the incredible scene of fifteen to twenty women climbing the prison's fences: some caught in the razor ribbon, others leaping to branches on nearby trees, some using their own bodies as ladders up the fence or as mats on the wire so that other women could clamber over them to freedom. There were guards hanging onto the feet of women who were trying to pick their way through the razor ribbon. Around the grounds there were groups of inmates shouting encouragement to their sisters who were 'hitting the fence' and guards trying to herd them back into their dorms for lock-down. It was all over in a matter of minutes.

Stephen still couldn't believe his eyes. Several police cars were pulling up to the gates and some officers jumped out of their vehicles and began giving chase to the escapees. As Travis approached the gate, both Captain Waller and Warden Nifong were barking orders at gathered guards. When Nifong saw Travis, she took him by the arm and said: "We need every able-bodied person to help round up these women—including you."

"Excuse me?" queried a baffled Travis.

"No, I won't excuse you," snapped Nifong, her face flushed with adrenalin and rage. "There are at least twenty women who've gone over the fence and I need everybody's help to round them up. Where's your car?"

"*I'm not going*," said Travis.

Nifong turned and glared at him. "*What* did you say?"

"*I'm not going*," repeated Travis evenly. Before the warden could speak again, Travis added: "Mrs. Nifong, if I go on this 'round-up,' I'll never be able to work with these women again. No one would trust me. I'm a chaplain for goodness sake, not a security officer."

Nifong was breathing rapidly and deeply, almost hyperventilating. By now Waller was listening in on their conversation, and as Nifong lifted her hand, the index finger pointing towards Stephen's chest, readying herself to speak, Waller cut in. "Warden—he's right. A chaplain's got no business doing custody work. I'm sure you'd rather he went into some of the dorms and helped to calm things down. Right?"

Nifong studied Waller for a moment, thought better of what she was about to say and quickly nodded her head: "Fine." And then to Travis, "Captain Waller's right. You're excused from this prisoner round-up. See what you can do to help settle the situation here." She turned to Waller and said, "Come on." They headed towards a waiting car outside the front gate. Waller looked over his shoulder and winked at Travis.

Stephen was still trying to come to terms with the fact that he had stood firm against 'Pumps & Pearls'—he didn't know whether to feel triumphant or concerned for his future in that institution. But at the moment he could dwell on neither feeling as the prison was still in turmoil. Travis decided to head to the prison infirmary first, as many of the women had incurred serious cuts from the razor ribbon on the perimeter fence.

As he entered the infirmary, he first passed by the maternity ward. It occurred to him what a shock it had been during his first week's orientation to see a maternity ward in a prison—even though it was a women's prison. Somehow the wholesome image of motherhood was so incongruous with these barred surroundings, that seeing the pink and blue cuddly toys and mobiles over the babies' cribs had emotionally 'winded' him. Yes, some women came to prison pregnant and it was part of human nature that other women got pregnant while behind bars—more often than not they were those who worked outside the prison gates. Some women got pregnant due to utter carelessness and desperation for sex; others through sheer ignorance of human biology. Travis had gotten used to the stories of young women from rural North Carolina who were told by the men with whom they worked, that "you can't get pregnant in the dark while standing up." Travis wondered how many children had been fathered in the broom closet of the state governor's mansion, where many inmates on Work Release—male and female—had jobs. It didn't bear thinking about.

Stephen made his way into the main ward. The women who were able, were sitting up on their beds, chatting excitedly and looking out the windows. Seated on a row of chairs was a group of inmates being treated for open wounds obtained in their gambit for freedom. Several, whose wounds had been cleaned, but not stitched, were holding deep red compresses to arms, legs and torsos. Despite the amount of blood lost, the women weren't showing visible signs of distress; rather they were laughing energetically—still fuelled by adrenaline—as they discussed who had made it over the wire, who kicked OC in the face ("Didja see the look on that honky's face?! Blood everywhere!"), and how Pumps & Pearls nearly wet herself while screaming at the women to "get off that fence and come back this minute!" Travis was reminded of his high school days in the locker room after a successful baseball game. Although these women were obviously hurt—and would certainly feel their wounds later—

they were nevertheless buoyed by the triumph of their will towards freedom. None seemed depressed at the fact that she hadn't been among those who had escaped. They had the collective satisfaction of their defiant act of sisterhood—of *personhood*—that would not be obliterated by being convicted, numbered and categorized either by courts or the system meant to hold them. Travis absorbed all this during the few seconds it took to enter the ward and cast his eyes around the room. It was the 'patients' who noticed him first. "Hey, Rev! You catch all the action out there?" Martine raised her injured arms with pride. The others laughed.

"Yeah, I caught some of it," smiled Travis. "I was in Dorm C when I heard the alarms. Are y'all okay?" Travis motioned towards their bandages and the two nurses busily stitching them up and dressing their wounds.

"Well, they're not going to die," grumbled the hard-working nurse, Thelma Miller, "but what a mess!"

"Don't you worry 'bout us," laughed Martine, "but Pumps & Pearls prob'ly gonna be in here with heart attack 'fore long!" All the inmates laughed at that.

Another inmate popped up: "She the reason so many women hit the fence in the first place. Just dyin' to get outta this place!"

"Wouldn't be so bad here if it wasn't for her," added Martine. The women all 'amened' that.

The front door of the infirmary slammed and they all turned to see two guards bringing in another few injured inmates. The women were laughing as they were escorted in. "Don't know what y'all are laughin' about," growled OC, who was one of the escorting officers. "Y'all are jutht gonna have to thpend more time behind barth!"

OC's face was caked with coagulated blood; his nose had a swollen, clownish look about it. Travis had a hard time stifling a laugh as he thought to himself: "Schmuck." The three would-be escapees joined the queue waiting for treatment.

OC's colleague said: "See ya later," and headed back out into prison yard. OC stood for a moment taking in the collateral damage from what was the largest breakout in the history of the women's correctional facility. Then he pointed at his nose and like an adolescent with a bad cold said: "Warden thaid I need to have thith looked at."

"Well, we lookin' at it!" blurted out Martine, at which all the others roared with laughter.

OC reached for a canister of tear gas spray that was on his belt. "I oughta thpray the lot of you! Then we'll thee whoth laughin'!"

Nurse Miller spun around from the patient she was attending. "You even *think* of spraying that gas in here, OC, and I swear when I'm through with you, you won't know whether to shit or go blind!"

OC stepped back involuntarily at the outburst from Nurse Miller—both from the unexpected vehemence as well as hearing her use his hated moniker, 'OC.' Travis looked on with both amusement and amazement. Thelma went back to the inmate she was treating, all the while mumbling to herself: "As though I haven't got *enough* to deal with right now, *that* dumbass redneck has to come mouthing off in here." The women laughed.

Like a man in a dream who finds he is standing stark naked in a public place, OC turned and hustled for the door, saying "My nothe will wait 'til later." And with that he was gone. Again the women howled with laughter. Travis was beginning to realize just how cathartic had been this day's mass dash for freedom. He had barely noticed that he too was howling.

Over the next three days, all of the escapees were captured and returned to the Correctional Center for Women. As with most prison escapes, after the first few hours of adrenaline and exhilaration wear off, the problem of 'where to go?' raises its querulous and insistent head. In the majority of instances people head for home—or whatever passed for home: the houses of parents, grandparents, boyfriends, etc. The prison officers knew that, as did the city and state police. Often they were waiting for the escaped inmates to arrive at their places of supposed haven. In certain instances, the fugitives were waiting for the police—having found that they were no longer welcomed at home or that their 'people' had moved on. One forlorn woman appeared at the front gate after spending thirty-six hours out-of-doors with nothing to eat. Like the Israelites longing for the fleshpots of Egypt, prison at least promised three square meals a day and a roof over one's head. After all, what constituted 'home' was relative to the misery each woman had suffered on the outside.

The stories of the 'great escape' carried the inmate population over the next several weeks, helping them to cope with their suspension of privileges. Dorm C was now full-to-bursting with its normal complement of prisoners plus all those who had been deemed the 'ring-leaders' of the mass escape. Warden Nifong had been called to the head office for the North Carolina Department of Correction. A team of 'experts' was called in to interview both inmates and staff as to the root causes of the discontent—as though simply being in prison didn't count for anything. However, as the days rolled on—and very little was seen of Nifong—it seemed that the prison grapevine was correct in its deduction that the warden's days were numbered. Meanwhile, Capt. Waller stood in for the disgraced warden while the team of experts finished their work and prepared their recommendations.

One of the last orders given by Nifong before her extended 'absence' was for a prison 'shake-down.' Pumps & Pearls felt certain that the 'great escape' could not have taken place without various sorts of contraband, and her imagination had run wild: cash for going on the run, schedules of the guards' shifts, maps, wire-cutters—who could know? In obedience to his 'superior'—in the chain of command only—Capt. Waller carried out the shake-down during the afternoon shift change—keeping the first shift on for an extra hour so that there would be plenty of hands for this lightning raid on the inmates' quarters and property. The choice of afternoon also assured that most inmates would be working or in educational classes, and thus unable to hide anything or warn others.

The guards set about their work with alacrity. Truth to tell, it was a welcome break from their normal routine—even for those who had to stay over the extra hour. For some, like Officer Chickenshit, it was payback time to particular inmates who had riled them, as they could go through their few private possessions, make a mess of them, and leave the clean-up to the owners. There was also the added thrill of an illicit find. However, such thrills were few and far between during this shake-down; so if Warden Nifong had pinned her hopes for survival on the successful recovery of knives, money, tunneling equipment, and uniforms converted into civilian clothes (à la a World War II POW film), she would have been gravely disappointed. Her fate had been sealed before she was called to the head office.

However, there had been one spectacular find in the minimum custody section—and that occurred in the room of Death Dyke's special 'friend,' Arletta Boykin. The women in minimum security were allowed private rooms and more furnishings than those enjoyed by their compatriots in medium and maximum custody. Therefore, two officers were making the searches in order to speed along the process. Naturally they searched the spaces for hanging clothes, removed drawers from their chests-of-drawers, opened bottles of shampoo, poked inside pillow cases and looked under beds. It was only when Officer Marilou Wolfe decided she needed to rest her bones and sat down on Arletta's bed, that the discovery was made. Even though she had lifted the mattress only moments before, nothing was revealed as untoward until she sat on it. She called to her partner and said: "Something's wrong here. Come sit on this bed."

Her colleague sat down and said: "This thing's all lumpy and uneven."

Together they stripped the blankets and sheets, and started to feel and prod the mattress. "Something's sorta rustling in here," remarked Marilou.

"Unh-huh," came her partner's laconic reply.

As the bed was placed alongside a wall, they lifted the mattress away from the wall and onto its side. Marilou ran her fingers along the edge that had been nearer the wall and cried: "The seam's been cut! I can stick my fingers inside it." She felt around inside for a few seconds and said quizzically: "There's paper in it—?!"

"Well, pull some out, so we can see what it is," suggested her partner.

When Marilou was able to extricate some of the paper, neither was expecting what they had found. "Money!" they exclaimed together. At that, they both began to tear at the loosely sewn mattress seam. What greeted their eyes was a sight neither had ever seen in one place: thousands of dollars—mainly singles—rolled into small bundles, bound by rubber bands, and shoved between the remaining top and bottom layers of mattress stuffing. Both were momentarily stupefied. They were brought around from the shock of their discovery by the sound of Lt. Jenkins' voice. He and one of the sergeants were making rounds to see how the shake-down was going.

Officer Wolfe shouted out: "Lieutenant Jenkins—in here!"

"Where?!" came Jenkins' reply. "In Arletta Boykin's room."

By the time Jenkins had popped his head into the door, both officers were standing with mouths agape and hands full of dollar bills. Even Jimmy Jenkins did a double-take. He pulled his uniform cap off and ran his hand through his hair. "Well, well," he chuckled, "what has our Ms. Boykin been up to?" Jenkins went over to the mattress, still being held on its side by the two officers, and peered inside. "Go-od Lord!" he blurted. Jenkins noticed that most of the bundles had small scraps of paper inserted between the rubber bands and the money. He pulled one out and read aloud the scrawled writing: "This dont belong to me—its Janet Whittles money."

Sergeant Samson, who had been accompanying Jenkins on their supervisory rounds looked in as well. "Somebody printing money here?" he asked—only half-jokingly.

Taking charge of the situation, Jenkins said to Sgt. Samson: "Go get Janet Whittle from the sewing room, and find Arletta Boykin; bring 'em both here—but don't say why. Got it?"

"Yes sir, Lieutenant Jenkins," replied Samson and immediately departed.

"Now you two," Jenkins turned his attention to Officer Wolfe and colleague. "One of you gets locked in here and the other waits outside while I go fetch Capt. Waller from the administration building. Okay? Don't breathe a word to *any*body about this. Understood?"

"Yes sir," they both replied.

As Jenkins headed down the corridor he let out a long whistle, and could be heard to say: "At least one woman's earned herself a one-way ticket to Dorm C..."

In the days that followed the shake-down, an investigation was held to determine just how DD, and/or Arletta, had amassed well over three-thousand dollars in small bills. Arletta pleaded—not unconvincingly—that the money was not hers, but that she had been threatened into submission by DD to keep it for her; thus the message Arletta had appended to many of the bundles. It didn't take a lot of questioning among the general inmate population to condemn Janet Whittle—especially after they found out that DD was securely ensconced in Dorm C. Boykin, as the investigation established, had indeed merely been a flunky, scared for her own safety. Dozens of inmates were all-too-relieved to be able to relate the fear and intimidation they had experienced at the hands of DD and her cronies. Most of it had taken place during the early periods of their incarceration—before the women had the protection of a family or friends. However, not one mentioned to the interrogating officers the money that had been extorted from the women who ran the still over in medium security. After all, the investigation had all the facts it needed to keep DD out of general circulation to the end of her appeal process—however it might turn out. In any event, her reign of terror was over, and in addition, her supervisor's job in the sewing room went to Lillian Walker. Everyone in the prison breathed a sigh of relief—except the one in Dorm C, who fumed in her solitary confinement.

February had yielded to the bright, breezy days of March. Frumpy found herself sitting in the afternoon sunshine watching Sally and a few of her tutees tending the flower beds with surgical precision. Several of the white women had hiked their skirts up around their knees and opened their blouses, as much as discipline allowed, in order to catch the sun's rays on their skin—something that would have been jumped on immediately had Warden Nifong still been in charge—which she wasn't. Nifong had been given the unceremonious boot once it had been determined that she, in fact, had been the root cause of the 'great escape.' The new warden was seemingly appointed on the basis of institutional-think: if one thing doesn't work, try its opposite. Replace the white female with a black male. However, more by luck than judgment, the departmental bureaucrats in the state capital had got it right. Warren Beasley was as suited to work with women in prison as anyone could be. He kept a cool head, thought through what needed to be done, took the counsel of others, and when a decision was reached, he acted. Beasley was dedicated to three things: his family, his work in the Department of Correction, and fishing. Happily they were not mutually exclusive—in fact, they were complementary. Beasley saw the dynamics of the women's prison as one large family: more was gained by mutual respect and personal accountability than by draconian rules and threats. And his fishing had taught him that you stand to lose when you try to drag in a catch too fast. Thus he allowed the women some 'slack in the line' as regarded dress codes. He referred to them as his 'ladies'—not in a patronizing way, but in a way that highlighted the fact that, though they were in prison, they were still women—even ladies. Thus, sunning sessions on pleasant afternoons went a long way to restoring the peace and smooth operation of the prison in his charge.

As the women took advantage of the more relaxed regime on this particular day, they lazily greeted a few of the inmates who had finished their kitchen duty and were making their way back to the dormitories after having mopped and cleaned the dining hall. Frumpy first noticed that they were all bunched unusually close together and secondly, that the gaggle of inmates was gathered rather tightly around 'Big Bertha' Hairston. Bertha was walking like a goose about to lay an oversized egg. Watching the woman lumber along, Frumpy couldn't help speaking her thoughts aloud: "Why is Bertha walking like *that*?" she asked—of no one in particular.

"Because she **big**—*too* big," laughed one of the spectators.

"Yes, but even so, she doesn't normally walk *like that* ..." mused Frumpy.

"Hush your mouth, girl," interrupted Violet Dixon, "before somebody hear you!" The group of kitchen workers drew near and, as they passed by, there were winks and knowing smiles.

"What's going on?" inquired Frumpy.

Violet leaned close to Frumpy and then pulled the young woman closer still. With her mouth right against Frumpy's ear Violet whispered: "We gonna be holdin' us a little celebration now that DD's in Dorm C. Bertha be carrying a five-pound bag of sugar between them thighs of hers. That's what she doing."

"*What*?!" exclaimed Frumpy, unintentionally loud.

"Damn girl! Hush your mouth!" interjected Violet while a few others grimaced at Frumpy. "We gonna make us some hooch with that sugar! We done collected us some fruit and potato peelings—be using that mop bucket in the back of the cleaning cupboard. The one you *never see* on cleaning days. In this heat, that stuff'll ferment nicely in a day or two; then we be getting high as kites!"

Frumpy listened in amazement. Her fellow inmates' ingenuity reminded her of the hi-jinx she had watched on "Hogan's Heroes." Here were prisoners talking about operating a still under the noses of their guards. Although she had no interest in drinking their concoction, Frumpy had to admit to herself that she was one-hundred percent behind them in wishing for their success. Her nearly ten months behind bars had proved to be a very interesting alternative educational system.

Some of the women retreated inside the dormitory to help in the process of turning Bertha Hairston's ill-gotten sugar into hooch. About a half-dozen of the women remained on the benches and steps watching Sally patiently tend her flowers. It was then that Stephen Travis came walking by. He saw Frumpy sitting with the small group and greeted her.

At that point Nelly Walker called to Travis. Nelly was a loud, middle-aged, stock-car fan with teased hair, who fancied herself irresistible to all men. She spoke with a nasally twang and added an 'h' to certain initial vowels. She began by asking: "Chaplain Travis? D'ju go to the state fire when hit was in town?"

Somewhat nonplussed by the question, Stephen stammered his reply: "Uh… the state *fair*? Well, um…yes, Nelly, I did."

"Well, was Joie Chitwood's Hell Drivers there this year?"

"Uh, gosh, Nelly, to tell the truth, I don't know."

"Now, Chaplain, how can you go to the state fire and not watch Joie Chitwood?"

Travis resisted the urge to say 'easy.' "Guess I just got too busy doing other things."

"You take a *girl* with you?" inquired Nelly.

Travis blushed. At this point Frumpy gave Nelly a firm, but gentle, nudge with the toe of her shoe. "Leave him alone. That's none of your business."

Nelly turned towards Frumpy, "Well now, you work with him, don'tcha Sweetie—did he sneak you out?"

Now it was Frumpy's turn to blush, but still she replied: "As though he would or could."

"Yeah, Nelly, I took a date, and that's all I have to say about it."

"Okay, Chaplain, hit don't make no never-mind," replied Nelly, "'cause you just listen here to me. When I get outta here, you and me's going to the state fire together. And I'm gonna make sure you see Joie Chitwood. Then we're going on the double Ferris wheel, gonna have some cotton candy, and just have us a good ol' time. You just wait and see!"

"I will, Nelly. But meanwhile, I've got my work to do. Bye for now." Travis knew that Nelly's plans were merely wishful thinking, but even so, as he walked away, he had to resist the urge to shudder as a picture was conjured in his head of Nelly and himself high in the air on the double Ferris wheel eating cotton candy.

As April unfolded, the signs of spring were everywhere. Chaplain Travis had all the windows rolled down in his old Chevrolet Biscayne so he could drink in the rich aromas of a Southern spring—particularly his favorite: wisteria mixed with honeysuckle. As he turned down the road leading towards the women's prison he found his way partially blocked by a tall black man who was trying to hitch a ride in the opposite direction—from the *middle* of the road. As Travis slowed the car, the man heard his approach and immediately spun around—nearly falling over in the process—and began trying to hitch a ride in the direction Travis was taking. Stephen came to a stop by the man, to ask whether there might be a problem; at which point the fellow in question nearly fell through the driver's window. It was now clear that the man was totally inebriated. Propping himself up on the car door, with head, shoulders and arms within the passenger compartment, the man blurted out, with intoxicated diphthongs: "Ah needs a ri-ide to Wa-ayland."

Travis couldn't help but turn his head from the blast of one-hundred-and-fifty proof breath. It quickly flashed through his mind that, had he been a smoker, the vapors from the drunk's breath would have ignited. "I'm not going to Wayland," replied Travis. "I work up the road, at the women's prison."

Undeterred the man continued with a plaintive: "I work so-o ha-ard."

"Yes, well, don't we all?" smiled Travis weakly—now wishing that he hadn't stopped.

"My name's Hubert: H-U-B-E-R-T," he spelled. "I lives on Cal-e-donia Road, in Wayland." At this point the inebriate's legs nearly gave way and he grasped Stephen's shoulder and the car door to regain his stance. "I—I ain't gonna hurt you…an- an- and you ain't gonna hurt me. Ain't no harm…naw, ain't no reason in the world…" His speech drifted off with his drunken thoughts as he shook his head. Cars had slowly been going around Stephen and Hubert as they carried on their largely one-way conversation in the middle of the street. "I work so-o ha-ard," Hubert began again, dropping his head in self-pity. He then perked up: "I will buy you a can of beer! I—I do not have any beer—but I will buy you a can of beer!"

"Look, Hubert, I don't want any beer, okay? I…I gotta get to work."

"I'm Hubert! H-U-B-E-R-T," he spelt once more, "I live in Wayland on Ca-al-e-donia."

"Yes, you've told me—."

"I will buy you a can of beer…I—I do not have any beer… I have a fifth of Paul Jones. But I will buy you a can of beer. I'm Hubert—."

"Oh get in!" commanded Travis. He could see that the situation was hopeless.

Hubert pushed himself up from the open car window and drunkenly sauntered around to the passenger door. Once open, he flopped into the seat. "I live on Caledonia—."

"Yeah, in Wayland. I know," mumbled Stephen. "You think you could direct me to Caledonia Road once we get to Wayland, Hubert?"

"I'm Hubert," came the reply, "H-U-B-E-R-T. I ain't gonna hurt you, you ain't gonna hurt me. Ain't no harm…ain't no reason in the world."

"There sure ain't," simmered Travis, "reason disappeared from this world a long time ago."

Hubert's repetitive monologue continued throughout the eight-mile journey to Wayland. Despite his drunkenness, Hubert had enough of a homing instinct to guide Travis to his house on Caledonia Road. When Stephen had pulled into the sandy driveway and come to a stop, Hubert took him by the shoulder, belched and said: "I will buy you a can of beer. I do not—."

"Have any beer. Yeah, I know, Hubert. But you know what? I don't *want* any beer—or Paul Jones. I have to go to work now."

Stephen had freed himself from Hubert's grasp and was now headed around the car to help Hubert get out. As he got to the passenger door, Hubert said, "I work so-o ha-ard."

"Hubert?! Dat you?" A woman's voice came from behind the screened, front door. Her head bobbed out from behind the screen and looked Travis up and down. "Who're you? —Whass wrong with Hubert?" Both questions rolled into one.

Answering in reverse order, as he struggled to pull Hubert up from the seat, Stephen grunted: "He's drunk—I guess. I'm a chaplain at the prison—"

"Prison?! Whass Hubert done?" She was now fully out on the front steps, wiping her hands on her apron. Slowly she placed each hand in a balled fist on her hips as she looked suspiciously at Travis.

"No. No, ma'am. I *work* in the *women's* prison—it's nothing to do with Hubert. It's just that I was on my way there when Hubert kinda stopped me…in the middle of the road. He said he wanted a ride home. I—I just gave him a ride home."

Hubert was now out of the car and clapping Stephen on the shoulder like they were the oldest and best of friends. Hubert's monologue was still in full swing as the young chaplain guided his charge to the front door and Hubert's less-than-amused wife. Together they got Hubert up the three concrete steps that led to the living room.

"You a rev'rund, huh?"

"Yes, ma'am, I am," said Travis, "And I really need to get to work."

Hubert's wife softened. "Hubert, he work at the chicken processin' plant there around the corner from that prison…if he *still got* a job, that is." She rolled her eyes and looked at Hubert with both disgust and disapprobation. Then the woman and Travis looked at one another. "Thank you for bringing him home."

Despite Hubert's now hanging over one of her substantial shoulders, she offered Travis her hand. He took it. In the one second that their eyes connected—*really connected*—they passed over centuries of slavery, across continents, racial barriers, social injustice, bad schooling and worse housing to a place of common humanity. Travis nodded at her and turned to leave. As he walked back to his car, through the screen door he heard: "I will buy you a can of beer…"

Nearly an hour after he had first encountered Hubert, Travis was walking to his office from the administration building. He noticed two cars—unmarked, but all the more noticeable as a result—parked in front of the main gate. Men in suits and sunglasses were talking with Capt. Waller. The cars, their suits and shades all announced:

"Feds." Stephen wondered what might be going on, but reckoned he'd find out sooner or later. The tall pines on the prison grounds were swaying gently from a soft, balmy breeze. With the breeze were carried the strains of Prokofiev's *Romeo & Juliet*—specifically the love dance from Scene Two. This happened to be one of Travis' favorite pieces and prison was the last place he ever expected to hear it. He followed the music until he came to one of the smaller meeting rooms across the corridor from the auditorium. The curtains were drawn, but—due to the warmth of the day—the windows were opened wide. As the curtains flapped in the breeze Travis could see a screen on which flickered Rudolph Nureyev and Margot Fonteyn in a *pas de deux*. A small group of women sat transfixed at the screen; most having never seen a ballet. Travis made his way inside and opened the door to the meeting room. He saw Peggy Ainsley, one of the teachers from the nearby community college. She taught fine arts and English literature in the extension program at the women's prison. She waved to him and then Travis signaled with his hands: 'may I come in?' Peggy nodded and waved him in. Travis gave a little wave to the gathered audience and noticed Frumpy sitting in the front row.

Once the film was over, Peggy invited the chaplain to stick around for the discussion if he had the time. Stephen said that as long as she had his secretary in the group he might as well stay—but first asked if it would be all right with the ladies. They all agreed that they wanted to hear what the 'Rev' had to say. Peggy led a wide-ranging discussion that went from Dante to Shakespeare and from Diaghilev and Prokofiev to Nureyev and Fonteyn. Peggy did a good job of explaining who each was and how all played an important part in the story they had seen danced on screen. Travis was enjoying the low-key lecture and discussion as much as anyone when Peggy turned to him and asked: "Now Chaplain Travis, what drew you in here to watch this ballet with us?"

Caught off guard and put on the spot, Travis did what he always did: he blushed. Peggy saw his predicament and effected a rescue by asking whether he knew the ballet, and if so, what he liked about it. Travis paused before answering. "I think it's one of the most beautiful pieces of music I have ever heard. I mean…from the very first time I can remember hearing Prokofiev's score for the ballet, I fell in love with it…I mean, it really moved me."

Ever the good pedagogue, Peggy said: "Tell us about that—why did it 'move you?'"

"Gosh, well… It's got everything, hasn't it? The music brings to life the story of Romeo and Juliet—there's passion (a few women mmh'ed their assent), violence, humor, love, tragedy, sorrow. I don't know…the music takes me through just about every human emotion, I guess. And the movement in the ballet enhances it all."

The women nodded and chatted about his comments for a moment. Then Frumpy asked Travis: "Have you ever seen the ballet?—in real life?"

"Yes, I have," replied Travis. "It was in London—."

"You mean *England*?" asked one of the women. Coming to do time in the Correctional Center for Women was probably as far from home as she had ever travelled.

"Yes, in England," continued Travis. "I was in London as a student—during college. Anyway, I tried to go to as many cultural events as possible while I was there, and one of them happened to be Prokofiev's *Romeo & Juliet*. I saw it at the Royal Festival Hall."

Now even Peggy was drawn in: "Tell us about it!"

Having now lost all self-consciousness, Travis related the winter's evening that he, and the young woman he was dating, went to the Festival Hall. Eager to sate their desire for details, he described the building ("Not very attractive, really"), the lobby, the good seats they had—and which had cost him dearly: the exchange rate was $2.46 to £1!—the set, the costumes, the dancers and the orchestra. Stephen's eyes glowed from the good memories.

He finished speaking and looked at the faces turned attentively towards him, each transported—if only for a few brief minutes—well beyond the confines of this prison. Peggy broke the silence: "How did it make you feel?"

Without hesitation, Travis said: "I cried." No one said anything as his words sank in. "Yes, I cried. Juliet died, the orchestra played those final brooding bars, the performance ended, lights came up and there I sat crying." He shook his head as though he himself couldn't believe it.

Frumpy was the first inmate to speak again: "Why did you cry?"

"Because—," Travis let out a deep breath and then started again: "Because it was all so beautiful…and so poignant. I mean the music, staging, dancing, etc. were exquisite—but the story itself is so tragic. It's silly, I know. I have read *Romeo & Juliet* in school and have seen the play on TV, on stage and at the movies. I *know* how the story ends—and yet…and yet I still hope against hope that Juliet will wake up before Romeo kills himself. And somehow, seeing it in dance form, accompanied by Prokofiev's powerful score… Well, it packs an emotional punch." Travis was unused to such self-disclosure—particularly in his professional role, but he felt it was a risk worth taking.

"Maybe that's what Shakespeare wanted us to do," chimed in Peggy, "make us want to change the story's ending—if not in Romeo's & Juliet's lives, then perhaps in our own life stories." The inmates were unusually silent and pensive. "Okay, ladies. That's your homework for next time: Is *Romeo & Juliet* meant to be a wake-up call to us?—a challenge to get our acts together in our relationships with other people? Write me about five-hundred words on that topic. See you next week."

As Travis headed for the door, Peggy touched him on the arm and asked him if he could remain for a moment. "Sure," he replied, and then to Frumpy: "See you in the office in two minutes." Frumpy smiled and passed through the doorway.

As the last inmate left and closed the door behind her, Peggy turned to Travis and said, "Thank you for that, Stephen—for what you said."

"Yeah, well, I was afraid that maybe I said too much." Travis blushed.

"I don't think so," Peggy replied. Her face became quite serious and she continued: "If you don't mind my saying it: You know what sorts of experiences most of these women have had with men. *Not* good."

Stephen raised his eyebrows and said, "Amen to that. I hear things in this place that almost make me ashamed to be a man."

"But that's the point, Stephen—you are a man. And there are a lot more men like you out there beyond these bars and fences than most of these women would ever dream. They need to hear the voices of men who do not abuse and belittle women. It's good that you're here—that you even *want* to be here. So thanks."

Stephen smiled, nodded towards Peggy and said, "Not a problem. Glad it was useful." Glancing at the clock on the wall, he said: "And now, after nearly two hours, I might actually set foot in my office!" He smiled at Peggy and left.

Frumpy was arranging the intra-office and inmates' mail for Travis when he got to his desk. Sheepishly, Frumpy stood up and handed Travis both piles. On top of the inmates' post lay a letter, scrawled in a childish hand with large letters. "I'm sorry Chaplain Travis; I couldn't help but see that Lola Rogers has written to you again. It's just been delivered." The note began:

Dear Chaplin Travis,

You sorry son-of-a-bitch. I am going to kill you one day but you wont know when or where but I will get you you lousy bastard...

Travis glanced quickly at the letter and said: "Don't worry about it, Frumpy. She'd stick it in an envelope if she didn't want anyone to see it." He scanned the letter front and back. "Lola must want a visit. I wonder what's up?" He thought about the 'Feds' at the main gate, but thought "Nah." Frumpy had hesitated near Travis' desk. "You do know you are allowed to sit down on this job, Frumpy?" She was still hovering over Travis' desk, and rolled her eyes self-mockingly in nervous recognition of that fact.

Frumpy plopped back into her chair. They looked at one another for a brief moment. Frumpy drew a deep breath: "Did you *really* cry when you saw *Romeo & Juliet*? Or did you say that, well...just for us?"

Travis crinkled his face and pulled back in his chair as if to say: "Where'd this come from?"

"Well...I never saw Carl cry—not that we were together all that long." Frumpy was now twisting her wedding ring and staring at it intently. She still wore it despite the impending divorce. "I never saw my daddy cry... But he made my mama cry—a *lot*...and me. He got angry a lot...and he hit us. I used to ask mama why, but she would just say that he didn't like his job or that he sometimes drank too much. But I don't know. I just think he didn't like *us*—that he didn't want to be married to mama... or have me. I think that's why I wanted to be with Carl. I thought things would be different. Carl really seemed to like me...I...I *thought* he loved me and that maybe that would be enough. But now we're both in prison—*thanks to him*—and waiting for the divorce to come through." Frumpy looked up at Travis and said: "I'll bet your family wasn't anything like that."

"No, it wasn't," answered Travis. "And working here has sure made me thank God for the good upbringing I had." He paused and then asked: "Where's your father now?"

Frumpy sighed deeply and said: "In hell—probably. In any case, he's dead."

"How?" asked Travis.

"He was shot dead…by my grandfather—my grandfather was the county sheriff…it was after he had attacked my mama…and me." Frumpy suddenly stood up. "Chaplain Travis, look what time it is! And I haven't even let you get to your mail or paperwork. Got any typing you want me to do?"

With his limited experience as a chaplain, Travis couldn't intuit whether Frumpy had firmly closed the door on her self-revelation or whether it was still open, and only waiting for him to lean upon it. Recognizing his lack of skill in such situations, Travis' indecision as to how to proceed soon combined with the pregnant silence between them, such that the room began to feel airless; thus he opted to give Frumpy her privacy—something that prison ill afforded. "Right!" Stephen quickly got to his feet. "Yes, I have some letters here that need typing." Stephen always wrote his letters by hand, as he found it easier than dictating them. He handed Frumpy a half-dozen sheets of paper, adding: "When they're finished, please take them to Administration for posting. I'm heading over to Dorm C. See you tomorrow."

Travis headed outside and across the main yard. There was a faster way to the Control Center but he was curious to see whether his supposed 'Feds' were still about. Their cars were still by the front gate. When Travis got to the Control Center, it was unusually busy. Capt. Waller was there speaking to Lt. Jenkins and several of the guards. There was a mixture of muffled laughter and exasperated head-shaking as Stephen entered the building. Everyone turned towards him as he joined them in the small area that served to oversee prison security.

"Hi. Sorry to interrupt," began Travis.

The security staff acknowledged his entrance with nods until Waller finished speaking. Jenkins smiled and winked at Travis. Waller turned to Travis: "Guess you've heard then?"

Travis proffered a Gallic shrug and shook his head: "Heard *what?*"

"About our little visit from the Secret Service. They've discovered a *big* security threat right here at our institution. Seems we got us someone here who constitutes a threat to the President of the United States." All the guards laughed.

One of them nudged Waller and said: "You think the Chaplain's in on it?" More laughter. Stephen was still puzzled. Waller turned, picked up a sheaf of papers on his desk and handed them to Stephen. The latter could see that they were photocopies of hand-written letters addressed to President Ford—and the script was all-too-familiar to Stephen.

Dear President Ford,
 You goddamned son-of-a-bitch...

"These are all from Lola Rogers!" exclaimed Travis.

"You got it," chuckled Waller. "Problem is, she sent him a batch just about the time his election campaign was due to bring him to Raleigh. Secret Service boys thought they'd better pay a visit to the return address to discover for themselves just who this Lola Rogers was and what—*if any*—security threat she posed."

Travis handed the photocopies back to Waller. "Reckon she hoped to get a visit from the president?" joked Travis. "I guess they were a bit surprised to find out that her street address led them to the women's prison—and that Lola is safely locked up in maximum security!" Now it was Travis' turn to join the laughter. "That's unbelievable! Did they actually go see Lola?"

"Sure did!" threw in Jenkins, "*and* she popped her eye out, and had it peekin' outta her hand like this." Jenkins cupped his hand, knuckles up, with his thumb and forefinger making an aperture for the peeking eye. "Freaked the shit outta one of the Feds! Oops— sorry there, Chaplain!"

Travis was laughing: "No apology necessary, Jimmy. That Lola is a trip, isn't she? Say, speaking of which—can you notify Dorm C that I'm on my way to see her now?"

"You got it," said Jenkins. "But don't let her take you hostage as a bid to get out and assassinate President Ford!"

"I'll do my best," replied Stephen as he headed out the door towards the security gate for Dorm C.

Once he was at Lola's cell, Stephen prepared himself in case her eye was missing or about to pop up in an odd location. He had to admit that it gave him a queasy feeling. Lola was lying on her bunk, face to the wall. "Lola? It's me, Chaplain Travis. Got your letter."

Lola turned and smiled broadly at Travis. "Hey," she said before going all coy and shy.

"It sounds like you've had a busy day," grinned Travis. "I hear you've had the President's security men here for a visit." Lola positively beamed and nodded her head in assent. "I don't suppose President Ford came with them, huh?"

"No-o," she drawled and then giggled. Despite all the attention-seeking, Lola never really shared much about herself. She tended to keep conversations in the present—what little she said. Lola was just happy to be visited on occasion, but mostly liked being left to herself. For her, the cell in Dorm C was probably more desirable than a suite at the Ritz—and certainly the security was better.

The next morning, on his way to work, curiosity got the better of Travis. He pulled his car into the front parking lot for the chicken processing plant where Hubert's wife said he worked. "This is crazy," Travis muttered to himself as he approached the front office.

Once inside he noticed a young woman behind a desk bearing the sign: "Reception". Next to it, there were tacky smiling chickens framing her name plate: "Vicky". Travis waited while the receptionist finished a call. When she hung up, she smiled at Stephen and asked,

"May, I he'p yew?" Vicky had a bouffant hairdo that looked too much like cotton candy, pale waxy skin and very red rouge and lipstick.

"Yeah, sure—I hope so," began Stephen. "Vicky, is there someone here that I could talk to about, ah, one of your employees?"

"Is there a prob-blim?" inquired the young lady as she cocked her head forty-five degrees to one side. Stephen had to fight the urge to tilt his head to meet her gaze.

"Uh, no. No, there's not a problem. I just needed to ask about someone."

"Way-yell, oka-ay then. Hold on just a min-nit." Stephen watched as her overly manicured hands lifted the receiver and dialed an extension. Her nails looked as though she had taken them to Earl Scheib, the nation's king of the quick car paint-job. "Hey, Sharon, there's a man here who—what's your name, Sugar?"

"Travis. Stephen Travis."

"There's a Mr. Travis here who wants to ask about one of our employees. No. He says there ain't a prob-blim." She smiled sweetly at Stephen and he shook his head and waved his hands to emphasize the fact there was nothing to worry about. Vicky put the phone down and smiled at Stephen: "Way-yell, Mr. Travis," she drawled, "just go down that hallway there and you'll find Sharon in the first office on the right. She's our personnel director."

"Great. Thanks a lot." As Stephen as he made his way to see Sharon, he thought to himself: "This is crazy!" The door was open, so Stephen tapped lightly as he stepped inside. The personnel director was smartly dressed in a two-piece suit, had a short Afro hairdo and coffee-brown skin. She stood and extended her hand. "Mr. Travis, I'm Sharon. How may I help you?" Travis began to speak, but Sharon interrupted: "Please, have a seat."

They both sat and Travis began again. "I'm sorry to bother you, but I have a question about one of your employees—I realize you might not be able to tell me anything. But…ah…"

Sharon rested her chin on her hand and looked curiously at Travis: "Is there some kind of problem?"

"No. No—it's just that yesterday, as I was driving to the prison (I'm a chaplain there), I met a guy in the middle of the road who was—uh—a little worse for wear. When I slowed down, he nearly fell in through my window. Told me his name was 'Hubert' and asked me to give him a ride to Wayland. So I did. I guess I'm just wondering whether he's okay." Sharon's face had broken into a wide grin as the story emerged. She was laughing by the time Travis finished.

Shaking her head with amused incredulity, Sharon said, "Oh Hubert's just *fi-ine*. Hung over, but just fine!" Sharon kept sniggering at what seemed to be a private joke, as though trying to decide whether or not to share it. Looking over at Travis she asked: "You gave Hubert a ride home yesterday?"

"Yes, ma'am. To Wayland."

Sharon laughed out loud and then said: "I sent Hubert home yesterday after his section manager told me he was drunk. Don't need him getting chopped up back there in the plant and ending up as chicken cuts at somebody's barbecue!" Sharon snorted a laugh full of gusto. "When Hubert got into work this morning I had him report to me. These little 'incidents' got to go on his personnel record, ya know. Well, when he got here he tells me that he had *absolutely no idea* how he got home yesterday!" Sharon gave a great belly laugh. "Crazy fool's wife had already left for her cleaning job, so he wakes up not knowing how he got from here back home—*and into bed*!" They both enjoyed a laugh. "You want me to send for Hubert?—so he can thank you?"

"Oh—no, that's not why I came. I just wanted to make sure that he was…okay—and that he hadn't, uh, been fired. I think Hubert's wife was afraid he'd get fired for going to work drunk."

"Listen, honey," Sharon took on a more personal and confidential tone with Travis, "It doesn't take a genius to know that ninety-nine percent of our employees are not college graduates—killing, plucking and preparing chickens all day?—shoot! And it ain't air-conditioned back there either." Sharon's thumb jerked towards the wall behind her desk, the other side of which lay Hubert's workplace. "I reckon I'd take a drink or two myself if I had to work in *that mess.* Mmh-mmh." Sharon was silent for a minute. Then, more to herself than to Travis, she said: "Man can't read or write. Worked like a slave all his life. He and his wife raised up six kids. I went to St. Augustine's College with one of their sons—he's a teacher now in Randolph County. I guess I have a secret liking for the man—even though he can be a mess!"

Travis stood up to leave. "Well, thanks for your time. I'm just glad he's all right." Travis' eyes twinkled and smiled: "Please don't tell him about my visit—okay? Let's leave him wondering how he got home—might help to keep him sober!"

Sharon's laughter pealed again: "Oh you go ahead on! You're a mess too!" They shook hands again and Stephen left.

It was about 11:00 a.m. when Stephen Travis pulled his old Chevy into the parking lot of the women's prison. By agreement with the senior chaplain, he often arrived at different times of the day so as to get to know the different shifts of guards, as well as to have access to women who worked outside the prison during the day, or who were in school or working at different jobs within the prison. But as Travis got out of his car and locked it, he could see that this was not going to be an ordinary day. Goodman was also in the parking lot, but in handcuffs and being led to a state police car by two armed officers. Travis was too stunned to say anything as he walked by the scene. Goodman kept his head down and looked at no one; his face was tear-stained. Warden Beasley was heading back into the administration building with Captain Waller. The police car drove away and Travis stopped, as though caught in a vacuum between Goodman's departure and Beasley's determined gait in the opposite direction. As the state police car sped up along the main road fronting the prison, Travis noticed that he was the only member of staff watching it disappear. A few inmates in the front yard between reception and the main gate were standing like statues, watching Goodman's exit.

Travis entered the administration building. People were standing in little groups of two or three, chattering and tittering with one another. As they noticed Travis, they quickly ceased their talk and nervously greeted him, "G'mornin' Chaplain Travis," several said—a little too cheerily. After Travis had walked through the metal detector, which led through to the main grounds, they began laughing, thinking him to be out of earshot. "Who's gonna tell *him*?" was the last thing he made out. Travis felt himself blushing and going all rubbery legged—the way he did whenever he had to cross the grounds in front of too many women on a sultry day and suffer their comments. Only this time it wasn't about him—*or was it*? He entered his office building, where a few social workers and case managers stood in the hallway, chatting and laughing. They stopped when they espied Travis. Travis fairly fled into his small office and closed the door behind him. He flopped into his desk chair and dropped his briefcase. He was sweating now. "What the hell was going on?" he wondered to himself. No sooner had he begun to compose himself than he heard a quick double knock at his door.

"Chaplain Travis?" The voice was Kate McIntyre's and the 'Chaplain Travis' had been for the benefit of those in the adjoining offices.

Travis was on his feet like a shot and opened the door. Kate was accompanied by Captain Waller. His face was as long as his six-foot-four frame. "Stephen, may we come in?"

"Sure. Sure." Travis replied. He pulled two chairs together and then spun his desk chair round to face them.

Kate and Bob faced Travis and both looked to the other to begin. Waller nodded at Kate. She took a deep breath and began. "Stephen…

I don't know quite how to say this, but Chaplain Goodman has been...*arrested.*"

She paused and waited for Travis' reaction. He uttered a low "Wow," and then: "I saw him being taken away as I was coming in this morning. What happened? What's wrong?"

Now it was Kate's turn to look at Bob Waller. The captain drew his large frame up in his chair, ran his finger inside his collar and said: "He got caught with one of the residents...having sex."

"Sex? How?...I mean, *where?*" McIntyre and Waller eyed one another sheepishly, and then to Travis' astonishment, they burst into laughter—gut-wrenching laughter. Kate had let loose first, quickly followed by Waller. The solemnity of the moment was lost forever. Kate was covering her mouth and holding her belly, but each time she saw Capt. Waller's huge frame convulsing with laughter, she let go again. Tears were flowing from Kate's eyes and Waller was spraying saliva whenever he tried to close his mouth. Travis was now laughing at the pair of them—but without knowing the source of the hilarity. Slowly both Bob and Kate regained their composure. Travis offered them both tissues to wipe their eyes—and lips, in Waller's case.

"Oh dear," said Kate, as she tried to catch her breath. "Oh dear. It was just *too* funny. Sorry, Stephen, sorry." Kate sat upright, smoothed her dress and said, "He was in the kitchen's storage freezer..." Now it was Kate who was spewing spittle at her colleagues as the laughter returned.

Travis looked incredulously at both Kate and Bob, and slowly exclaimed: "In the *freezer?*"

"Yep. Can you believe it?" nodded Capt. Waller, who was nearly on the floor as he heaved with laughter, "In the damn freezer—of all places!" Now it was Stephen's turn to laugh. Waller continued, "Yeah, I guess he thought nobody'd expect such carryings-on in there..."—splutter—"and it seems it wasn't the first time, either." More laughter. "One of the kitchen helpers tipped off Officers Sampson and McCall. They radioed me and asked me to be there as a further witness. And—there—he—was..."—splutter—"with Rosalee Mason, trousers down around his ankles, and huffin' an' puffin' like a dog on a bitch in heat—oh, sorry Kate—uh, you too, Chaplain."

"Don't worry," said Kate, "We're all adults here. But look, I have to go now." She wiped the tears of laughter which had run down her cheeks. "May I leave this between the two of you?" Both Travis and Waller nodded approval. As Kate started through the door, she paused briefly and said to Travis, "I am sorry," and left. As the sound of Kate's footsteps receded, Stephen thought about what Sally Wilkins had said to him—how she and some of the other women would take care of 'Quickshot' Goodman. It seemed they had certainly done that.

Waller and Travis both stared at Kate's empty chair for a moment, and then the captain turned his attention to Travis. "Stephen, I'm sorry as hell this had to happen—and right before Easter." Stephen just raised his eyebrows and let out a puff of breath. Waller continued: "How do you feel about holding the fort here? The women still need a chaplain; services still need to go ahead. I've already had a brief word with Warden Beasley, and he feels you've got the respect of most staff and inmates. Believe it or not, even ol' Pumps & Pearls had a grudging respect for you and left a letter in your file saying so—even after the way you refused to help in the inmate round-up after the 'great escape.' Beasley's read it."

Travis thought for a moment before he spoke. "Well, I still have part of this intern year left—and I want to finish it. Who'd be my supervisor? That's part of the arrangement for my being here."

"Don't you worry about that," said Waller. "Warden Beasley will get in touch with Ralph Martin at the Chaplaincy Department and let him know that he values your services and needs you here—we need some stability until this thing settles down.

"Okay, sure," said Travis, and then—under his breath to himself: "Guess the church'll de-frock him."

"What's that?" asked Waller, standing up to leave.

"I said, I guess the Church will de-frock Goodman—after what he's done."

"Ha!" came Waller's response, "guess he's done the de-frocking already!—in the freezer!" And then, more seriously: "He'll be damned lucky if he doesn't do some time himself." Waller shook his head at Goodman's predicament and then departed.

Travis thought about Waller's parting words. Could someone like Goodman—*a chaplain*—actually get sentenced to prison? Then he thought about the events of the last couple of years following the Watergate break-in: the trials and convictions of Nixon's cronies. Travis whistled softly and then said to himself, "Well, if it could happen to them…"

Exit Time

Thus the whirligig of time brings in his revenges.

Twelfth Night

The weeks following Goodman's ignominious departure saw Travis putting in more hours—trying both to cover more of the counseling needs as well as the regular worship services. In the aftermath of Goodman's departure, his secretary, Marla Thompkins, decided to leave the chaplains' office for another assignment in the prison. Despite Stephen's being the only chaplain at present, the administrative duties remained the same as when Goodman was around. Thus he approached Frumpy about taking on another three to four hours per week of secretarial and administrative work. She said she would be happy to help if Travis would speak with her case worker, Charlene Walker. In addition, Ralph Martin made sure that chaplains from two nearby correctional facilities would be available to help with some of the increased work load over Easter. Stephen felt he could just about see daylight through all the smoke and dust generated by the Goodman fiasco. His feeling was undergirded by Charlene's stopping by his office to tell him that Frumpy would indeed be able to take on more secretarial work. Breathing an audible sigh of relief after Charlene's visit, Travis put his hands behind his head and leaned back in his creaky desk chair.

As the office door was opened to allow fresh air into the windowless room, there was no courtesy knock before an inmate appeared:

Sharon Moore. Sharon had been a regular visitor to the chaplains' office and had been on Goodman's counseling list. Sharon was about thirty years of age, slim, with strawberry-blond hair and moved in a feline manner which bespoke a lurking danger to Stephen. The male guards' eyes followed her movements around the grounds for more than security reasons. The spring sunshine had brought out faint freckles on her skin, which was moist with perspiration. Sharon's hair was pulled back into a rough plait, but there were long wisps floating about her face, giving her a sensual—even sexual—appearance. Like most of the inmates on these sultry spring days she had both top buttons of her blouse undone. She smiled as she entered the office and then asked: "May I come in?"

"As you're already in—yes," Travis returned the smile.

"Mind if I close the door?" The door was shut even before Sharon finished asking. She glided over to a chair and, in her cat-like manner, didn't so much sit as perch upon it. Still smiling at Travis, Sharon gathered up her loose hair and plait and said: "It's very hot today, isn't it?" She pushed out her bottom lip and blew at a wayward strand of hair, then let her hair fall as she fanned her face. "I don't know how you can stand it in this hot office—especially with no windows."

Travis shrugged and said matter-of-factly: "It's what the prison gives me for an office. I don't suppose they worry about my comfort any more than yours. Anyway, the tax-payers would probably riot if they thought any prison buildings had air-conditioning."

"Well, *I'm* hot. Aren't you?" Sharon looked directly at Travis' eyes. Now it became crystal clear why he had felt Sharon to be dangerous—at some point since her entry (and he hadn't noticed when) a third button had been unfastened and her cleavage was plainly in view. She swiveled back and forth on the desk chair. "Chaplain Travis, I don't have any cigarette money." Sharon kept her eyes fixed on the chaplain's as though waiting to see if they lowered to her chest.

Travis could feel sweat starting to form on his upper lip and the back of his neck. He tried to remain calm. His brain was working overtime because he knew—at a certain male level—that he found Sharon to be an attractive woman. But in the back of his mind he could hear the knowing voice of Stanley Kowalski in *A Streetcar Named Desire*: "I never met a dame yet that didn't know if she was good-looking." Still, Travis was thinking clearly enough to know that he was in an explosive situation—especially after what had recently transpired with Goodman. Professionalism triumphed over any trace of libidinous curiosity. She was playing him. "Well, Sharon, you know the rules. There's nothing I can do about your inmate trust account."

Sharon cocked her head to one side and pouted: "That's not what Chaplain Goodman would have said."

"Yeah, well, Goodman's gone, as you well know. Maybe you should bum a few cigarettes from your friends until you get some money in your account. Or," Travis struggled to lighten the atmosphere, "perhaps you could use this as an incentive to give up smoking."

Sharon rolled her eyes back at the suggestion. "So I don't suppose you know about the little 'trust fund' that Chaplain Goodman kept in that desk? *He* didn't mind helping out inmates in need." Involuntarily Travis turned to look at the old wooden desk behind him. "See the three drawers on the left? Pull out the middle one." Travis felt a rivulet of sweat run down his scalp and along his spine until it was absorbed in his cotton shirt. He pulled the drawer out and looked inside. He started to riffle through the contents when Sharon rolled her chair closer and said: "All the way out." When Travis had it fully extracted he felt, and then saw, a small manila envelope stuck onto the back of the drawer with thumb tacks. In the meantime, Sharon had kicked off her left shoe and drawn her foot up onto the chair seat. "Now you've found it!" she beamed triumphantly.

To Travis' fingers, it felt as though there were dollar bills waded up inside the envelope. His mouth and throat became dry as he fumbled to open it. What greeted his sight left him startled: Condoms. A dozen or more condoms. Stephen's heart started beating harder as he tried to think of what to say in order to hide his perplexity. He glanced sideways at Sharon. "This is…uh…this is *not* money, Sharon."

Ignoring his statement, Sharon reached over to wipe the gathering sweat from Travis' brow. "You really are *hot*—and nervous too."

Stephen quickly pushed his chair back from Sharon, bumping loudly into the desk. "Look, Sharon. I—I don't know what this is all about." He held the envelope as evidence of his bafflement.

"It's a sort of deposit, silly." Sharon laughed and sought to move close again.

Stephen stood up, threw the envelope onto the desk and paced around. "A *deposit*? For what?"

Sharon moved quickly from her chair, reached around Stephen, brushing against him in the process and picked up one of the condom packets. Flopping back in her chair, she waved the packet in front of Stephen, tossed her hair back and tilted her head to one side. "Haven't you ever used one of these before?" she queried. Stephen remained stone silent. Sharon then shrugged and said: "I can show you how." She began to tear open the condom packet.

"God no! I *know* what they are Sharon. What I don't understand is *why* they are *here* and how *you know* they're here!"

Sharon's countenance began to change from playful-seductive to business-like. She pulled the condom out of its wrapping and dangled it between her thumb and forefinger. "Look, it's simple. *This* (she waved the condom in front of him) goes on *that* (she pointed toward Travis' crotch). *That* (she pointed again at his groin) goes in *here* (she lifted her skirt, revealing her white panties and indicated her pudendum). *And then fifteen dollars goes into my account so that I can buy me some goddamn cigarettes.*" Sharon blew out her breath in an impatient, heavy sigh: "Are we gonna do this thing or aren't we?"

Travis' dark hair looked like a deflated thundercloud which had let loose all its moisture. The sweat was pouring down his face, trickling into his ears, and his shirt was now sodden. His throat was so dry he could barely speak, but still he managed to croak: "I'll have that," indicating the condom.

"It's about time!" huffed Sharon, as she handed Travis the condom. And then, having taken the wrong meaning: "Where do you want me?"

At that moment there was a bump against the office door, followed by a light tapping. Stephen quickly mopped his brow with his shirt sleeves and headed for the door.

"Great," harrumphed Sharon, spinning the desk chair around.

As Stephen opened the door, he was greeted with the vision of Frumpy carrying two large cardboard boxes from the American Bible Society. She was keeping the top one in place with her chin and trying to rest the lower box on her thigh so that her right hand would be free to turn the doorknob. "Ooh, sanks!" she grunted throatily through her clenched teeth. She then caught sight of Sharon's back in the desk chair. "Mi intrupting innisang?" she queried.

"No. No—not at all! In fact, Sharon was just leaving; weren't you, Sharon?"

"Yeah, sure," Sharon said languidly as she stood to leave. She took one last, peevish look at Travis as she made for the door. "Bye, Chaplain Travis," she said lethargically and then ambled away.

Meanwhile Frumpy was still precariously clutching the two large boxes. "Oh here, l-let me help," stammered Stephen. Once he had placed the box on a nearby table he virtually fell forward across it, exhaling deeply. "Thank you for coming in, Frumpy. Thank you! Bless you!" Having placed the second box on her work desk, Frumpy turned to look at Travis. His arms were draped over either side of the box and his face was turned to the side. Travis' back was rising and falling from his near hyperventilation.

"Chaplain Travis? Are you okay?" Frumpy drew near to look at him more closely.

"Yeah. I think so. But could you go get me a glass of water?"

"You're soaked with sweat—are you feverish? Or is it heat exhaustion?" Frumpy was becoming more solicitous in her concern for the chaplain.

"No. I'll be all right," rasped Travis. "I could just use some water."

"Oka-ay," said Frumpy hesitantly, "but shouldn't I go get someone?"

"No. No really. I'll be fine." Stephen lifted his head and smiled weakly at Frumpy. "Really. I'll be okay. I just need some water. Please." Frumpy nodded, picked up the beaker from Travis' desk and quickly marched out into the hallway for the water fountain. When she returned, Stephen was sitting in his chair, wiping his face and neck with his handkerchief. He looked pale. Frumpy proffered the beaker of water and looked him over in studious fashion. "Thanks." Stephen took the beaker and drank most of it in a few swift gulps. He then poured some into his hand and splashed it across his face. Frumpy looked at him curiously, but Stephen just shrugged, held out the empty beaker and asked: "Would you mind?" Frumpy smiled and shook her head 'no' and stepped out into the hallway once more. Upon her second return Stephen had the color back in his face. He thankfully received the second drink of water and, between gulps, asked Frumpy to close the door. When she had turned from the door, Stephen motioned towards her chair, but without speaking. Taking the hint, Frumpy sat down and waited. Stephen was leaning forward, elbows on his knees, looking into the half-empty glass, as though divining what to say. He swished the water round a few times and then inhaled deeply through his nostrils. Frumpy took this as an indication Travis was about to speak and straightened herself in her seat. Stephen lifted his head slightly, looked at Frumpy and smiled.

"Do you...*trust* me?" he asked. He lifted his eyebrows as though to reiterate his question.

Not quite sure where he was going with his question, Frumpy paused for second and then drawled, "Well, of course, Chaplain Travis."

Stephen started again: "I mean, do you trust that the things you have told me over the months we have known each other will remain with me?—in confidence?"

"Yes. Certainly."

Stephen nodded and his head dropped as he studied the water sloshing around in the beaker. Without looking up he asked: "Can I trust *you*, if I told you something?" He raised his head and look at her steadily. Frumpy returned his gaze and nodded assent. Travis took another long gulp of water, started to speak, but then shook his head, as though doubting his own thoughts. He frowned at his inability to get his words organized into sentences, but then launched in with a question: "Frumpy, do you have any idea what's been going on in here—between Chaplain Goodman and some of the inmates?"

Frumpy thought briefly and then replied: "Some. I mean, everybody knows why he got fired—especially how he got caught— and from the few things I've heard, it sounds like that's not the only time he's had sex with an inmate...and since he left I've heard some of the women laughing and talking about him. And then he tried that nonsense with me back before Christmas... That's really about all." Frumpy saw from Travis' furrowed brow the frustration he must be feeling within. "Sorry I can't be more helpful," she offered.

"No, Frumpy, that's all right. It's just that..." Travis shook his head again as if trying to clear a mental fog. "It's just that *today*—just before you walked in—Sharon Moore told me that Goodman used to put money in women's trust accounts if they had sex with him. 'Cigarette money,' she called it. And: *they did it here!*" Travis waved his arm about as an expression of his disbelief. Frumpy didn't know how to respond, but Travis wasn't finished: "And that's not all!" He struggled to keep his voice down. "And that's not all!" he repeated as he spun his chair around and picked up the envelope containing the condoms. "She even knew where these were hidden! And what's worse: she expected me to do the same as Goodman!" Travis spilled several of the packets into his open hand and stared at them himself for a moment, before looking up at Frumpy as though to confirm he was not hallucinating.

Frumpy was trying to keep up with all of the startling revelations and could only summon one word: "Gosh."

Stephen then showed her where the envelope had been fixed to the back of the desk drawer with thumb tacks. He turned back to Frumpy. "Jeez, I just can't believe what this guy's been up to!" He dropped his forehead into the palms of his hands. "And you've never been told about this by anyone?" Frumpy shook her head. "I mean…well…apart from your encounter with him last December; he never tried it with you, did he?" Stephen didn't know whether he was crossing some professional boundary or not, but at this point he didn't really care. His head was still spinning from the shock of his visit from Sharon.

"Heavens no!" responded Frumpy. "I had already smacked him once!" She started to say something else but stopped herself as her fingers tapped her thighs. Finally she said: "Hmm, I wonder…" Frumpy had Travis' full attention as she asked: "But do you think this is why Marla Thompkins was so keen to quit working here?"

Travis raised his arms in a Gallic shrug. "Goodness knows," he said, "But it all ends now—it's got to. I can't hack going through the same mess with other women that I've just had with Sharon; it's too much." Travis looked at the envelope on his lap and the condoms he had shown Frumpy. "Right," he said with determination, "These have got to go. I'll take them out with me tonight. But how do I prevent another 'Sharon' episode?" Travis turned to Frumpy. "Look, can you help me with this? I mean, I can't just stick up a notice that says (and here Travis took on a TV announcer's public service voice):

'All women who gave Marv Goodman sexual favors for donations to their trust accounts are now hereby informed that this service is terminated.' But, Frumpy, you know how things work on the inside. Maybe you could just drop a word or two with the right people... let them know that Goodman—and everything that went with him—is *gone, finished, kaput*. What do you think? Please, could you help me?"

As Frumpy listened to Travis, she felt something shift inside her. For the first time in her life, here was a man soliciting her help—he wasn't making false protestations of love designed to get her between the sheets, not asking her to become the unwitting driver of a getaway car, not seeking her to take a beating in order to heal the rage which burned inside his soul—this man's entreaties were simply from one human being to another. He actually needed her help and wasn't afraid to say so. Travis couldn't have begun to know what had coursed through Frumpy's mind in the few seconds since he had asked for her help in dissuading other women from seeking the 'Goodman solution' to their money problems. And Frumpy's thoughts flowed in one direction: "Yes," she almost blurted out, "Yes, I'll help you. I'd hate for anyone to think that you'd do any of the things that Chaplain Goodman has done."

Travis exhaled a long breath of tension released, which served to make Frumpy realize that—even though there was a power imbalance in the relationship—Travis had by no means simply taken her assistance for granted. "Wow," Travis wiped his brow, symbolically removing the worry, "That would be a great help. I couldn't bear to have another scene like today's!" Travis stood up from his chair, shook loose his tense muscles and stretched. "Man! What a day! I need to go for a walk." Nodding towards the boxes Frumpy had brought with her, Stephen asked: "Will you be okay with getting those unpacked for a few minutes?"

"Sure, Steph—uh, Chaplain Travis," Frumpy smiled and slight color appeared in her cheeks. "I'll get started right away."

⧗

When Stephen returned to his office, Frumpy had nearly finished going through the boxes of material sent by the American Bible Society in anticipation of Holy Week, which was nearly upon them. There were Bibles, New Testaments, and single Gospel tracts stacked in neat piles; there were also the strip-cartoon style pamphlets of the Easter story—for the less literate inmates. "Hey, Frumpy. How's it going?"

"Just fine," she replied, "I'm getting there. But two more boxes and these letters arrived about five minutes after you left. Seems someone in the administration building hadn't noticed they were for the chaplains' office."

"Right then, let me help you." Travis began tearing at the packing tape. "Man, it's hot in here," he interjected, "I don't suppose a window would be too much to ask? This place is an oven!" He mopped his brow with the back of his hand and then checked the result, as though to make his point.

"Oh—Martha Price is waiting for you to get back. She's out by the basketball court. You want me to go get her?"

"Did she say what she wanted?" asked Travis distractedly, as he thumbed through the mail. "I've really got to get the Good Friday and Easter services organized."

"No, but I could ask her, if you like," offered Frumpy.

"Nah—thanks anyway," said Travis as he tossed the post back onto his desk. "I'll go find her. At least there's a bit of a breeze outside."

Martha was seated on a bench along the courtside, watching a few women lazily shooting hoops. Travis came alongside and then plopped down on the place beside her. "Martha, hi. Frumpy tells me you wanted to see me."

"Yes-sir, I do." Martha was from a poor, working class background in one of North Carolina's many mill towns. She spoke slowly at the best of times, but the heat of the day seemed to exaggerate the lethargic pace even more. "I…I'd like to see me some of the lit-tra-ture you got 'bout Jesus, an' Easter an' all. Is that aw-right?"

"Yes, Martha, of course it's all right; that's why we have it. Want to come with me to the office and we'll see what you might like?"

"That'd be jest fi-ine," came her reply.

They both stood up and made their way towards the chaplains' office. As they entered, Frumpy was dusting her hands, having emptied the last box. She waved her hands at the neat piles of reading materials. "Ta-da!" she sang out with a flourish. "All done. Okay if I leave you now? I got my fine arts class in fifteen minutes."

"No problem. Thanks for the help—*all of it.*" Travis nodded towards Frumpy as she closed the door behind her, and then motioned for Martha to take a seat. "Now, Martha, what may I do for you?"

Martha was eyeing the stacks of literature on the table and the secretary's desk. "Well… I'd sho' like to look at them pamphlets." She nodded towards the small, comic-style pamphlets which illustrated the Easter story.

"Fine, fine," Travis replied. "Why don't you have a look and take what you like?"

Martha nodded and got up. She slowly and methodically looked through the materials which contained illustrations. "Chaplain Travis?"

"Yes, Martha?"

"Chaplain Travis…I…I cain't read too good." Travis was not sure how he should reply, but needn't have worried, as Martha quickly spoke up again: "How'd it be if I sat here with you…an- and read out loud? Could you help me? Would that be all right with you?"

Travis thought about the services that needed preparation and the time they would take. Then he felt churlish for even having that thought: "Yeah, all right. I can give you half-an-hour, is that okay?"

"That'd be je-est fi-ine," came the drawled reply.

Martha had picked up a *Good News* selection from Mark's Gospel in which the crucifixion of Jesus was described. She began to read, stumbling over long and multi-syllabic words. Travis corrected her whenever she got stuck and looked to him for help. The sultry day and Martha's slow monotone conspired to put Travis in a soporific state. "On the way…the-ey met a man…na-named Si-…Si-…" Travis realized Martha was looking at him for help.

"Uh… Simon; his name was Simon."

Martha went back to the text and, while she wasn't looking, Travis licked his fingers and wiped them across his sleepy eyes—anything to help keep him from falling asleep.

"This was Si-mon [Martha looked up triumphantly] from Ki-… uh… mmh… Cry-?" She looked to Travis again.

"Cy-re-ne," he enunciated slowly.

Martha smiled and started once more, only to be stymied by "Alexander and Rufus." Travis next helped her with "Golgotha" and then found himself being lulled into a waking doze, in which he was seeing Hubert plucking chickens. With eyes opened, but glazed, in the background Travis could still make out words coming like drips of water from a slow leak: "So they na-… nai-led him to the cross…"

Travis' head was just dropping to his chest when he heard a loud shout. "*The sons-of-bitches killed him!*"

Travis not only became fully awake, he shot halfway out of his chair. "Wh-what?!"

"They killed him! The sons-of-bitches killed him!" cried Martha.

Travis had never heard her so animated. "W-well, yeah, they did; they killed him—."

"Well, *what did they do that for?*" demanded Martha. "He didn't do *nothin'* to *them*! Did he?"

"No. No, you're absolutely right. He didn't do anything to them. It's terrible, isn't it?"

"Damn right," shot back Martha. "I mean, you know, Chaplain Travis, I de-serve to be in here—jest like them criminals that got kilt with Jesus—they got what they de-served. But Jesus ain't done nothin' wrong." Martha sighed heavily and then shook her head. "All right if I take this with me?" She proffered the small pamphlet.

"That's fine, Martha. It's yours to keep. You let me know if you need anything else, okay?"

As he opened the door for Martha to leave he saw Charlene Walker's inquisitive face peering out of her office. She smiled and nodded at Martha as she left, clutching her Bible tract. "Everything okay in there, Stephen?"

"Yeah. Yeah, everything's fine. Martha just got a little excited about something." Stephen paused. "Have you got a minute Charlene? You might be interested in what just happened in here."

"For you? Sure," came the reply. "I don't have to see anybody else for another twenty minutes or so. You like a cup of tea?"

"You bet!" said Travis, "Anything to help me stay awake!" Charlene looked over her reading spectacles at Travis: "Late night, Reverend?"

"Gosh, no!" blushed Travis. "It's the heat—and an office with no windows or air-conditioning."

"Air-conditioning?! In *prison*? You're not one of these people who want to coddle the criminals, are you?" asked Charlene in mock horror.

"Well...if not the inmates—how about the *staff*?" pleaded Travis.

"Because, Chaplain Travis, this gives you sol-i-dar-ity with the inmates—and a bit of credibility—since we get to suffer some of the same conditions they have to live with," teased Charlene, who quickly added: "Only we get to go home at night."

"Mmh," considered Travis.

"So, you want to tell me what Martha was shoutin' about?" queried Charlene. She had already set her small electric kettle to boil and was fishing out some tea bags and mugs.

"Yeah," began Travis, as he tried to clear his thoughts. Then he smiled and said: "I think Martha was just helping me with my Good Friday sermon."

"Come again?" Martha was once again peering at him over the half-lenses as she made the tea. Travis then related what had just transpired: How Martha was reading the story of Jesus' crucifixion and, in the process, putting Travis to sleep, and then her outburst.

"Ok-a-ay…?" uttered Charlene, not quite following what Travis was getting at.

"Here's the point, Charlene. You're a Christian, right?"

"Baptized when I was ten!" She lifted her right hand as though 'testifying.'

"Okay, so both of us have heard the story of Jesus' crucifixion how many times? Dozens? Hundreds?" Charlene nodded. "And how *angry* does it make us? Does the fact that Jesus gets nailed up ever *piss you off*?" Charlene made a disapproving face at Travis for his choice of words. "No, Charlene, I'm not trying to be rude or vulgar. What I'm saying is that we've listened to these Bible accounts so many times that we tend not to *hear* them; we tend to take them for granted, don't we? We don't even get astonished when we hear about the miracles—I mean: have you ever seen anyone walk on water? And have you *ever* heard *anyone* in church get angry and shout out at the account of Jesus' crucifixion?!"

Charlene now cocked her head to one side and looked thoughtfully at Travis. "No. Can't say I have."

"Well that's the point!" exclaimed Travis. "Martha got so worked up at what she was reading that she got *really pissed off*—to the point she started shouting and swearing about it. It's like she was actually *there*! That's what you heard coming from my office."

Charlene was now smiling at Travis. "Now I see. You have got you a good sermon for Good Friday, haven't you? Don't ever let anybody tell you that you can't get an education behind these bars!"

Easter week was only second to Christmas for depression, suicide attempts, and emotional outbursts in the women's prison. This was despite the fact that it was mid-April, days were growing longer and the world was renewing itself: oaks, sycamores and poplars were showing off their new greenery; Dogwood trees were full of blossoms; wisteria was flowering and, not to be left out: the many pine trees were showering everyone and everything with a fine blanket of yellow pollen. Travis could understand why Christmastide saw the greatest numbers of depressed and suicidal inmates: after all, that season saw the longest nights and shortest days of the year; it was also early winter, with more to follow. Yet here was spring bursting out all over and the blues were as contagious as measles. Travis decided to duck into Ben Katz's office to see whether he could shed any 'clinical light' on this conundrum.

When Travis got to Katz's office the door was partially open; he could see Ben seated at his desk and speaking on the telephone. Stephen tapped lightly on the door and Katz waved him in, motioning to a chair. When Ben wasn't rubbing his bald spot with his free hand, he was animatedly gesturing—making his point to the unseen listener. As the conversation reached its end, Ben's voice rose in exasperation: "Yeah, yeah—I heard you. Got it. Fine. G'bye." And then as the phone reached the cradle, he spat: "Putz!" He shook his head as he smiled at Travis, "Bureaucrats! Who needs 'em? I mean, why is it that people who have *never worked* in a prison—and rarely visit them—can set our budgets and *tell us* what is needed or not— can you answer me that?"

"Beats me," replied Stephen.

"Anyway, *Rabbi* Travis," Katz winked, "What brings you to my *shtetl*?"

"Oh, just need to pick your psychologist's brain…and just wondering whether you're getting as many depressed people through your door as I am."

Katz snorted a short laugh; picked up a pencil and started wagging it nervously between his right thumb and forefinger. "Well, ya know…this resort ain't up to its previous standards. Since the warden took away the polo ponies and driving range…"

"Yeah, yeah, Ben. I got ya," retorted Stephen, "It's a prison. But even for a prison, there seems to be a lot of depression and talk of hitting the fence. Why now?—especially with this beautiful, warm weather."

Katz tapped the knuckles of his left hand with the pencil before speaking. "Look Stephen, if it's statistics and long-winded psychological explanations of why women in here get depressed this time of year, then Kate McIntyre's your woman. She keeps all the journals and professional articles and could point you in the right direction. As for me," Katz shrugged, "it's all down to the birds and bees."

"How so?" queried a puzzled Travis.

"Simple," grinned Katz, "it's mating season. The sap's rising. Birds are building nests and everybody and everything seems to be 'making whoopee'—all except our 'clients.'" Katz grinned mischievously: "Especially since your boss went!"

Stephen rolled his eyes and said, "Yeah, don't remind me."

They both sat in comfortable silence for a few minutes, their energies slackened by the heat and humidity of the day. Stephen finally spoke up: "So it's all down to horniness is it?"

"We-e-ell, yay-yus…and no-o," Katz mimicked a Southern drawl. "On the 'yes' side is the fact that many of these women are of child-bearing age. So apart from the odd 'accident', it ain't going to happen here. It's also a fact that we're all human—these inmates being no exception. Why do so many hold hands and 'marry' each other and create 'families' in this joint?—it's certainly not because they're lesbians. There are scant few real lesbians in this institution. Nah, it's their way of nest-building—even if they won't be laying any eggs or raising any chicks. And that, my friend, is depressing."

"So what's on the 'no' side of horniness?" queried Stephen.

"Well, if we think in terms of archetype or symbolism, a lot of ancient and so-called 'primitive' societies observed their new year festivals in the springtime…"

"Except the Hebrews!" quipped Travis.

"Contrariness is our gift to the world," retorted Katz magnanimously and without missing a beat. "It makes sense after all: the world is renewing itself—all by itself—and we go along for the ride. But as with any new year, it also makes us conscious of the years that are now behind us." At that, Ben drew his hand across his balding head, cast his eyes futilely towards his scalp and uttered: "Oi!" He then continued: "I mean, why do people sing 'Auld Lang Syne' at New Year's parties? Same difference. There's always a little wistfulness as we mark the passing of another year in our lives, never to return. Who was the poet who wrote: 'All music stops when death doth lead the dance?'" Stephen shook his head; he liked it when Katz was in full-flow. "Well," Katz continued, "in the music of springtime, there is also the strain of lost time and of lost days *to come*—of another stifling summer behind bars." Katz paused for a breath and looked at Travis. "And let's face it," Katz leaned forward opening his palms towards Stephen, "before you Christians get to Easter you have the rather distasteful events of Good Friday to pass through. And even for us Jews, Pesach is a festival of laughter amidst the tears." Katz sat back in his chair and emitted one of his short bursts of laughter. "*Nu*, have I missed anything?"

"Whew!" laughed Stephen as he interlaced his fingers and stretched his arms over his head. "No, Ben, I think you've just about covered everything." Travis then got to his feet. "In fact, Ben, if you have any rope, I think I'd like to go hang myself now."

Laughing, Travis dodged Katz's foot as it came up to kick his bottom. "*Lekh lekah!*" growled Katz, in mock anger.

"I'm gone!" called Stephen as he sped out the door, but his shoes squeaked as he stopped in his tracks. He turned and said, "Hey, Ben?"

"What?!" fired back Ben, still in mock rage and looking at some papers on his desk.

"Thanks."

"*Al lo davar,*" Ben smiled to himself and waved to Travis without looking up.

Easter Sunday was a visiting day, just like any other Sunday— except that it was more frenetic. Visiting relatives and friends brought cakes, chocolates and the like, so the security officers were working like mad to check for possible contraband. And just like any other visiting day, the auditorium was reverberating with a mixture of chatter, weeping and laughter. Travis was slowly making his way around the auditorium, greeting an inmate here and a staff member there. Sometimes he sat with a family, and occasionally he was asked to pray with them. Stephen was about to take a break when he saw Frumpy waving to him and motioning him to come over where she was sitting with two women. The older of the two wore her hair tied back into an old-fashioned bun; the other had shoulder-length, slightly graying, auburn hair in a loose pony-tail. As he drew closer, Travis immediately saw a resemblance between the second woman and Frumpy. In the instant his eyes took in Colleen, he noticed slight, long-healed scars on the bridge of her nose, above her right temple and long her scalp-line. Stephen's mind quickly churned out the brief account Frumpy had given him months ago, of how her father had attacked both mother and daughter. Travis rightly assumed the other woman to be Frumpy's grandmother. Frumpy proudly stood up to introduce them. "Chaplain Travis, I'd like you to meet my..."

"Mother and grandmother?" said Travis with a twinkle in his eye.

"W-well, yes," stammered an upstaged, but delighted Frumpy.

Stephen laid his hand on her shoulder and said: "The likeness would be hard to miss. Glad to meet you all, and Happy Easter— that is, I *hope* it is a happy one for you?"

"Oh yes," beamed Colleen. "It's just so good to see my Annabel Lee. And despite the fact that she's *here*," Colleen's eyes made a furtive dart round, "she seems to be making the most of her time. I guess that's all we can ask for. And we're ever so thankful that she's been able to work for you—it has been such a boon for her—and for Mama and me."

Ginny nodded her agreement and smiled at Travis. He joined in adding his agreement: "She's been a big help to me, I can tell you."

For some reason, at that very moment, Frumpy had a picture flash through her mind: of herself and her mother at parents' evening, after a particularly good school semester, and the young Frumpy beaming at her teachers' praise. She shook the thought from her mind and returned to the present moment. Frumpy went to fetch a spare chair for Travis. When she returned, Ginny was in mid-sentence, speaking to the chaplain: "...has nearly served out the minimum requirement of her sentence and...well....we're all hoping that the parole board will see fit to let her out just as soon as possible."

"Oh Grandma," interrupted Frumpy, "Chaplain Travis *isn't* on the parole board!"

"It's okay, Fru—*Annabel Lee*," Travis hoped he had caught himself just in time. He repeated her name again and caught a glint in her eyes when he did so. "It's natural that families want to know when their loved ones will get out of here. And while it's true that I am not on the parole board, and cannot say anything definitively, it's also true that you will have gained nearly one hundred—or more—days off your sentence. For the benefit of Frumpy's relatives, Travis added: "That's called 'good time.'" He nodded towards Colleen and Ginny (and then smiled at Frumpy): "for good conduct and no disciplinary action." Travis turned back towards Colleen and Ginny and saw their approving smiles. He continued: "And then there's also what's called 'gained time,'" pausing to make sure Colleen and Ginny were following his explanation, "for the work you've been doing in the chaplains' office (he looked once more at Frumpy)—but I can never remember how the percentages of time off your sentence work! You'd need to talk with Charlene Walker about that." Travis turned to Frumpy's mother and grandmother: "Charlene Walker is Annabel Lee's case worker—but maybe you knew that?" Whether they did or didn't wasn't said; all Colleen and Ginny could do was to effuse over the fact that Frumpy's time behind bars might well be drawing near its end.

Travis saw this as a natural time to make his exit and to continue his rounds in the auditorium. "Look," he offered as he stood to leave, "all I can assure you is that I will support Annabel Lee's application whenever her case worker puts it forward." He winked at Annabel Lee. "It's not that I'm trying to get rid of a good secretary, mind you! But I think your skills and intelligence are bettered used elsewhere! Don't you?" Frumpy laughed and nodded.

Colleen stood and shook Travis' hand warmly. She held it for a moment longer and hoarsely whispered, "Thank you," with tears in her eyes.

As he then reached for Ginny's hand, she was using the back of it to wipe her eyes. She sniffed a little laugh as she apologized for giving him a damp hand. Travis laughed it off as he took the elderly woman's hand in both of his. "Y'all have a good young lady here," he nodded towards Frumpy, "I'm glad she has you to support her."

They said their goodbyes and Travis carried on his way. As Frumpy, Colleen and Ginny continued their visit, Ginny nudged Colleen saying, "*When* are you going to tell this girl *your news?*"

"Now, Mama, don't you spoil it this time! I was just waiting for the right moment."

"Well git on with it," chided Ginny humorously.

"What?" Frumpy squirmed in her seat with anticipation. "*What*?!"

Colleen began: "You know how I've been doing some part-time teaching since last fall?" Frumpy nodded. "Well," Colleen teasingly paused for dramatic effect, "I've been offered a full-time job again!"

"Oh, Mama! That's wonderful!" Mother and daughter embraced and broke into tears of joy.

"But that ain't all," interjected Ginny.

"There you go again, Ginny McNair!" Colleen shook her forefinger at her mother-in-law in mock anger.

"Well, they ain't gonna let us stay here all day," remarked Ginny, "so you might as well spill the beans now."

Buoyed by the news of her mother's job, Frumpy now bounced up and down on her chair like a ten-year-old. "What else?!" she exclaimed.

Colleen started to speak, but found herself at a loss for words; instead she started to turn crimson. She fanned herself, saying: "Is it hot in here or is it me?"

"You're too young for the 'change,'" chimed in Ginny; and then she blurted: "Your mother's been dating again."

At this, Frumpy squealed with delight and clapped her hands together. "Who is he?" she inquired.

"Ray Wilkins," replied Ginny—Colleen nodded, patting her moist face with her handkerchief. "Your mother and him used to teach together at the high school—back 'fore you were born. His—"

"Thank you, Mama," interjected Colleen, "I can take it from here."

"Ray's wife died of cancer a few years back. He remembered me from when I used to teach at the high school..."

"He ought to," interrupted Ginny, "your husband punched him in the nose!"

"Now, Mama, we don't need to go into all that. Anyway, it was *me* he remembered! So, where was I? Yes, well, we got to talking in the teachers' lounge at break times…and over lunch, and…well…he asked me out!"

"Fantastic! What's he like?" queried Frumpy.

"He's gentle," began Colleen, almost savoring the word on her tongue like a fine wine. "He's quiet—he likes to listen to me! He enjoys reading and music… Ray's just a lovely man. What can I say?"

"You can say you're in love!" announced Ginny. "Your mama's like a school girl whenever he calls. But, Lord knows, she deserves it." Ginny smiled as she said this, and patted Colleen on the knee. Colleen took her mother-in-law's hand and squeezed it.

"Oh Mama, I'm so happy for you. I'd really like to meet him, but…" Frumpy paused and looked at her surroundings, "but maybe it ought to wait until I'm out of here, huh? I mean…does he…does Ray know I'm in prison?"

"Yes, darling, Ray knows; most people around Bransford know you're here; but those folk who know us and love us *know* that you *shouldn't be here*. Anyway, Ray asked me to convey his greetings to you." Frumpy nodded thoughtfully at her mother's words.

At that same moment, OC came walking by. He stopped and ostentatiously looked at the clock on the auditorium wall, and then he checked his watch. Tapping his wrist, he said: "Time for y'all to wind it up."

Amazing even herself, Frumpy quipped: "You figure that out all by yourself, OC?" OC's nostrils flared and his freckles seemed to rise from his skin, but seeing the cool gaze of Ginny and Colleen, he—for once—thought better of losing his cool. He just looked menacingly at Frumpy, snorted and moved off.

"OC?" queried Colleen as Bain shuffled away.

"Officer Chickenshit," replied Frumpy in a stage whisper. Both Colleen and Ginny had to cover their mouths as they giggled. OC twitched and wriggled his neck as he kept moving—but his neck took on a reddish hue all the same.

"Y'all are just a fuckin' freak show!" Fred Bain was losing his patience with the inmates in Dorm C. It was laundry day and, having been tipped off that it was OC's day as laundry officer, they had prepared many surprises for him: sheets with feces smeared on them, others with the bloody evidence of recent menstruation.

"Here, catch!" they brightly shouted as they tossed the sheets to Bain.

"Hot a'mighty!" Bain averted his face, which was already screwed up in disgust and red with anger. "Filthy pigs!" he grunted as he pushed the large laundry cart into which the past week's bed linens were being thrown.

Officer Bradford, who often oversaw security in Dorm C from the front office, shouted down the corridor for Bain to 'cool it and just get on with the job.' Another female officer, Paula Ayers, was both assisting Bain in laundry collection and escorting women to and from the showers. As Bain approached Lola's cell, he cautiously checked her eyes. Lola's plump, pink, Buddha-like self was sitting calmly on her stripped bed. The sheets and pillow case were folded and sitting next to her. Bain unlocked the cell, not taking his eyes off Lola. He was always unsettled by her glass eye and was never certain of which eye was actually looking at him. "Wanna hand me your sheets?" Bain's questions were never requests. Lola nodded assent but didn't budge. Fred stepped testily towards Lola at which she dropped her head to her chest. "Fat freak," he muttered at Lola as he reached for the sheets. While Bain leaned down to pick up her sheets, he hadn't noticed Lola's right hand removing her glass eye. Lola sprang into action, her arm like a one-eyed tentacle seeking out its quarry's face. "Jesus Christ!" shouted Bain as he threw up his arms to shield himself from the one-eyed monster and backed towards the cell door. Surprisingly nimble, Lola kept pace with him and edged him away from the door, back into her cell. "Get that damn thing away from me!" shrieked Bain.

Lola just smiled at Bain and quietly said: "Motherfucker."

From the other cells came cheering from Lola's fellow inmates when they heard Bain's shouting in fear. This only served to infuriate Officer Chickenshit all the more. Because Lola had to turn her head to keep up with Bain's weaving about the cell, OC was able to slip past her, and with one stiff-arm push, shoved Lola onto her bed. He then made for the cell door, slamming it behind him as he slipped through. Embarrassed by his unmanly flight, Bain put his face up to the bars and growled at Lola: "Yew gawddamned weirdo bitch! I'll see to it that you spend yer entire sentence in this shit-hole!"

"Cocksucking sombitch!" fired back Lola as she loosed a side-armed pitch with her glass eye. Officer Bradford was just rounding the corner of Lola's end of the cell block when the glass eyeball connected with Bain's forehead, but the thud was audible to her from fifteen feet away. Bain stumbled back against the laundry cart, which went scooting away from OC's rearward momentum. Officer Bradford was there to slip an arm around and support him; she was quickly joined by Ayers, who had heard all of the commotion.

"Lawdy mercy, Bain! When you gonna learn not to rile the inmates?" chided Bradford. Ayers had to bite her lip to keep from smiling and left Bradford to help Bain.

Bain shook his head in dazed disbelief. Lola's eye had fallen to the floor and spun around a few times before turning its taunting leer towards him. While holding the growing lump on his forehead, Bain kicked at the eye and sent it rebounding around Lola's cell. "You might oughta have that looked at," offered Bradford. Bain then took note of the strong black arm that was supporting him and shook himself free without acknowledging the assistance. The whites of

Bradford's eyes grew saucer-like against her midnight skin as she said, "OC, man, you just plain nasty! Shoulda let your honky ass fall flat on the floor. Mebbe that hard concrete mighta knocked some sense into your head."

Bain 'harrumphed' and shoved the laundry cart towards the last of the cells. He was sullen and close-lipped as he received the remainder of their linens and insults. He pushed the cart like it was a hearse meant for his funeral, silently staring into the middle distance. When he got to the front security desk he simply stood there until Officer Bradford opened the door for him. Arms folded over her ample breasts, she pursed her lips and studied Bain's exit. For all intents and purposes, Bain had the look of a defeated man. Then she shook her head in an attitude of 'don't that beat all?' and locked the door.

Short Time

The end crowns all,
And that old common arbitrator, Time,
Will one day end it.
Troilus and Cressida

Frumpy sat back in her desk chair and smiled at the ceiling. Then she gaily spun the desk chair round in a circle and laughed. She chuckled again at both Officer Bain's predicament and the ingenuity of one of her sister inmates—in not only escaping from Dorm C—but also the prison! Frumpy had been doing time long enough now to absorb some of the 'us vs. them' mentality present in so many prisoners, and thus derive vicarious pleasure from a fellow inmate's escape—even if that individual had been in maximum security. Frumpy spun in her chair again and replayed the mental tape of what she had seen the previous day. While Frumpy had been in her English class, the alarm was raised that there had been an escape from Dorm C. Even the course's teacher had joined the inmates in looking out the windows at all the frantic activity as uniformed staff ran hither and yon trying to determine whether or not the escapee was still on the prison grounds. After things had settled down a bit, one of Frumpy's classmates said; "Hey, look! Something's up!" Once more they adjourned their lesson for the drama on the prison yard. Captain Waller was escorting Officers Bradford, Bain and Ayers to the administration building. None looked very happy.

In typical fashion, within twenty-four hours the inmates knew the true facts of the escape—long before the security staff. They learned the details from the women who helped transfer meals from the kitchen to Dorm C. It seems that Diane McLeod, serving time for illegal gambling, bootlegging and counterfeiting, had decided to shorten her sentence by a few years by staging the 'laundry assault' on Bain. Like so many long-timers, she had had plenty of time to study the staff and find a weak link. Bain was not only a racist, but a misogynist as well—and he was a hot-head. Through whispered messages, cell to cell, the plan was laid. The women were to soil their linens with various excreta—the more visible the better. First of all, this would be certain to piss off Officer Chickenshit, but secondly—and more importantly—he would be very unlikely to search the contents of the laundry cart once Diane McLeod had dived in and burrowed herself to the bottom. Getting Lola and her removable glass eye to play into the scheme was the *pièce de résistance*. To cap it all, it was Bain himself who had rolled the cart and all of its contents—*unchecked*—out of the main gate to the waiting state laundry truck.

It was a day later before the security staff was able to fit together all the pieces of the escape. When the truck driver had returned to the state laundry, he had discovered one of the rear doors to be open. He assumed that he hadn't properly latched it on one of his stops. Nothing had fallen out, and all of the linens were within their carts, so he hadn't thought any more of it until his line manager had received a call from the women's prison. However, once Diane McLeod was outside those prison walls, she just kept moving and beat the odds of being caught and returned within a matter of hours. Rumor had it that she had stashed away more than ten-thousand dollars against the day when she might really need it. Apparently that day had come.

It didn't take Warden Beasley and Captain Waller two minutes to fire Fred "OC" Bain. Because Officer Ayers had remained in Dorm

C on shower escort duty, and thus was not ultimately responsible for checking the laundry cart, she received only a mild reprimand. The facts were all there: Bain had been negligent in his duties. Despite his years of government service in the Marines, both Waller and Beasley considered him to be a liability both to prison moral and—with this latest incident—to security. Rarely are decisions taken by wardens and heads of security which bring such unity—and amity—between both inmates and staff. Inmates could share their enjoyment of the incident with staff and not worry about being rebuffed. Everyone greeted each other with: "Didja hear the news?" This was typically followed by wide grins, laughter, head-shaking and shoulder slapping. Frumpy was no exception.

Frumpy was in mid-spin again in her chair as Stephen entered the office. He was thumbing through some mail and looked up in surprise at Frumpy. "Hey, Frumpy. It's not your afternoon to work, is it?" Travis gave the office calendar a quick glance. Frumpy shook her head, still wearing a broad grin. "You look mighty happy," noted Travis, "got a secret?"

"Just the same one everybody else has, I guess," smiled Frumpy.

"Which is?" asked the still somewhat-distracted Travis.

"Oh, Officer Bain and Diane McLeod's escape—all of that. What do you think about it?"

"I suppose it depends on what 'it' is—Diane's escape or Bain's getting fired."

"Maybe both," suggested Frumpy.

"Seriously?" asked Travis.

"Yes, seriously," came the reply.

"Well, I didn't have much time for either one of them. Diane always seemed duplicitous—I never felt I was getting a straight answer from her—or even a straight question for that matter. And as for Bain… *We-e-ell,*" Stephen paused, and then spoke declaratively:

"The guy's a jerk. Prison's better off without him. There. Is that a serious enough answer for you?"

Frumpy's smile broadened as she nodded—then she added quickly: "But you have to admit—it really is too rich: Bain rolling Diane right out the front gate of the prison without even knowing it!"

"Yes, it is that. How would Shakespeare have put it?: 'Hoist by his own petard?'" They both laughed—something that was always welcome behind bars.

As their laughter subsided, Frumpy started to speak, but hesitated. Travis plopped himself into his chair, stretched, and then cocked an eye at Frumpy: "Something on your mind?"

"Have you got a few minutes? I mean…if you've got things to do, I can come back another time."

"Not at all," smiled Travis, "What may I do for you?" Stephen tossed the mail on his desk and focused himself on Frumpy.

Frumpy straightened herself in her chair, smoothed her blue prison dress and then began to wring her fingers. She looked up at Chaplain Travis, smiled, then laughed nervously, and looked back down at her intertwined fingers.

Sensing her obvious discomfort, Travis leaned forward in his chair and gently asked: "Is there something the matter, Frumpy?"

"Well…*yes*." She paused, "And *no*." Frumpy blushed deeply, looked up at Travis and shrugged.

"Frumpy, you've worked with me long enough to know that I don't bite, and…and well, I've heard a lot of things since I've been here, so don't think that I'll be shocked or start judging you or anything."

"I know." Frumpy's words came quietly. "And I suppose that's why I'm here."

"Is what you want to tell me difficult because I'm a man?" inquired Travis.

"Well, *yes*...........and *no*." Frumpy laughed at herself now and flushed deeper than Travis thought possible—and he knew something about blushing. They both sat in silence for a few minutes, after which, Frumpy took a deep breath and began. "Chaplain Travis... You're not a regular—I mean—*ordinary* man." Frumpy paused again and risked looking Travis in the eye, to see how her words were being received. This made her flush again; her neck was beet red. "Don't get me wrong...I mean you *are* a man..."

"Last time I checked," quipped Travis. They both laughed. Frumpy gazed at Travis for a moment and began laughing again, clapping her hands on her thighs. "Well, gosh, Frumpy. Maybe you'd better let me in on the joke here?"

"It's not a joke, Chaplain Travis...it's *this*." Frumpy gestured to the two of them and their surroundings.

"Not sure what you mean," offered Travis.

"It's being here, like this..." Frumpy measured her words, "with *you*...a *man*...and it all seems so...*normal*...and natural."

"Oka-a-ay," responded Travis, "but can you help me out a bit here? I'm not sure I follow you."

Frumpy was gaining confidence now and pressed ahead. "Chaplain Travis, all the men who have been close to me...have *hurt* me." Frumpy checked in with Travis' eyes again. "My daddy hurt me. He hurt Mama, too. He beat her up something awful from as early as I can remember... And she was so beautiful too—outside and in. You've met her, so you know. I don't know why my daddy did that. It seemed Mama and I could never get it right with him."

"Get *what* right, Frumpy?" asked Travis.

After a long pause: "Anything." They sat in reverent silence for several minutes. Frumpy shifted in her seat, looked up at Travis and said, "I suppose you have other people to see and things to do?" Stephen simply held her gaze and shook his head 'no.' The silence in the room was so complete that Frumpy could hear the sound of the blood coursing through her ears. The weight of the silence seemed to suppress her ability to speak, but then she heard her voice quietly speaking: "My daddy did something awful to me—I mean, *really* awful; something no father should ever do to his daughter." Frumpy's eyes welled up with tears. "He raped me." The young woman gulped audibly, sniffed back the mucous, wiped her eyes with the backs of her hands, and looked at Travis.

"I'm sorry," replied Travis, "I'm truly sorry that happened to you." He reached for a box of tissues and handed them to Frumpy, as sacredly as passing the host at the Eucharist. Frumpy took one, nodded her thanks and began to dab her eyes and wipe her nose. "And you're right," Travis continued, "No *father* should *ever* do that to his daughter."

"You see," she began to cry once more; "*this* is what I meant about your not being an *ordinary* man." Her upturned hands mimed her exasperation. "I've never talked to a man the way I talk to you...*any man*. Not even Carl, my soon-to-be ex-husband." Frumpy looked at Travis as though awaiting some explanation.

"Frumpy, I'm a chaplain, a minister...I mean, it's what I do—what I feel *called* to do."

"No," interjected Frumpy, "it's *more* than that." Another long pause. With her eyes firmly fixed on her clasped fingers, Frumpy demanded: "*Why* do men beat up women?"

Travis leaned forward, placed his elbows on his knees and looked earnestly at Frumpy. She returned his gaze, and now seemed to be *studying* Travis' eyes—for any hint of deceit. "They don't, Frumpy. Not all men beat up women. And, in case you're wondering: I've never laid a hand on a woman." Without blinking, Frumpy kept her eyes on Travis'. "My father didn't beat my mother," Travis continued, "He never hit her—or my sisters. Frumpy, *most* men *don't* beat up women. I—I know it doesn't help you, maybe, in your situation...with what you've been through. But you've been...well...*very* unlucky..." Travis thought how weak and inadequate his words sounded. He lifted his hands, palms upwards, towards Frumpy, offering her the only and best gift he had: the truth. "*Some* men are shits…but we're not *all* that way." The fact that Chaplain Travis had used a swear word seemed somehow both apposite and served as a seal on her confession and this moment of self-revelation.

Like pieces of a magnetized puzzle, which heretofore had been indecipherable, an image slowly brought itself together in her mind. She considered each word of her incipient thoughts: Women were *not* made to be beaten and abused by men… Not *all* men beat their wives, daughters or girlfriends. Frumpy cocked her head while continuing to look intently at Travis, as though a different angle might undo his words and her thoughts; but they remained firm. After a moment, Travis, now somewhat embarrassed and at a loss, shrugged his shoulders and asked: "*What?*"

A look of deep calm now pervaded Frumpy's face. "Nothing!" she shook her head and smiled. "Nothing, Chaplain Travis. But thank you. *Thank you.*" She extended her right hand. As Travis took it in his, she smiled. She smiled in a way that transformed her face—or perhaps she smiled in a way that revealed her for who she truly was—or had been—a long, long time ago. Travis looked at her deeply for a moment. Now it was Frumpy's turn to ask, "*What?*"

"I don't know how you ever got your nickname, but you're not 'frumpy' at all, *Annabel Lee*—that's what."

Annabel Lee slowly stood and withdrew her right hand; she held it in her left and considered it for a moment. She looked at Travis and again said 'thank you.' As she left the office, she was somehow more erect than Travis had ever seen her, and at the same time she seemed almost to glide.

Travis took a deep breath and exhaled slowly as he settled back in his chair. He picked up a pencil and lightly tapped the desk as he thought deeply about his conversation with Annabel Lee. He wondered who had gained the most out of their conversation. After nearly a year of working behind bars, it occurred to him that he was finally beginning to understand what being a chaplain was all about:

it was simply offering the time to be *present* with another human being—a sheer human *presence*, accompanying those in a place where they would rather not be.

Travis slumped back into his chair, slowly and deliberately placed both hands behind his head and interlaced his fingers. He rested his head in the nest of his hands, closed his eyes and began to reflect on the events of the past few days, leading up to this moment. Diane McLeod's escape from prison, OC's expulsion from prison, and Annabel Lee's from her inner prison. A smile spread across Travis' face from ear to ear. With a loud "Ha!" he flicked both of his heels and set his chair spinning.

The following morning, not long after arriving in his office, Travis answered a light knock on the door. It was Annabel Lee's case worker Charlene. "May I come in?" she asked in a cheery manner.

"Certainly," replied Travis. "Take a seat." He motioned towards the chair normally used by Annabel Lee.

"Well, now," began Charlene, "What do you want first: the good news or the bad news?"

"Bad news, I guess," said Travis.

"Looks like you're going to need a new secretary before long."

Perplexed and off-guard, Travis grunted: "Huh? Why?"

With a flourish Charlene produced a letter for Travis to read. "Here's the good news."

Stephen took the letter and began reading. Before he had finished it, he looked up and said, "Charlene, that's wonderful! The parole board is going to give Frump-, uh, Annabel Lee a release hearing. But when?"

"Calm down and keep reading," smiled Charlene.

"Okay, so in about ninety days," mused Travis.

"Right," said Charlene, "It's so her parole case analyst can hear from me, the warden, some of the security staff, and from you, of course. After all, you've been her boss for the better part of a year. It's working with you that gives her a lot of gained time on top of her good time. Anyway, you'll need to write a letter for her file jacket. I'll speak with Frumpy about her home and job plan, but I believe she's going home to her mother and grandmother, and then on to Appalachian State; so there shouldn't be any problem there." Charlene stood up to leave. "So Chaplain Travis, you got about three months to be finding yourself another secretary."

Stephen's voice took on a serious note: "You seem fairly sure about this, Charlene. Do you think it will be that simple?"

"Stephen," beamed Charlene, "I couldn't be more certain." She tapped the side of her nose with her index finger, grinned mischievously and left.

Stephen's head was fairly spinning from the last hour: the session with Annabel Lee, and now this news from Charlene. He had the urge to shake his head, and then wondered why people shook their heads at receiving certain types of news—did it re-jig their brains? Stephen laughed and gave his head a shake. But then he started to calculate timings: his intern year was due to end this summer—or at least before the autumn term began. Whether he would stay on at the prison as a part-timer wasn't yet clear. All he knew was that he had another year of full-time study to complete his Master of Divinity. And all being well, Annabel Lee would be out in late July—early August at the latest—so he should still be here. This was one release Stephen wanted to witness. He decided to get cracking on the letter to Annabel Lee's parole analyst.

April slipped seamlessly into May, with days growing warmer and the humidity helping to transmit the intoxicating aroma of wisteria over the prison grounds. Fed up with his stuffy office, Stephen decided to get some of the fresh spring air into his lungs and left the building to stretch his legs around the grounds. As he neared the fence surrounding Dorm C, he heard Lt. Jenkins calling to him. "Hey, Chaplain! Over here!"

Travis looked over his shoulder and saw Jenkins in a loose huddle with Captain Waller and Warden Beasley near the front gate guard post. Stephen changed direction and headed over to join them. As he approached the three men, their conversation was ending.

Beasley gave Travis a wave and said: "How's it going, Chaplain?" while turning towards the administration building.

Waller greeted Stephen and shook his hand. "Got some news about your former boss."

"Goodman?" queried Travis. Both Waller and Jenkins nodded.

"Yeah," began Waller, "seems the reverend's got himself in need of a chaplain now."

"How so?" inquired Stephen.

"Why don't you fill him in, Jimmy?" Waller nodded towards Jenkins. "I need to get down to the Control Center."

"So what's up?" Stephen asked Jenkins.

The lieutenant took off his uniform cap and ran his fingers through his sweat-dampened hair. "We-ell," he drawled, "After ol' Goodman got caught doing the dirty a couple months back, and after Beasley and the Captain started doing their investigation, a lot of shit started coming out. Women in here started talking—*and* women out on parole. Most of us knew that Goodman had himself some rental properties—and we knew that some of them housed former inmates... but *damn*! That ol' boy was having those women work as prostitutes in order to pay their rent!" Jenkins slowly shook his head.

"Man! I've heard it all now. And *he* was supposed to be *helping* these women!" Travis couldn't find the words to express his thoughts about the matter. He whistled slowly through his teeth and stared out through the front gate of the prison.

Jenkins laid his hand on Travis' shoulder: "Off the record—and just between me and you—did you ever get wind of any of Goodman's shenanigans?"

Travis slowly turned his gaze from the houses across the road from the prison and back to Jenkins. "Not really. I mean—certainly not the prostitution business. I did hear from one or two inmates about his sexual hi-jinks, but it seemed that no one was willing to report him. I didn't know what to believe at first, and wasn't sure what I could do—especially if no one was willing to come forward." Stephen paused as he traced his thoughts about Goodman backwards. His eye caught a dart of bright red as a Cardinal flew easily through the chain-link fence. "Goodman played grab-ass with my secretary once—and got his face slapped."

"Frumpy did that?" asked a surprised Jenkins.

"Yep. She did," replied Travis.

"Well, he ain't going to be playing grab-ass where he's going—or he'll get a *lot more* than he bargained for!" averred Jenkins.

"What do you mean?" asked Travis.

"Well, as the Warden was telling Capt. Waller and me—just when I called you over—Goodman's got himself booked into a Federal prison for the next two years."

Travis let out a puff of breath: "Whoa!" and then queried: "Why Federal?"

"It's standard procedure when someone who's worked in the state prison system gets convicted. It's for his own protection."

Travis considered Jenkins words and then responded: "Jimmy, I can understand sending a former prison guard to Federal prison, but why a chaplain?"

"Same reason, Stephen. A lot of the ladies here got men doing time in other units. Word gets out about Goodman's…umm…'extra-curricular' activities and Goodman could soon find himself in a world of hurt. It's also his first conviction. And…" Jenkins was toeing the loose gravel which ran alongside the security fence, "you mustn't underestimate the fact that Goodman's female tenants serviced a number of parties attended by esteemed members of the judiciary and state legislature—among others. They've given him the best deal he could hope for. Almost enough to make you lose your religion, ain't it?" Jenkins shot Stephen a quick wink.

They both laughed at the irony, injustice and idiocy of the situation, and then stood in silence for a minute until Stephen said: "Quickshot."

"Beg your pardon?" responded Jenkins.

"Sally Wilkins once told me that some of the women called Goodman 'Quickshot.'"

"How's that?" asked a curious Jenkins. Travis mimicked a gunfighter pulling his gun and firing, but then let his finger droop. "Ha! I got it!" laughed Jenkins.

"Jimmy?" reflected Travis, "Isn't this one crazy place to spend time?!"

"I s'pose it is," came Jenkins' laconic reply. "But when you get right down to it, we're all doing some kind of time. Me—I've been here going on eight years now. I spend nine, maybe ten, hours a day here. Add 'em up and that would mean I've done over two years behind bars! I guess what matters is not *where* you do your time, but *how* you do it…and why."

Travis carefully weighed Jenkins' words before uttering: "Ain't *that* the truth."

Annabel Lee's time behind bars was growing short. Travis noticed, however, that rather than becoming lighter of spirit, a palpable heaviness clung to Annabel Lee like a magnet collecting metal shavings. She seemed distracted when she was working in the office. Annabel Lee was still friendly enough—that hadn't changed—but neither was she exhibiting any visible, joyful anticipation. Travis found this hard to comprehend. And she was always evasive whenever Stephen broached the subject of parole. He had heard nothing since sending his letter to the parole analyst. Charlene Walker kept Travis informed whenever she received telephone calls from the case analyst—but they had only been for points of clarification, nothing more. Stephen queried whether this had any significance, but Charlene had told him just to be patient, everything would work out.

Yet Stephen wanted to share in the joy—because for the first time since he had come to this institution, he was really caught up in the release of an inmate. Thus, like a chipped tooth, Travis found the topic hard to ignore.

When July 1, 1976 rolled around, Stephen couldn't help remarking: "It's the anniversary of my starting date."

The typewriter at which Annabel Lee worked was clattering away. "Mmh?" was the only reply Stephen received.

"I said," repeated Stephen, as Annabel Lee paused from her typing, "that today is the anniversary of my coming to work here. It's hard to believe a year's gone by."

"My 'anniversary'—if you want to call it that—was four days ago," shrugged Annabel Lee.

Travis spun round in his chair to look at Annabel Lee. "I don't think I had ever realized that we both arrived here at roughly the same time—although under very different circumstances."

"That's true," said Annabel Lee as she went back to tapping at the keys.

Travis continued to look at Annabel Lee: "We could both be leaving around the same," he mused aloud.

His office-mate simply shrugged again and said softly: "We'll see."

"Right," said Stephen, and turned back to the papers on his desk. After ten minutes passed he became aware that he was reading the same words over and over again. Annabel Lee was still typing his hand-written letters. Annabel Lee's refusal to discuss her imminent release was clawing at him and prevented him from thinking about anything else. Stephen pushed his chair back from the desk and sprang to his feet. He stretched, rolled his shoulders and quickly said: "I gotta go out. See you later."

Amidst the chattering of keys he heard Annabel Lee's faint: "Okay."

Travis exited his building and breathed in the humid air. He could feel himself starting to perspire under the punishing Southern sun. He walked purposefully—but aimlessly—for a moment or two, then heeled about and headed for Kate McIntyre's office. He hoped to catch her in one of those rare times when she wasn't running an orientation group or seeing an inmate. Travis entered the diagnostics building and saw that Kate's door was partially open. As he went to knock, he could hear Ben Katz speaking. Travis tapped gently and heard Kate's voice beckon him in. The two colleagues were sharing a cup of coffee.

Katz quickly changed tack and said: "Stop talking dirty to me, Kate! The holy man's here!"

"Aw, shucks!" complained Stephen, "Could I go back to the door and just listen in?"

They all enjoyed a laugh—to the point that Katz spilled some coffee on his leg. "Oi! You see?! Punished for having a filthy mind!"

"Okay if I interrupt?"

"You already have!" jibed Katz in his abrupt Yankee manner.

Kate just smiled and said: "Not at all, Stephen. Never mind my rude guest—he's a foreigner in these parts!"

Not one to let Katz get the upper hand, Stephen leapt in: "Oh, he loves it down here. He just has to keep up the Yankee act. But I do have it on good authority that his mother gave him a supply of matzoth so he could leave a trail to find his way home—and he has yet to use it!"

"Do you mind?!" interjected Ben, "Let's leave my mother out of it! *Nu*, are you just here to schmooze or what?"

"Probably 'or'" quipped Travis.

"May I grab a chair?" Kate nodded to her right, still amused at the repartee between the chaplain and psychologist. "In fact," continued Stephen, "It's probably good I've got the two of you for the price of one. I need your professional insight."

Katz parodied tidying himself, sat up straight and dropped his eyeglasses—which had been resting on his balding head—onto his nose. "There! I'm ready."

"Thank you, Dr. Freud," said Stephen, bowing towards Katz, and then quickly became serious: "It's about Annabel Lee—Frumpy? She's up for parole. I suppose one, or both, of you have been asked for an assessment?" Katz deferred to Kate. Kate had drawn her fingertips together as she listened and simply smiled assent. Stephen continued: "What I can't understand is that Annabel Lee refuses even to discuss the possibility of parole. If I bring it up in conversation, she changes the subject or just shrugs it off; and her mood has changed—you know how upbeat she generally is."

"She's a short-timer. Got the pre-release jitters," stated Katz matter-of-factly.

Kate nodded agreement, saying, "Ben's probably right, Stephen. It's not unusual. Let me ask you something: Have you ever been so closely involved with an inmate before her release?"

Stephen thought for a moment before saying: "Guess not. Annabel Lee's the first—and, of course, she works as my clerical assistant. She's also the first inmate for whom I've been asked to write a letter to the parole analyst."

"Prison changes nearly everything in a person's life," said Kate.

"Come in married; leave divorced," stated Katz.

"Come in a mother with children; leave with them under the care of social services in a foster home," added Kate. She continued: "And don't underestimate the reality of 'institutionalization'. I know the law and order brigade see it as a lame excuse for recidivism, but until you've worked or done time in a place like this, you really are in no place to judge."

Katz interjected: "I wish every judge in the land had to spend at least two weeks in a prison as part of the training—we'd soon see a change in sentencing."

Both Kate and Stephen gave their assent, but Kate saw that Stephen's questions remained un-answered and returned to Annabel Lee's situation. "Look, Stephen. Pre-release is a very stressful time for most inmates. The longer a woman spends in here, the harder it is to contemplate leaving. That's why the long-timers usually go to the halfway house across the street before they fully exit to parole."

"And then there's your friend, Lola," put in Katz. "She's an extreme case, mind you, but she's always a mess before parole—and if she doesn't get her time extended before she's set free, she's always back fairly soon."

"Don't I know it," replied Stephen.

Kate resumed: "You're to be forgiven thinking that Fru—*Annabel Lee*—should be chomping at the bit to get out of here. But she's going to be thinking about how her friends, family and townsfolk will see her. Too many prospective employers don't look farther than 'spent time in prison.' While it's true that ninety-nine percent of women don't *want* to be in here..."

"That same ninety-nine percent are probably scared shitless at the thought of getting out." Katz finished Kate's sentence.

"That's right," agreed Kate. "So, as keen as you are to see Annabel Lee get parole; if you really want to help her, then let her deal with it in her own way and in her own time."

Stephen bowed deferentially towards Kate and then Ben. "Sorry, guys. I really hadn't realized..."

"Oh Stephen, there's no need to apologize—we've all been through it," Kate interrupted.

"And that's why we enjoy watching you make a schmuck of yourself!" jibed Katz. "It makes us feel powerful."

Stephen mimed a slug to the jaw and said, "Thanks, Doc. I needed that," as he rubbed his chin and stood to go.

"Anytime," smiled Kate warmly.

"Now would you go back to your cell so Kate can resume talking dirty to me?" grinned Katz.

"I'll close the door behind me, shall I?" said Travis, as he laughed and gave a little wave over his shoulder.

When Stephen arrived back at his office, Annabel Lee was just gathering her things and getting ready to leave. "Oh, Chaplain Travis—will you be here on the Fourth of July?—for the picnic?"

"I wouldn't miss it," chirped Travis. "There was a lot of good food here last year from all of the visiting families. I've got to admit it surprised me—I wasn't exactly expecting family picnics within a prison—"

"Well, it's only once a year," broke in Annabel Lee. "Anyway, it's just that I'd like for you to meet the man that...well, that my mother's been dating—it sounds so weird to talk about *my...mother... dating!*" Annabel Lee gave each word emphasis. "She's been seeing him—Ray's his name—since sometime before Easter. They both teach at the local high school. Her letters are full of news about him." She paused for a few seconds. "Mama told me about Ray when she was here at Easter—and I was really excited for her. But now, I just wonder..." Annabel Lee became more pensive, "well, if they might get...*together.*"

"Do you mean *married?*" asked Travis. Annabel Lee just nodded. "I suppose all kinds of things have changed since you came here, haven't they?" Again a nod. "Well, how can I say 'no' to my number one secretary?" asked Stephen cheerfully.

"You're *only* secretary," mocked Annabel Lee, breaking into a smile.

"Yeah, but *what* a secretary!" teased Travis. Then he swung their conversation back to Ray: "So, *if I may ask,* why are you so anxious that I should meet your mother's new man?" Travis raised his eyebrows comically.

Annabel Lee raised hers in mock exasperation. She drew patterns with the toe of her shoe on the linoleum and stared at their invisible outlines. "I don't know," she mused, "it just feels *right*. We've—I mean—*I've* been through so much here. And you've been *here*... with me... during this time." Annabel Lee stared in front of herself as though looking at an album of her life. "I don't want *anything* to be like it was before—that's all. And so far, you're the only man I've been able to trust." Annabel Lee raised her eyes and met Stephen's.

"Okay then," he said, "I'll make sure I meet up with your family—and Ray. Just as long as you understand that I can't see inside his soul. But Annabel Lee?"

"Yes?"

"Try to trust your mother's judgment, okay? From what you've told me, she's been down a hard road too. I don't expect she wants to repeat past experiences any more than you do."

"Guess you're right," agreed Annabel Lee. "And thanks; I *will* try to bear it in mind."

On the Fourth of July, scores of cars and taxis converged on the Correctional Center for Women. It was midday on the one day of the year in which families were allowed onto the grounds of the prison—and they didn't scrimp on the cornucopia of home-cooked food. Because so many people were allowed into the prison grounds, Warden Beasley and Captain Waller made certain there were enough guards—virtually two full shifts—for all the contraband searches required by the number of bodies and picnic baskets. Tables had been set up in the reception area of the administration building to hold the kitchen knives and other table-ware which—though unwittingly packed—were not allowed into the prison. Happily the day had dawned fine, as no one—neither staff nor inmate—wanted to contemplate squeezing several hundred people into the auditorium. American flags festooned doors, gates, light posts, guard posts and more.

For Chaplain Travis, this—his second—Fourth of July celebration at the women's prison was positively surreal when compared with his first one the previous year. His experience last year had simply seemed incongruous with his naïve, stereotyped vision of prison, fed by Hollywood gangster films starring George Raft and Jimmy Cagney. But on this occasion, as Stephen walked the grounds greeting inmates, meeting their loved ones, tasting secret family recipes for fried chicken, potato salad and cherry cobbler—the three-hundred-and-sixty-four preceding days were thrown into high relief. The tears, depression, violence, escapes, fear, births, grief of separation—and so much more—made the few millimeters of wire seem more like the Atlantic Ocean, so great was the gulf between what was happening today, in freedom, and the abject lack of that same freedom the rest of the year.

Fighting to keep his mind on the present reality, Stephen heard his name being called. He turned in the direction of the voice and saw Annabel Lee standing and energetically waving at him. Seated on the ground, on a checkered picnic blanket were two women and a man. As Travis made his way towards them he recognized Ginny right away—despite her straw sun hat, but it took him a few seconds to recognize Colleen. Her auburn hair was down and, though streaked with grey, its luster caught the sun's rays; she also wore make-up and was looking intently at the man seated next to her. Travis could now truly see the source of Annabel Lee's beauty. The man with whom Colleen was speaking had mid-length, salt-and-pepper hair and a moustache. He laughed while holding the gaze of the woman he obviously loved. Annabel Lee was the most animated Travis had seen for some weeks—ever since news of her parole review became known. As Travis approached the foursome, the man—whom Stephen rightly supposed to be Ray Wilkins—

stood up to greet him. Stephen waved to him to remain seated, but this bit of social protocol was not to be ignored and Ray fairly sprang to his feet. "You must be Chaplain Travis?"

"That's right," said Stephen as they shook hands.

"Well, I'm certainly glad to meet you. Annabel Lee's told us a lot about you. I believe you know everyone else here," Ray motioned towards the seated ladies.

"Hey, Reverend," offered Ginny. "Don't expect me to do no jumping up like this 'un." She playfully slapped Ray's leg. "This crazy feller gets up at dawn and *runs*—can you believe that? As though he ain't got enough work to do, he *runs!*"

"I keep telling Ginny it's just so I can keep up with her!" teased Ray, "And this one, of course."

Ray turned to Colleen, who was saying to Ginny: "Oh, Mama! You know it's just that Ray wants to keep fit and healthy!" And then quickly turning to Stephen, she offered her right hand and shielded her eyes from the July sun with her left. "Good to see you again, Chaplain Travis." The joy radiating from her face rivaled the sun's beams and was infectious.

Travis smiled broadly and said: "It's really good to see you all. I know Annabel Lee's been looking forward to it."

"That's for sure!" interjected Annabel Lee, who up to this point had been unable to get a word in. "And Grandma's been looking forward to feeding you some of her fried chicken and buttermilk cornbread, so I hope you brought your appetite."

"After last the Fourth of July here, I decided to skip breakfast this year! I'd be glad to join you." Annabel Lee, Ray and Stephen all squeezed themselves onto the blanket.

Ginny's weathered—but strong—hand took hold of Travis' and warmly pressed it in hers. "Reckon you ought to be the one to ask the Lord's blessing on this food."

"Glad to," said Travis. Still clasping Stephen's hand, Ginny reached and took Ray's left hand. Ray, in turn, took Colleen's hand who—with eyes already closed—found her daughter's hand. Annabel Lee shifted her position so that she could close the circle and extended her hand to Stephen. Stephen's eyes were firmly shut and he was just about to start his prayer when he felt Annabel Lee's fingers seek his. Stephen was surprised by the pang which he experienced in his chest, but let his hand enfold Annabel Lee's as words began to tumble from his mind to his tongue. "Lord God, we are gathered here on this special day—a special day for this family and other families at the women's prison—and a special day for our country. It's a day which speaks of freedom...a gift which perhaps means most to those who have lost it." Travis felt Ginny's hand tighten on his, as he continued: "Therefore help us to treasure our freedom. And Lord, you are the God who led your people to freedom, despite many perils, and led them to a land flowing with milk and honey. So we ask that you bless this food, no less given from your hand, and prepared by loving hands for this gathering today. And if it be your will, may it be the last time this family gathers in this place. Amen."

"Amen," echoed the others, as three generations of tears flowed silently at the finish of Travis' prayer.

Ginny's strong hand drew him close so that she could kiss him on the cheek. "Thank you," she croaked.

Annabel Lee and Colleen nestled their heads against one another. With a final squeeze the party released each other's hands. As matriarch, Ginny handed out the paper plates and began to pass the food around. She wiped her glistening eyes and wordlessly pointed at the equally glistening gallon jug of lemonade, sweating from the noonday July sun. Ray opened the jug and began filling Dixie cups with the homemade mixture. Conversation soon resumed with compliments on Ginny's cooking, amplified by the smacking of lips.

"Oh Grandma," sighed Annabel Lee, after finishing a piece of cornbread with lashings of butter made soft by the heat of the day, "I wish you could cook for us here!"

"No thanks!" cried Ginny. "You just get yourself back home and let me feed you there."

"That's a deal!" replied Annabel Lee as she tucked into a drumstick.

As the food disappeared, they talked of the current dry weather, whether Jimmy Carter had a chance to win the presidential election and events back in Bransford County. A combination of full stomachs and mid-summer heat led to languidness that curtailed their previously animated banter. In the lull, Colleen spoke up: "Chaplain? Is there any word yet?" She looked at Travis with hopeful eyes.

"Don't put the man on the spot, Honey." Ray gently squeezed Colleen's shoulder.

"It's okay," replied Travis wiping his mouth with a paper napkin. "I can understand why she's anxious to know. I wish I could tell you something, but it's all in the hands of the parole board now. Charlene Walker might be able to give you an idea of timing—she's coordinating most of Annabel Lee's case material for the parole analyst." Travis craned his neck to scan the grounds. "I think I can see her over by the basketball court—shall I fetch her for you?"

"Not before you've tried my strawberry pie," said Ginny. "Got to have your dessert first!"

"Yes, ma'am!" replied a compliant Travis. "But look, I'll see if I can catch her and send her over to you *after* I've had my dessert." Stephen turned and winked at Ginny.

"Well, I 'spect that will be all aright," assented Ginny. Travis extolled the pie as he downed it in a half-dozen bites. "See there, Ray? The chaplain knows how to eat! He's had two pieces of chicken, cole slaw, corn bread *and* some of my pie!"

"Mama," said a drowsy Ray, whose head now rested on Colleen's lap, "If I ate like that I'd have to run twice as far—or I'd be the size of your tobacco barn. 'Sides, the chaplain is a good deal younger than I am—no disrespect, Stephen."

"None taken," laughed Stephen, "but I had better stop eating now so that I can still walk around and visit other folk." Stephen had noticed how Annabel Lee's head had turned sharply when Ray had called Ginny 'Mama.' As he stood to leave, Stephen asked: "Do y'all mind if I speak with my secretary for a moment?"

"Doesn't your secretary deserve a day off? It's a national holiday, if you haven't noticed." jibed Ginny.

"Is it?" joked Travis, "I plumb near forgot! I'll only keep her a moment." Then wiping his brow—as much for effect as for necessity of the sweat collecting under the midday sun—Stephen said to Annabel Lee: "Let's find us some shade! I'm about to melt." He guided her to a tree next to the diagnostic center. Stephen placed himself so that Annabel Lee's back would be to her mother and Ray. "Before you ask, yep, I noticed how close your mother and Ray are. And 'no' I can't vouch for the man's character—but he seems like a genuinely decent guy."

"But he called Grandma 'Mama,'" Annabel Lee stated almost pleadingly.

"Yep. He did. It seems he's not only feeling close to your mother, but your grandmother as well."

"But…calling her '*Mama*'—you *know* what that means?"

"Indeed I do," noted Travis, "but you know what?" Annabel Lee shook her head: "Your Grandma Ginny wouldn't have let him call her that if *she* didn't like it." Travis lowered his gaze and looked Annabel Lee straight in the eye. Annabel Lee considered Travis' words for a moment and then nodded. "And you know what else?" asked Travis. Annabel Lee shrugged and shook her head. "It's clear to me that your mother and grandmother are looking out for each other—that's what."

Annabel Lee exhaled a heavy sigh and said in a low voice: "That's true."

Travis started to leave, but then said: "Oh—one more thing. From what I can see: you've probably changed as much while you've been in here as their lives have changed out there. You've all got to make room—and time—for each other to adjust. Okay?"

Annabel Lee's face slowly reflected a change from consternation to cautious acceptance. "Okay," she said, and then, as Travis turned to go: "Thanks, Stephen."

Stephen felt another short, sharp pang upon hearing his first name. He waved over his shoulder and said: "I'll try to find Charlene Walker for your mother."

As Annabel Lee returned to her family's picnic blanket, she felt a sense of quiet calm pervade her thoughts and emotions. Colleen and Ray were laughing about something, and it occurred to Annabel Lee that she hadn't seen such a beatific countenance on her mother since she was a small child. She felt her own spirits lift. As she took her place on the blanket, Ginny tugged Annabel Lee closer to her and said: "That chaplain's a good man. He seems to care about you right much."

Annabel Lee nodded: "He is a good man...*very* different from most of the men I've known." She lay back and let her grandmother stroke her fine auburn hair. "It's odd," she mused aloud.

"What's that, child?" asked Ginny.

"It's odd that I had to come to prison to meet a *good* man." Annabel Lee laughed at the sudden revelation.

"That's true," agreed Ginny, "We just don't know how the good Lord wants us to learn things. Bible's right when it says that his ways aren't our ways. If we knowed half the things that would happen to us in this life, we'd probably think we couldn't cope and throw ourselves in the river and drown..." Ginny's voice halted at the realization of what she had said. Even Colleen's and Ray's quiet conversation came to a halt. Annabel Lee drew closer to her grandmother and squeezed her tightly. Her mind drifted to the day she received the news of Wyatt's death—she had just married Carl, who had seemed to fill so much of her life; and life with him had seemed so full of promise. Could that have been only just over a *year* ago? And now, Carl was barely a footnote in her life—her time in prison being the only legacy of their union.

Aware that a heavy silence had settled over what was meant to be a happy day, Annabel Lee said: "Hey, everybody! I have an announcement." Ray sat up, while Colleen and Ginny turned to face her. "I am a *free* woman!" proclaimed Annabel Lee, flinging her arms open wide. Seeing that she was met by looks of puzzlement, Annabel Lee went on: "I know I'm still an inmate in this fine state institution, but nevertheless: *I am free!* The final divorce papers arrived last week. All I had to do was sign them and send them back—which I did! So now you see, I am a *free* woman...despite the gift my former husband gave me of a year's free vacation here in Fairborn."

Unsure whether Annabel Lee's comments were born of mere sarcasm or false bravado, Colleen gently inquired: "Honey? ...Are you *sure* you're all right?"

"Well, apart from being here," Annabel Lee looked around her, "I am perfectly *all right*. Carl was—*is*—a jerk! And I'm *glad* to be free of him. I was saying to Grandma just a few minutes ago how ironic it is that I had to come to prison to meet a *good* man—Chaplain Travis; and the other great irony is that being a *prisoner* here has also made me *free*—both now and when I get out of here."

It was Ray who broke through the bewildered uncertainty of the two McNair women: "I say let's drink to Annabel Lee's freedom! Just like the chaplain's prayer: there's nothing finer that we could celebrate on this day!" Ray collected the ladies' cups and began to fill them with the now tepid lemonade. Ray held his cup high and said: "Ladies, lift your cups! A toast to Annabel Lee's freedom!" The three women joined in the toast and then enjoyed the gift of laughter.

Travis had left Annabel Lee and company in search of Charlene, but as on any visitation day, he hadn't got very far when he again heard his name being called. It was Sally Wilkins. Sally was sitting on the ground with her back against a pin oak, enjoying both its support and shade. She motioned Travis over, saying, "Come pull up a spot of cool earth!" Stephen acknowledged the invitation with a wave and sat down, cross-legged, with Sally. "No visitors today?" he inquired.

"N-a-aw," drawled Sally, "You know me: the black sheep of the family." Sally was surrounded by several small paper plates with a selection of different foods.

"Well, it looks like you've been taken care of food-wise," noted Travis.

"Yeah, the sisters look after me pretty well. Got my own smorgasbord! Sorry I can't offer you any."

Travis patted his stomach and said: "No need to! I've been amply fed and watered."

Sally took her plastic fork and toyed with some potato salad. With a sly smile she looked up at Travis and asked: "Heard the news about your former boss: Doc-tuh Marv *Good*-man?"

"Yeah, Sally, I have. Do I assume from that smile on your face that you are fully informed?" Sally snorted with laughter and said: "I told you we'd get that peckerwood, didn't I?"

"You certainly did!" replied Travis, "But in the *freezer?*—who cooked that one up?"

"Oh, Rosalee Mason, one or two others, myself—and one of the guards—*whose name you don't need to know!*" Sally had seen the look of surprise on Stephen's face when he heard that a guard was involved in Goodman's downfall and departure. "Goodman might not have been as obnoxious as Fred Bain, but he wasn't liked much better…maybe worse—after all, he was *supposed* to be a man of God. Anyway, his *cock*erel is cooked," cracked Sally.

"Yeah, but only for two years," interjected Travis, "He'll probably be out in a year or less."

"Thrue," lisped Sally as she licked potato salad from her lower lip. She reached for a napkin and wiped her mouth. "True. But he's had his wings clipped—even had to give up his rent-a-brothel business. He'll be a lot less of a threat to women now. And who knows? Maybe some muscle-bound ape will nail him in the prison freezer—now *that would be funny*! Oh—sorry Chaplain. That's not very Christian of me."

"No need to apologize, Sally. Goodman's earned what's coming to him. I believe hell—and for that matter, heaven—begin right here on earth. He's shared enough hell with others; time he got a taste of his own medicine. Goodman's left a lot for me, and other prison chaplains, to live down. Maybe the afterlife is when we get the time we really deserve." Sally nodded in silence as she stabbed at a plate of dumplings. "Well," said Stephen as he stood and wiped the gathering perspiration from his brow, "I've got to be on my way. Need to find Charlene Walker."

Stephen hesitated and then sat back on his haunches for a moment: "Sally, I want you to know something." Sally looked up from her dumplings and squarely into Travis' eyes. "I want you to know—despite all of the injustices that have happened to people here—that when you took care of Goodman: at least some justice was done—and I mean that."

"The Lone Ranger—that's me," smiled Sally. And then more quietly: "Apart from my flowers, what else have I got to do with my time?"

Having been informed by Chaplain Travis that Annabel Lee's mother wanted to see her, Charlene wended her way through the park-like appearance of the prison grounds. Those that were able had squeezed into what little shade remained from the sun's relentless rays. Others succumbed to the lethargy-inducing heat and dozed with sun hats or newspapers over their faces. Thanks to Stephen's accurate directions, Charlene easily found her way to Annabel Lee and family. Their meal long-finished, Ray—who had driven the three of them from Bransford County—now slept soundly next to Colleen, who gently stroked his head. Annabel Lee talked quietly with Colleen and Ginny. Not wanting to disturb Ray, Charlene whispered her greetings and knelt down beside the three women. Annabel Lee introduced her to Colleen and Ginny. Ray stirred and then snored softly. Colleen smiled at her man and turned her attention to Charlene. "I'm sorry if I have interrupted your day—and I suppose you have to answer this sort of question a lot—but is there any news about my daughter's parole?"

"Heavens, don't apologize," replied a jovial Charlene. "It's just part of my job; and the good Lord knows that if I had a child in here, I'd sure be asking when she was getting out! There—*that's* the easy bit. Next bit is kinda tricky 'cause these things never happen in a set amount of time—usually somewhere between three and four months. The good news is that all the paperwork is in, and nearly three months have gone by—so really (Charlene looked at Annabel Lee) you should be hearing something fairly soon."

"And when I know," continued Annabel Lee, "you'll be the very next person to hear."

Colleen mulled this over for a minute and then asked, "But what if...well if..."

"Your daughter is turned down?" Charlene finished the unpleasant thought. "It's highly unlikely. Not impossible, mind you; but highly unlikely. It's Frumpy's—" Charlene halted when she noticed the looks given her by both Colleen and Ginny. "My apologies. It's Annabel Lee's first conviction and she's been an exemplary inmate. I've worked here nearly two decades and it's been almost unheard of for someone like Annabel Lee to be denied parole. And truth to tell, with this being the main prison for women in North Carolina, there's always a need for space. Sad, but true."

"You hear that, Mama?" interjected Annabel Lee, "There's nothing to be concerned about."

"That's right, Colleen," chimed in Ginny, "Listen to your young'un and Miss Charlene here. They ought to know."

"I'm sure you're both right," said Colleen, "It's just so hard waiting—that's all."

At that point Ray stirred again and muttered, "We're nearly there…next exit…" and drifted back into calm sleep.

"Bless him," said Colleen, "He got up at four this morning to drive us here. Guess he's still driving."

Annabel Lee looked at Ray—perhaps for the first time—for the person he was, and not as the potential threat he posed. She turned her gaze to her mother and smiled.

Annabel Lee laid the small suitcase on her bunk and opened it. It was the same case she had used as a child. Though nearly empty of contents, it seemed full to overflowing with memories. In it were the garments of freedom, brought to her by her mother: a plain cotton blouse and a floral print dress—clothes from another time, and an earlier life. Annabel Lee picked them up and pressed them close to her face. They smelled of Ginny's favorite washing powder and fresh mountain breezes. It seemed to Annabel Lee that everything she did now was in slow-motion—as though she were making indelible mental pictures for…*for what*? And why? So that this moment—this day—would never be forgotten? Perhaps. She unbuttoned her prison blouse and removed it. Next she slipped out of the prison skirt and laid both on the bed. She studied them for a moment: her uniform for just over a year—the skin that had defined her in the eyes of the law. She smiled to herself, feeling she now knew how snakes must feel in the spring. She had often collected their sloughed-off skins on her grandparents' farm and taken them to 'show and tell' at school. Annabel Lee now luxuriated in donning her new skin. She nuzzled her nose into her shoulder and again breathed in the smell of home. Next she gathered her few possessions: toiletries, her Bible and few books, letters from home, writing paper and pen, placing them carefully into the suitcase. Finally she picked up the manila envelope containing her divorce decree and laid it on top. As she closed the case and snapped it shut, it occurred to her that she had closed the case on childhood, a marriage and nearly fourteen months in prison. So much time in such a small case!

Lillian and a few others from her prison family sat or stood at a respectful distance. Even Alfreda—with whom Annabel Lee had worked in the sewing room when she first began her time—had managed to get there to say goodbye. Some of them had been through this ritual more than once. It was no less sacred for the repetition. None of them said a thing until Annabel Lee was finished. They watched her stand quietly over the suitcase. Only when Annabel Lee said, "There! That's it," did they move towards her and speak. The siblings, parents and grandparents cried, hugged and laughed. Annabel Lee gave them pieces of paper with her address written on them. Lillian wise-cracked that she reckoned Annabel Lee would know where to send their letters. They all laughed, and just as quickly the tears flowed once more. They embraced in one large huddle.

It was Lillian who finally said: "Best you get going!" Annabel Lee nodded and wiped the tears from her cheeks and eyes. "Everything taken care of now?" asked Lillian.

"Mmh-hmm," nodded Annabel Lee again. And then added: "Well, just one more thing: I need to go by the chaplains' office."

As had happened long months before, the women all began to tease her. "Bet she breaks parole just to come back and work with Chaplain Travis!"

"No wonder that girl put in extra hours!"

"What? You mean he's not in her suitcase?"

Annabel Lee laughed through her tears and returned the joke: "No. I'm afraid he's all yours now. But you look after him for me!"

"Let's go," said Lillian, and they all moved towards the door.

Annabel Lee said goodbye to the officer on duty in her dormitory and stepped outside into the sultry August day. It was cloudy, and steam was still rising from an earlier rain shower. In surveying the now familiar prison grounds, Annabel Lee thought to herself: Had it really only been a matter of weeks since she had sat out here and shared a picnic with her family on the Fourth of July? On that day, parole was still ahead of her—and an uncertainty at that. Sally Wilkins was out in front of the dormitory digging in the freshly watered earth. Two other inmates sat by her and listened to her description of the bedding plants.

"Bye Sally," said Annabel Lee as she walked past the small group.

Sally eyed Annabel Lee and her family for a moment and then grinned and said: "Y'all kick her butt outta here and make sure she stays out!" They all laughed, and then Sally said: "Don't y'all stand there looking at me! I got work to do!" However, they hadn't walked very far when Sally shouted out: "Take it easy, kid!"

As Annabel Lee's entourage approached the building that housed the auditorium, case workers' and chaplains' offices, Annabel Lee said, "All right, all of you! I think I can handle this by myself!"

"I just bet you can!" came a retort, and all the teasing began once more.

Annabel Lee waved her hand at them as she entered the building. Knowing that Charlene would be in the administration building preparing the final paperwork for her release, Annabel Lee turned down the corridor leading to her former workplace. The door was open and from within she heard Travis whistling and humming the Cowardly Lion's song from the film "The Wizard of Oz." She smiled to herself, as Travis had often cited that story as one of the best modern parables on life. "What if it were a hippopotamus?" he was mumbling to himself in his best Bert Lahr voice as she entered the doorway.

"I'd thrash him from top to bottomus!" answered Annabel Lee.

"Ha!" was Stephen's gleeful response: "And what if it were a brontosaurus?"

"I'd show 'im who's king of the forest!" laughed Annabel Lee.

"Ah, Dorothy! Have you got your ruby slippers? Today's the day!"

"Yes, they're on my feet, in case you haven't noticed."

"Well, just remember to click them together three times, and say, 'There's no place like home!' Think you can remember that?"

"Yes, Chaplain Travis, I think I can just about manage that." There was a slight musical quality to Annabel Lee's voice that Travis had never really heard before. "Well, just make sure you click those slippers no more and no less than three times, you hear, because I haven't got a hot air balloon to float you back to Kansas—or is it Bransford County? I forget." Annabel Lee stood looking at Stephen to the point that he became nervous: "What? Did you come for your typewriter? Because if so, it's state property—and besides it wouldn't fit into your suitcase."

Annabel Lee simply smiled and said: "No. I just wanted to see this office again… You know, it was a real haven for me during most of my time here."

"Oh!" said Stephen, feigning emotional hurt: "So you came to say goodbye to this office? Let me get out so as not to interrupt."

Annabel Lee shook her head and sighed deeply. "You know, Stephen, you're not making this any easier for me."

The use of his first name halted his manic joking. "I'm sorry, Annabel Lee. I've really enjoyed having you as my secretary—both for your good work and your company. Truth to tell, it has occurred to me that I am really going to miss you. And then I feel guilty for having the audacity to 'miss' someone for getting out of this place. I guess it means I feel that you never belonged here to begin with."

"Oddly enough," replied Annabel Lee, "It's not been as bad as you might think." They stood looking at one another. "Will you walk me to the gate? I know my mother and grandmother will want to see you—Ray's here as well."

"I'd be honored," said Travis giving a little bow, "This is one release I wouldn't want to miss." They turned, left the office and headed for the door which led out towards the administration building. A light drizzle had started.

"I need to say goodbye to my family and friends," said Annabel Lee.

"Take your time; I'll wait," replied Travis, sheltering beneath a tree.

Annabel Lee looked at the motley group of women who had become family by choice rather than by blood. Her eyes welled up with tears again as she said: "I don't know what to say."

"Try 'goodbye,' girl!" piped up Alfreda.

"She's right," agreed Lillian. "There's only one place for you now, and that's outta here! Chaplain Travis!" she cried, "Would you please show your *ex*-secretary the way out of this prison?"

"With pleasure," laughed Stephen. He gallantly stepped forward and offered his arm. The women all laughed, made their jokes and shouted their final well-wishes as Stephen escorted Annabel Lee towards the administration building. Neither said a word as they strode towards the building that was the last stop on Annabel Lee's journey towards freedom. Travis pressed the buzzer which notified the guard to open the last locked door for Annabel Lee. They moved through into the lobby where Charlene was talking with Colleen, Ginny and Ray, who were seated just inside the entrance door. Warden Beasley was talking with Captain Waller. When he saw Travis and Annabel Lee enter, he waved in acknowledgement. Whenever possible, Beasley tried to be available for the release of inmates from the Correctional Center for Women. Charlene came over to Beasley to take care of the last paperwork involving the parole and release papers, while a guard performed the last custodial duty: a search of Annabel Lee's suitcase. Satisfied that no state property had been unlawfully removed, and that all the paperwork was signed and in order, it remained only for Warden Beasley to shake Annabel Lee's hand and give his speech. Charlene motioned for Annabel Lee's family to join the ceremony.

Beasley cleared his throat and said: "Annabel Lee, although you are a bright and attractive young lady, *I really do not care to see you again...*" pause "*... here.*" Beasley produced his winning—but sincere—smile; then greeted Colleen, Ray and Ginny, who individually hugged and kissed Annabel Lee. Having stood tactfully to one side, Travis now came forward and congratulated them on having a reunited family. Ray shook Stephen's hand and told him that they had driven down from the mountains the previous evening just so that everyone would be fresh both for this special moment and for the long drive back home. Ginny and Colleen turned to speak to Travis.

Colleen took both of Stephen's hands in hers and said. "Thank you, Chaplain Travis. You don't know what a relief and help it has been for us to know that Annabel Lee had you to rely on."

"Words don't say enough," added Ginny, who grabbed Travis and hugged him tightly.

Stephen blushed slightly and said: "Well, it was a two-way street, you know: she was a great support to me in the office."

Warden Beasley bade the party farewell and followed Waller out onto the prison grounds. Charlene stepped forward and said: "I'm afraid it's my turn to get back to work." She gave Annabel Lee a quick hug and said: "Go get that degree, girl! You deserve it." Then to Ray, Colleen and Ginny, she offered: "Y'all drive carefully, hear?" and headed back to her office.

This left only Travis who nodded towards the front entrance and said: "I want to accompany you and this young lady *out that door.*"

"Lead on!" said Ray, as he picked up Annabel Lee's suitcase.

Annabel Lee, flanked by her mother and grandmother—each clinging tightly to one of her arms—followed Travis as he led them to the front door. He flung it open wide and held it for them as they made their exit. And then she was outside. Walking towards the adjacent parking lot, Annabel Lee suddenly stopped and looked back. Ray went ahead and unlocked the car. Colleen and Ginny stood back, instinctively knowing what their loved one needed to do. Annabel Lee's eyes drank in the panorama before her: this view of the prison which she had only seen once previously, on the day of her arrival. Women were coming and going on the prison grounds, just as she had done; the guards kept an eye on things—but no longer on her. She saw Warden Beasley and Captain Waller standing near the front gate. She surveyed the high fence topped with razor ribbon. And then Annabel Lee shut her eyes and lifted her face into the soft summer rain; standing motionless.

When she opened her eyes, Travis was standing near her. "How does it feel?" he quietly asked her.

"Like the time has been washed away...like I've been washed clean."

Travis looked at her for a long moment and then said: "Hang on to that." Annabel Lee and Travis looked at one another, speaking only with their eyes and from their shared experience.

"I'm no longer an inmate."

"No."

"You're no longer my chaplain or my boss." Stephen shook his head.

Annabel Lee stepped forward and embraced Stephen, who shared the embrace. She lightly kissed his cheek and then laid her head on his shoulder for a brief time. Stephen received the gift of her presence without restraint. Then, as though responding to a cue that only they heard, they released their embrace and Annabel Lee rejoined her mother and grandmother as they walked to the waiting car. Colleen joined Ray in the front, while Annabel Lee helped Ginny into the back seat and then took the seat next to her. The doors closed. Ray switched on the ignition, put the car in gear and reversed from the parking space. The windows were steamy from a combination of the day's heat and humidity; Travis could only see the vague outlines of the occupants' heads. The car then moved forward and around to the exit, where it halted, as a grey, department of correction bus passed by, drawing to a stop outside the front gate of the prison. Ray started to drive onto the road.

Annabel Lee leaned forward and laid her hand on Ray's shoulder. "Please wait a moment," she asked. No one said anything to her as Annabel Lee watched the gate open and the bus slowly pull up to the diagnostics center. The rain began to fall harder, so Ray switched on the wipers. The wipers squeaked gently as the rain beat a tattoo on the roof of the car. Annabel Lee's eyes took in the arrival of new inmates, but her inner eye took in so much more. After a short time she eased herself back in the seat and simply said, "Okay." As Ray drove out of the parking lot, Annabel Lee suddenly remembered Travis, and hastily wiped the foggy window and craned her neck. She saw his solitary figure, hunched against the rain, making his way back into the prison.

Breinigsville, PA USA
31 August 2010
244615BV00001B/30/P